Researching and Writing Across the Curriculum

Third Edition

Christine A. Hult
Utah State University

PEARSON
Longman

New York   San Francisco   Boston
London   Toronto   Sydney   Tokyo   Singapore   Madrid
Mexico City   Munich   Paris   Cape Town   Hong Kong   Montreal

Publisher: Joseph Opiela
Marketing Manager: Alexandra Smith
Production Manager: Charles Annis
Project Coordination, Text Design, and Electronic Page Makeup:
     Pre-Press Company, Inc.
Cover Design Manager: John Callahan
Cover Designer: Joe DePinho
Cover Illustration: Getty Images, Inc.
Manufacturing Buyer: Lucy Hebard
Printer and Binder: Courier Corporation
Cover Printer: Courier Corporation

Library of Congress Cataloging-in-Publication Data
Hult, Christine A.
   Researching and writing across the curriculum/Christine A. Hult.—3rd ed.
     p. cm.
   Includes bibliographical references and index.
   ISBN 0-321-33808-1
     1. Report writing. 2. Research. 3. Library resources. I. Title.

LB2369 .H84 2006
808'.02—dc22   2005004341

Please visit our website at http://www.ablongman.com

ISBN 0-321-33808-1

1 2 3 4 5 6 7 8 9 10—CRS—08 07 06 05

Contents

Preface   ix

PART ONE   RESEARCH METHODS

CHAPTER 1   College Research   1

Introduction   1

Research in the Disciplines   2

The Importance of Research   4

Thinking Critically   5
Establishing Your Purpose and Raising Questions   5
Analyzing the Topic   6
Synthesizing   7
Making Inferences   7
Evaluating   7

The General Process of Research   8
Preparation   9
Incubation   9
Illumination   10
Verification   10
A Physician Uses the Research Process   11

Engaging Critically and Actively in the Reading Process   13
Reading on Three Different Levels   14
Structuring Your Reading Process   17
Annotating the Text While Reading   18
Using Sources Responsibly and Avoiding Plagiarism   20

CHAPTER 2   Finding Library and Internet Resources   23

Introduction   23

Libraries and General Library Resources   24
The Library Reference Area   24
General Reference Works   25
Locating Library Books and Resources:
Computer Cataloging Systems   29

Locating Articles in Serials: Popular Periodicals   *35*
Locating Articles in Serials: Professional Journals   *37*
Locating Government Documents   *38*
Other Technologies   *39*
Electronic Full-text Databases   *40*

Internet Resources   41
Using Search Tools to Locate Information on Your Topic   *41*
Using Internet Library and Periodicals Collections   *44*
Bookmarking Important Sites   *48*

CHAPTER 3   Using Library and Internet Sources   51

Introduction   51

Preparation and Incubation   51
Finding a Topic   *52*

Selecting a Specific Topic   53

Narrowing and Focusing the Topic   53
Asking Research Questions   *53*
Developing a Hypothesis   *53*
Gathering Research Materials   *54*

Taking Notes with Photocopies and Printouts   56
Photocopies and Database Printouts   *56*
Printing Internet Sources   *56*
Downloading Internet Sources   *56*
Saving Online Sources   *57*
The Working Bibliography   *58*
Developing a Search Strategy   *61*
Outlining a Time Frame   *63*
Locating Sources   *65*
Evaluating Print and Electronic Sources   *65*
Working with Sources   *70*

Avoiding Plagiarism   71
Acknowledge Required   *71*
No Acknowledge Required   *72*
Unintentional Plagiarism   *72*
International Plagiarism   *72*

Illumination and Verification   77
Evaluation   *77*
Writing from Sources   *77*

CHAPTER 4   Planning and Writing Your Research Paper   91

Introduction   91

Planning Your Research Paper   91
Rhetorical Situation   92
Organization   95

Outlining and Drafting Your Research Paper   101
Constructing an Outline or Plan   101
Drafting Your Paper   102
Avoiding Writer's Block   107
Collaborating   108
Drafting with a Computer   109

CHAPTER 5   Revising and Formatting Your Research Paper   111

Introduction   111

Rewriting Your Research Paper   111
Rereading and Reviewing Your Draft   112
Revising for Structure and Style   112
Improving Paragraphs   114
Improving Sentences   114
Improving Words   115
Editing for Grammar, Punctuation, and Spelling   117
Rewriting Your Paper Using Word Processing   119
Incorporating Reference Materials   120
Incorporating Direct Quotations   121
Formatting and Printing Using Computers   123
Proofreading   123

Considering Formal Details   124
Word Processing   125
Line Spacing   125
Margins   125
Title Page   125
Numbering   126
Indentation and Word Spacing   126
The Abstract   126
The Endnote Page   126
The References Page   127
The Annotated Bibliography   127
The Appendix   128

Sample Student Paper   129

PART TWO MODEL RESEARCH PROJECTS

CHAPTER 6   Writing a Research Paper in the Humanities   147

Introduction   147

Reports and Research Papers   148

The Inquiry Process in the Humanities   149
The Importance of Texts in the Humanities   150
Research in the Humanities   151
Acceptable Evidence in the Humanities   153

Primary Research in the Humanities   156
Using Primary Texts   156
Life-History Interviewing   163

Organizing and Writing the Humanities Research Paper   166
Outlining   167
Writing the First Draft   169

Documentation in the Humanities: MLA Style   170
Internal Citation   170
The Reference List   173

Model References: Language and Literature (MLA)   175
Type of Reference   175

Footnote and Bibliography Style   183

Model Notes: Humanities   185
Type of Reference   185

Exercises and Research Project   187

Discipline-Specific Resources for Humanities   188
Technology and the Humanities   188
Resources for Humanities   188

Sample Research Paper: Humanities Format (MLA)   192

CHAPTER 7   Writing a Review Paper in Science and Technology   203

Introduction   203

The Inquiry Process in Science and Technology   204
The Importance of Observation in the Sciences   204
The Importance of Formulating and Testing Hypotheses   205
Critical Scientific Research   206
The Importance of Replicability and Scientific Debate   207

Primary Research in the Sciences   208
   Lab Experiments and Reports   208
   Field Observations and Reports   210

Organizing and Writing the Scientific Review Paper   216
   Arranging the Materials   217
   Writing the First Draft: Verification   218

Documentation in Science and Technology   218
   Internal Citation   219
   The Reference List   221

Model References: Natural and Physical Sciences
   (Number System) (CBE)   223

Exercises and Research Project   227

Discipline-Specific Resources for Science and Technology   228
   Resources for the Sciences and Technology   228

Sample Engineering Paper: Science Format (CBE)   233

**CHAPTER 8   Writing a Research Paper in
Social Science   253**

Introduction   253

The Inquiry Process in Social Science   254
   The Importance of Observing Human Behavior   255
   *The Importance of Understanding Human
   Consciousness   255*
   Objectivity versus Subjectivity   257

Primary Research in the Social Sciences   258
   Step 1—Problem and Hypothesis   258
   Step 2—Research Design   259
   Step 3—Gathering the Data   259
   Step 4—Analyzing the Data   259
   Step 5—Interpreting the Results   261
   Social Science Research Designs   261

Organizing and Writing the Social Science
   Research Paper   273
   Organizing Your Materials   274
   Planning and Outlining   274
   Writing the First Draft   275

Manuscript Preparation (APA Style)   277
   Title Page   277
   Abstract   278

Text   278
Introduction   278
Body   278
References Page   279
Appendix   279

Documentation in Social Science: The Author/Date
   Style (APA)   279
   Internal Citation   280
   The Reference List in APA Style   282

Model References: Social Science (APA)   282
   Type of Reference   282

Exercises and Research Project   290

Discipline-Specific Resources for Social Science   291
   Resources for the Social Sciences   291

Sample Research Paper: Social Science Format (APA)   295

**CHAPTER 9   Writing a Research Report
in Business   311**

Introduction   311

The Inquiry Process in Business   312
   Three Types of R & D   312
   Other Types of Business Research   313

Primary Research in Business   313
   Presenting Business Information   314
   Conducting a Survey in Business   314

Organizing and Writing the Business Report   319

Documentation in Business and Economics   320
   Internal Citations   320
   The Reference List   321

Model References: Business and Economics (Chicago)   322
   Type of Reference   322

Exercises and Research Project   326

Discipline-Specific Resources for Business and Economics   326
   Technology and Business   326

Sample Research Report: Business and Economics
   Format (Chicago)   329

Index   341

Preface

Researching and Writing Across the Curriculum, Third Edition, is an interdisciplinary research text that introduces you to research processes used in the sciences and technology, the social sciences, the humanities, and business. By reading this book you will gain experience in posing and solving problems common to an academic discipline, learning both primary research strategies and library and Internet research strategies. A comprehensive list of library and Internet resources is included in each chapter to provide you with access to the important tools used by researchers.

Also included, as examples, are model student reports and research papers from various disciplines to show you how your peers have solved research problems similar to yours. The exercises are designed to guide you through research processes and to teach the important supporting skills of summarizing, synthesizing, and critiquing source materials. Complete listings of citations show you how to document your sources within each discipline. In addition, this book stresses principles of research presentation and documentation common to all disciplines.

Perhaps you may feel a bit inadequate when thinking about college-level research. You may find you were introduced to various disciplines piecemeal and may be justifiably confused about the larger issue of research—its nature and use in the humanities, social sciences, sciences, and business. Furthermore, you may be confused about the relationships among academic disciplines. By providing you with an introduction to college writing, reading, thinking, and research, this book will show you important relationships among disciplines.

Many of the research guides now on the market fail to provide the broad introduction to research that you need. Traditional research texts are often focused very narrowly on the library "term paper." They discuss formal considerations at length, from the form of note cards and bibliography cards to the form of a completed term paper. But they do not explore the entire research process, which is an integral part of any successful research project. In contrast, *Researching and Writing Across the Curriculum* explains and fosters intellectual inquiry; compares research in the humanities with that in the sciences, social sciences, and business; and provides students with logical practice in research methodology.

Researching and Writing Across the Curriculum is divided into two main sections. Part One, Research Methods, contains five chapters of general information about research methods and resources in the academic disciplines. This part first introduces you to college research in general, and then to library and Internet resources and library and Internet research methods. Next, you'll find explicit instruction in the planning, writing, revising, and presentation of research papers in any field.

Part Two, Model Research Projects, offers specific guidance in writing research papers for humanities, science and technology, social science, and business. Exercises in Part Two are designed to help you conduct your own research projects in a systematic and organized fashion.

NEW TO THIS EDITION

In this edition, I have updated and expanded in several areas to make the book even more user-friendly. In Part One, I added a more attention-getting introduction that will draw students into the excitement of research and expanded the section on critical thinking and reading skills, describing in detail how to read a text closely and carefully. I expanded the discussion of educational values and academic honesty (avoiding plagiarism), since this is of ongoing concern to both teachers and students. I provide a balanced explanation of library and Internet resources so that students will see the need and place for both. The discussion of information resources—library databases and electronic full-text databases, electronic search engines, and keywords for searching—has been expanded considerably. I also go into more depth about the research process: selecting and narrowing a topic, summarizing and paraphrasing from sources, and taking notes with photocopies and printouts. Throughout this section, I stress the appropriate use and attribution of sources, particularly when working with Internet sources. In Part Two, I have expanded the number of models of electronic citations in each discipline. I have included new model papers in the humanities, social sciences, and sciences (engineering) that are student-friendly and accessible as well as timely and interesting. Throughout Part Two, I have highlighted the disciplinary aspects of writing and research in the humanities, science and technology, social sciences, and business.

Researching and Writing Across the Curriculum is both a comprehensive guide to research processes and an easy-to-use, complete reference tool designed to be used throughout your academic career and into your professional life. As with all research, my own work on this book has been a challenging process of discovery. I am grateful to the many researchers and theorists in the field of composition and rhetoric on whose work this book is built. Although I have cited in chapter notes only those authors whose ideas directly contributed to my own, many others contributed their ideas indirectly through journals, conferences, and textbooks. Teachers I have studied and worked with, students who have patiently tried my ideas, and friends and family who have supported me along the way have all helped in the genesis of this book. I wish to thank in particular the students who allowed me to use their work as models.

Finally, I am grateful to the editors and production team at Longman for their personal, professional attention, and to the reviewers of this edition of my manuscript.

Christine A. Hult

1

College Research

INTRODUCTION

As a college student, regardless of your major, you are probably taking courses in the sciences, such as geology or chemistry; in the social sciences, such as sociology or political science; and in the humanities, such as philosophy or English literature. You may also be taking "applied" courses in home economics, agriculture, or business. Each of these academic disciplines seeks understanding and knowledge in traditional ways; each shares with all other academic disciplines basic research processes. In this book, we explore the nature of college work in an effort to understand both the general processes of research and the particular research tools used in the disciplines. Exploring these important relationships among disciplines will help you to interpret and use the research methods and established ways of proceeding employed by researchers.

The effects of back surgery on worker's compensation patients; a multivoiced narrative on surviving breast cancer; the effectiveness of a cholesterol education class; the structure and function of a cardiac protein; a biogeography of South American aphids; the effects of a prescribed burn on wildlands; bicycle seat interface pressure; calibration of atomic oxygen instruments. This is a listing of research projects in many disciplines undertaken by undergraduate students much like you, carried out in a variety of disciplines. Research, and writing about that research, is invaluable for students' intellectual growth.

RESEARCH IN THE DISCIPLINES

What is research? Broadly defined, it is systematic inquiry designed to further our knowledge and understanding of a subject. Using this definition, nearly everything you do in college is "research." You seek to discover information about people, objects, and nature; to revise the information you discover in light of new information that comes to your attention; and to interpret your experience and communicate that interpretation to others. This is how learning proceeds both for individuals and for all human beings together as we search for knowledge and understanding of our world.

People are interpretive animals. In our interaction with the world, we seek to represent internally to ourselves what we have experienced externally. We generally assume that the universe is an orderly, reasonable, meaningful place, and that, if we but look, we will be able to discern that order. However, we may also be confronted with problematic experiences in the world. At such times, since we are inquiring animals, we seek to discover the cause or a reasonable explanation for that problematic experience; that is, we "research" the subject to discover its meaning.

In the accompanying cartoon, the character is confronted with a problematic experience. As he relaxes under the shady tree, he is rudely awakened from his reverie. In searching his own internal representation of the world, the character finds a "solution" to the problem. The humor of the cartoon is the result of its parody of Archimedes, who shouted "Eureka" when he discovered a new principle of physics, and of Newton, who deduced the principle of gravity from a falling apple. We recognize the circular reasoning the character has used in solving the problem. Because we are familiar with the orderly procedures people use to solve problems—procedures that this character has not used—we understand that his response is ludicrous.

FIGURE 1-1
Reprinted by permission of Johnny Hart and Creators Syndicate, Inc.

This same issue, concerning the falling apple, could be researched by a scientist, perhaps a physicist, who might ask, "Why does the apple fall?" "How fast does it fall?" "How long will it take to reach the ground?" Such questions involve broad issues about the nature of the physical universe and the "laws" that govern it. The physicist observes natural phenomena within reasonable limits and then develops a systematic body of principles to account for or predict other similar events in the universe. For example, physicists have deduced the following principle: Any object at a distance from the earth will be acted on by gravity, which is the force of mutual attraction among all bodies, proportional to the product of the masses of the bodies divided by the square of the distance between them.

A social scientist, perhaps an economist, researching the falling-apple issue might focus on the need for a reliable food source in a society, asking such questions as "How do people provide for their basic need for food?" "What laws of supply and demand operate on the production and distribution of food?" An economist also seeks to define the broad issues of how people in society structure their economic relationships. The economist develops a systematic body of ideas to be used in accounting for other similar economic systems or events. Responding to the falling-apple issue, the economist might make the following statement: "The increasingly prevalent view by consumers that food is a public good and that all citizens should be assured of an adequate and nutritious food supply, plus the fear of prolonged food shortages together have led to a growing demand for change in the agricultural policy of this nation."

A humanist, perhaps a historian, researching this issue would attempt to explain and explore the human experience of the character in the cartoon by asking such questions as "What is the significance of the event to this character and to others of his historical period?" "How does this event relate to other similar events?" The historian would account for, reconstruct, and narrate all the events related to this character's so-called discovery that apples cure hunger, relating the discovery to other more general cultural events. Then the historian might postulate the following explanation: The invention of agriculture was a significant historical event, often called the Neolithic Revolution. Occurring between 8000 and 3000 BC, the Neolithic Revolution involved a change from the gathering society (in which humans gathered wild grasses) to the agricultural society (in which humans prepared the soil and sowed seeds for harvesting).

In these examples, it is clear that researchers in different disciplines ask different questions about the same subject. What distinguishes them is the perspective of the researcher in each field.

THE IMPORTANCE OF RESEARCH

Researching, that is, exploring a problem systematically, is a crucial skill for an educated person. In college, you gain habits of mind that will serve you in every endeavor. Learning to research promotes careful, critical, systematic thinking. Learning to write promotes the effective communication of the ideas and insights gained in the research. Researching and research writing necessarily go together, with each building on and promoting the other.

Researching is different in kind from much of the work you did in high school and even from much of what you are probably doing in your introductory college courses. When you are first introduced to a new subject, you spend a great deal of time memorizing facts. However, once you move beyond that initial phase, you spend much of your time both in and out of the classroom discussing and examining the bases for current beliefs and claims in an academic discipline, claims that may seem questionable. This type of intellectual activity occurs in *addition to* and goes beyond the simple recall of material. College teachers are not concerned with simply imparting information; their main objective is to present and examine the basis on which the information or claim rests. Students and teachers together search out the justification for an accepted belief or claim. This search is research, because only such inquiry, not rote memorization, advances knowledge and understanding in an academic discipline.

As an example, suppose your roommate says to you, "Everybody knows that liberals are bleeding hearts who are soft on criminals." As with all claims, you would have to maintain reservations regarding this statement until you had reasons for believing it. To search out or research those reasons, you might begin by systematically exploring the basis or grounds for the claim. The "everybody knows" part of the statement implies that your roommate considers the claim to be common knowledge. But is it? Your roommate would need a pretty large research sample to justify the claim that "everybody knows. . . ." At the outset, then, you could reasonably discount the claim as unwarranted simply because it is overgeneralized.

What about the basis for equating liberalism with a softness on criminals? Perhaps your roommate is basing the equation on an assumption that being liberal means having a hyperactive social conscience. But perhaps your roommate is unaware that, as you find out from looking it up in the library, liberalism is a political and social philosophy that advocates individual freedom and the protection of civil liberties. A person may be liberal, you discover, and still advocate a strong system of criminal justice or even favor capital punishment. Consequently, the grounds on which your roommate made the claim are tenuous. As a rational person, once you have investigated—that is, researched—the particular grounds, you would have to reject the claim.

Similarly, much of the work you will be doing in college, and much of the work researchers do, involves looking into a particular claim. A second kind of research involves the exploration of a problem or event to arrive at a claim or hypothesis. Whether you are investigating a claim or hypothesis made by someone else or exploring a problem you have encountered to arrive at a hypothesis yourself, the research process will be much the same.

EXERCISE

Briefly describe a research project that you did in the past. What exactly did it involve? How did you feel about the project's success? What did you learn from it?

THINKING CRITICALLY

A term often used to describe the way in which educated people approach the knowledge building inherent in research is *critical thinking*. To think critically is to make a conscious effort to delve beneath the surface of things. Much of the process of achieving a college education is designed to help you become a more critical thinker. The term "critical" in this case does not mean the same as "criticize." Critical thinking does not imply a negative attitude; rather, critical thinking involves the ability to contemplate, question, and explore ideas in depth without accepting easy answers. When you identify the political propaganda in a political speech, you exhibit critical thinking. When you recognize the overblown claims for a product in an advertisement, you also exhibit critical thinking.

The processes involved in thinking critically are the same for all forms of communication—speaking and writing as well as listening and reading. They include (1) establishing your purpose and raising questions, (2) analyzing the topic, (3) synthesizing, (4) inferring unstated meanings, and (5) evaluating. Although they tend to occur in the order given, this is not a strict necessity. Critical insight can sometimes be gained by doing some of these processes simultaneously or by redoing previous steps.

Establishing Your Purpose and Raising Questions

The key first step in critical thinking is to have a clear sense of purpose. *Why* are you interested in this topic? Why do you want to learn about it in depth? What specific aspects of the topic most concern you? What is your goal? Having a clear sense of purpose is crucial, because it will guide you through the entire process of critical thinking. Even if your topic is assigned, rather than one you choose yourself, you must still establish a purpose of your own. Among other things, knowing your purpose will allow you to formulate more specific questions about the topic. And these questions themselves will help focus your exploration.

For example, let's say you're in the market for a used (or "pre-owned," as they say in the trade) car. If you're a careful buyer, you won't just head for the nearest used-car lot and let yourself be talked into the first car that catches your eye. It's more likely that you'll do some research—by reading *Consumer Reports,* talking to your parents or knowledgeable friends, showing the car to a trusted mechanic, and so on. And if you know what kind of car you're looking for and why, you'll probably ask the right kinds of questions to elicit the information you need to make a wise decision.

Analyzing the Topic

Analyzing something means mentally dividing it into its parts. Sometimes, when the subject being analyzed has obvious component parts, this dividing is straightforward. For example, a music reviewer will typically analyze a symphonic performance according to the symphony's different movements, and a drama critic will typically analyze a play according to its acts and scenes.

But critical analysis usually goes beyond such obvious procedures. Guided by particular purposes and questions, a critical analyst will often see *other* ways to dissect a subject. For example, the music reviewer may choose to analyze the performance of the symphony according to the different instrumentalists, and the drama critic may decide to focus on the acting, the costumes, or the sets. The mode of analysis, in short, is not necessarily predetermined by the object of analysis; more often it is governed by the purposes and interests of the analyst.

The purposes and interests of your sources of information should also be taken into account. Analysis often depends to some degree on information provided by other people, who have their own interests, biases, beliefs, and assumptions. As a critical thinker, you should always be aware of other people's orientations and try to keep them in mind as you absorb their information. Information from any source can lack objectivity, so it's a good idea to routinely gather information from multiple, independent sources and compare each source to the others.

Synthesizing

Synthesizing is the opposite of analyzing. Instead of taking something apart, synthesis puts things together. But this does not mean that synthesizing merely restores something to the way it was before analysis. Rather, synthesis seeks to find *new* ways of assembling things, *new* relationships among the parts, *new* combinations. Like analysis, this process is governed by the critical thinker's purposes.

For example, let's say you live in the northern part of the country and you're looking for a car that will get you back and forth to school through the winter. You have looked at various cars and analyzed them in various ways, but you're uncertain which one is best for you. As you ponder the situation, you realize that what matters most to you is not the purchase price or the fuel efficiency or the looks of a car, but rather how suitable it is for winter driving. You want a reliable car that has a good heating/defrosting system, a good ignition system, solid traction (either four-wheel drive or front-wheel drive), and all-weather tires in decent shape. Also, it should be a dark color (for better visibility in snow). A snowboard/ski rack would be a plus. This set of features would not emerge from any standard analysis. Rather, it is the result of synthesizing, guided by your own purposes and needs.

Making Inferences

Another important critical thinking skill is the ability to make inferences, or "read between the lines." People often do not say exactly what's on their mind. Sometimes their lack of candor is just an effort to be tactful, sometimes it's due to uncertainty about what to say, sometimes it's more deceptive than that. When you interpret what people don't say or don't say fully, you are making inferences. For example, if a used-car salesman evades your question about a car's heating system and you thereby infer that there's something wrong with the heating system, you are exhibiting an important kind of critical thinking. (Note how *purpose* once again plays a key role—in this case, the purpose or intent of the message producer.)

Evaluating

Once you've determined your purpose, analyzed your topic, synthesized new ideas, and made appropriate inferences, you are ready to "put it all together"—that is, to **evaluate** the results of these four steps. Evaluation involves examining everything you have done up to this point and determining what it all adds up to. In the case of buying a used car, you would review what you had learned from going through the first four steps; in particular, you would check to see if the information you had gathered consistently pointed to the same conclusion. If not, you would identify the contradictions and try to resolve them. Perhaps your sources of information were not as knowledgeable as you had thought; perhaps you didn't ask them the right questions. In any case, this evaluation itself is a form of critical thinking, which requires a willingness to confront and resolve inconsistencies in your reasoning and information-gathering.

If at this point there are still troubling inconsistencies in your thinking about the topic, you may want to "change the playing field"— that is, broaden your inquiry. This can be done in either of two ways. First, you can use additional sources of information: talk to more people, consult other publications, gain some more firsthand experience. Alternatively, you can reexamine the initial premises of your investigation. It could be that these have changed in the course of your inquiry— or were never quite accurate in the first place. For example, in your search for reliable transportation for winter weather, perhaps you assumed too quickly that you needed a used car when public transit might be just as good or even better. Sometimes it is only at this evaluation stage that nagging discrepancies and uncertainties are resolved and critical thinking is fully rewarded.

EXERCISES

The used-car case offers a good illustration of how different interests will cause people to analyze something in different ways.

1. How would a used-car salesman or other seller likely analyze (describe) a car?

2. How would an auto mechanic likely analyze that same car?

3. How would *you* analyze a car, if you were shopping for one today?

4. In each of the above cases, explain how a particular set of purposes gives rise to a particular basis of analysis.

THE GENERAL PROCESS OF RESEARCH

Many accounts of the process of research have been written by scientists, artists, and philosophers. Researchers generally agree about the outlines of the process regardless of the discipline. The process often begins with a troubled feeling about something observed or experienced, followed by a conscious probing for a solution to the problem, a time of subconscious activity, an intuition about the solution, and finally a systematic testing to verify the solution. This process may be described in a number of ways but may generally be divided into four stages: preparation, incubation, illumination, and verification.[1] We will examine these stages in order, but during a research project, each stage does not necessarily neatly follow the next. Quite probably the researcher moves back and forth freely among the stages and may even skip a stage for a time, but generally these four stages are present in most research projects.

Preparation

The preparation stage of the research process involves the first awareness by researchers that a problem or a question exists that needs systematic inquiry. Researchers formulate the problem and begin to explore it. As they attempt to articulate the exact dimensions and parameters of a particular problem, they use language or symbols of their discipline that can be more easily manipulated than unarticulated thoughts or the data itself. By stating the problem in a number of ways, looking at it from various angles, trying to define its distinctive characteristics, and attempting possible solutions, researchers come to define for themselves the subtleties of the problem. Preparation is generally systematic, but it may also include the researchers' prior experiences and the intuitions they have developed over time.

Incubation

The incubation stage usually follows the preparation stage and includes a period of intense subconscious activity that is hard to describe or define. Because incubation is so indistinct, people tend to discount it as unimportant, but the experience of many researchers shows that it is crucial to allow an idea to brew and simmer in the subconscious if a creative solution is to be reached. Perhaps you have had the experience of trying and failing to recall the name of a book you recently read. You tell your conversation partner, "Go ahead. It'll come to me." A few minutes later, when you are not consciously trying to recall the name but have gone on to other matters in your conversation, you announce, *"The Scarlet Letter,"* out of the blue. This is an example of the way your subconscious mind continues to work on a problem while your conscious mind has gone on to another activity.

We need to allow ourselves sufficient time for incubating. If you have ever watched a chicken egg in an incubator, you will have a sense of how this works. The egg rests in warmth and quiet; you see no action whatsoever, but you know that beneath that shell tremendous activity is going on. The first peck on the shell from the chick about to hatch comes as a surprise. The chick's first peck is analogous to the next stage of the process, illumination. You cannot really control the incubation of a problem, but you can prepare adequately and then give yourself enough time for subconscious activity.

Illumination

In the illumination stage, as with the hatching chick, there is an imaginative breakthrough. An idea begins to surface out of its concealing shell, perhaps a little at a time. Or the researcher leaps to a hypothesis, a possible solution to the problem, that seems intuitively to fit. Isaac Newton discovered the law of universal gravitation as he watched an apple fall, and Archimedes deduced his principle of the displacement of water while in the bathtub. The illumination of a hypothesis can come suddenly or gradually, after laborious effort or after an ordinary event that triggers the researcher's thinking along new lines. Remember, though, that the hypothesis comes only after the researcher has investigated the problem thoroughly. The egg must be prepared, fertilized, warmed, and cared for. The solution to a complex problem will come only after much conscious study and preparation in conjunction with subconscious intuition. Sometimes the solution will be not so much a breakthrough as a clearer understanding of the problem itself.

Verification

Once a researcher has arrived at a hypothesis, he or she must systematically test it to discern whether it adequately accounts for all occurrences. Sometimes, this testing requirement necessitates a formal laboratory research experiment; in other cases, only an informal check against the researcher's own experience is necessary. In the sciences, the verification stage tends to be highly rigorous, involved, and lengthy. One should also be prepared at the verification stage to discover that the original hypothesis is not valid. Although we are often reluctant to make mistakes, without a willingness to err we would never be led to make an original contribution. Research often progresses as a series of increasingly intelligent mistakes through which the researcher ultimately is led to a reasonable and workable solution. Sometimes hypothesis testing goes on for years and, for a particularly promising hypothesis, is performed by the research community in general. To be judged as sound, or verified, such a hypothesis must survive the critical scrutiny of the whole research community.

A Physician Uses the Research Process

In the following essay, Charles Nicolle, a physician and scientist of the early twentieth century, describes the research process he used to discover the mechanism that transmitted the disease typhus.[2] As you read the essay, pay particular attention to the research process Nicolle outlines.

The Mechanism of the Transmission of Typhus

Charles Nicolle

It is in this way that the mode of transmission of exanthematic typhus was revealed to me. Like all those who for many years frequented the Moslem hospital of Tunis, I could daily observe typhus patients bedded next to patients suffering from the most diverse complaints. Like those before me, I was the daily and unhappy witness of the strange fact that this lack of segregation, although inexcusable in the case of so contagious a disease, was nevertheless not followed by infection. Those next to the bed of a typhus patient did not contract the disease, while, almost daily, during epidemic outbreaks, I would diagnose contagion in the *douars* (the Arab quarters of the town), and amongst hospital staff dealing with the reception of patients. Doctors and nurses became contaminated in the country in Tunis, but never in the hospital wards. One day, just like any other, immersed no doubt in the puzzle of the process of contagion in typhus, in any case not thinking of it consciously (of this I am quite sure), I entered the doors of the hospital, when a body at the bottom of the passage arrested my attention.

It was a customary spectacle to see poor natives, suffering from typhus, delirious and febrile as they were, gain the landing and collapse on the last steps. As always I strode over the prostrate body. It was at this very moment that the light struck me. When, a moment later, I entered the hospital, I had solved the problem. I knew beyond all possible doubt that this was it. This prostrate body and the door in front of which he had fallen, had suddenly shown me the barrier by which typhus had been arrested. For it to have been arrested, and, contagious as it was in entire regions of the country and in Tunis, for it to have remained harmless once the patient had passed the Reception Office, the agent of infection must have been arrested at this point. Now, what passed through this point? The patient had already been stripped of his clothing and of his underwear; he had been shaved and washed. It was therefore something outside himself, something that he carried on himself, in his underwear, or on his skin, which caused the infection. This could be nothing but a louse. Indeed, it was a louse. The fact that I had ignored this point, that all those who had been observing typhus from the beginnings of history (for it belongs to the most ancient ages of humanity) had failed to notice the incontrovertible and immediately fruitful solution of the method of transmission, had suddenly been revealed to me. I feel somewhat embarrassed about thus putting myself into the picture. If I do so, nevertheless it is because I believe what happened to me is a very edifying and clear example, such as I have failed to find in the case of others. I developed my observation with less timidity. At the time it still had many shortcomings. These, too, appear instructive to me.

If this solution had come home to me with an intuition so sharp that it was almost foreign to me, or at least to my mind, my reason nevertheless told me that it required an experimental demonstration.

Typhus is too serious a disease for experiments on human subjects. Fortunately, however, I knew of the sensitivity of monkeys. Experiments were therefore possible. Had this not been the case I should have published my discoveries without delay, since it was of such immediate benefit to everybody. However, because I could support the discovery with a demonstration, I guarded my secret for some weeks even from those close to me, and made the necessary attempts to verify it. This work neither excited nor surprised me, and was brought to its conclusion within two months.

In the course of this very brief period I experienced what many other discoverers must undoubtedly have experienced also, viz. strange sentiments of the pointlessness of any demonstration, of complete detachment of the mind, and of wearisome boredom. The evidence was so strong, that it was impossible for me to take any interest in the experiments. Had it been of no concern to anybody but myself, I well believe that I should not have pursued this course. It was because of vanity and self-love that I continued. Other thoughts occupied me as well. I confess a failing. It did not arrest my research work. The latter, as I have recounted, led easily and without a single day's delay to the confirmation of the truth, which I had known ever since that revealing event, of which I have spoken.

Nicolle's struggle to discover a solution to the problem of typhus transmission illustrates a research process. Nicolle worked on the problem of typhus transmission both consciously and subconsciously; his "Eureka" experience came unexpectedly and forcefully. Nicolle was awarded the Nobel Prize for medicine in 1928 for his discovery and for the experiments that conclusively confirmed that typhus was indeed transmitted by parasites.

QUESTIONS FOR DISCUSSION

1. What stages of the research process outlined in this chapter are revealed in Nicolle's description?

2. What incongruity led Nicolle to research the question of typhus transmission?

3. What experience triggered the solution to the problem?

4. What procedures did Nicolle use to verify his hypothesis?

5. You may have noticed that Nicolle grew bored at points during his research. What kept him going?

EXERCISES

1. The four research stages discussed in this chapter come from words we often associate with different contexts. For example, we use the term *preparation* in connection with preparing dinner or preparing for a test. First, briefly describe a situation (other than research) commonly associated with each term. Then list any similarities between the connotation of each word in your situation and the particular research stage.

    A. To prepare:

    B. To incubate:

    C. To illuminate:

    D. To verify:

2. Think of an activity with which you are familiar, such as a sport (football or tennis), a hobby (cooking or gardening), or an art (painting or dancing). In one paragraph, describe the process you use when participating in the activity and relate the process to the research stages discussed in this chapter (preparation, incubation, illumination, and verification).

ENGAGING CRITICALLY AND ACTIVELY IN THE READING PROCESS

An important component of any research process is reading. A good reader reads critically; that is, he or she reads with an open mind and a questioning attitude. To be a critical reader, you need to go beyond understanding what the author is saying; you need to challenge or question the author. You may question the validity of the author's main point or ask whether the text agrees or disagrees with other writings on the same topic.

A good reader also reads actively. As you read, you make meaning out of the letters and numbers you encounter in the text. Your mind must be actively engaged with what your eyes see on the page or the computer screen. You may have had the experience of dozing off while reading; when this happens, your mind is not actively engaged, even though your eyes might be following the type. You need to pay close attention, or read actively, in order to understand what you are reading.

Reading on Three Different Levels

As you read critically and actively, you need to attend to three different levels of meaning in order to fully understand what you are reading. The three levels are literal meaning, interpretation, and criticism.

Reading for Literal Meaning

The literal meaning of a text is its explicit meaning as determined by the words on the page and their conventional meanings. Put another way, it is the "surface" meaning of a text. It comprises all those aspects of a text that are available to anyone who reads that text. Literal meaning does not include insinuations, satire, irony, subjective impressions, tone, or other implicit meanings that must be inferred by the reader. (This type of meaning is discussed later.)

When readers start reading a novel, a magazine article, a textbook, or another published text, they expect to move from sentence to sentence in a smooth flow of literal meaning. (Certain kinds of poems might be an exception to this.) Authors, of course, are aware of this and work hard to provide readable texts. Indeed, there seems to be an implicit understanding among readers and authors that the linguistic surface of a text should be coherent, meaningful, and accessible to all. Since the deeper meanings of a text (see later) are derivative of this literal meaning, before you can engage in interpretive or critical reading you must fully understand the literal meaning of a text. Use a good dictionary to help you with any words you don't know. At this stage, you should be a *compliant* reader trying to understand the text on its most basic terms. This is no different from a moviegoer enjoying a sci-fi film as sheer entertainment, rather than analyzing it as a movie critic would.

Reading for Interpretation

Once you have grasped the literal meaning of a text, you should go beyond it to the realm of interpretation. At this level, you are seeking a deeper understanding of the author's ideas, point of view, and attitude. You become more conscious of the author's role in construct-ing the text, giving it a certain "spin," and manipulating the reader. In short, you become a more detached, *resistant*, and analytical reader. You look for clues as to what the author has implied rather than overtly stated, what assumptions the author is making, what audience the au-thor seems to be addressing, and what the author's attitude seems to be as revealed by the tone of his or her writing.

This interpretative work should start with certain words, expres-sions, and statements found in the text, but instead of taking these tex-tual details at face value, you contrast them with alternative words, expressions, and statements that the author opted *not* to use. For exam-ple, if an author consistently used the term *fetus* where he or she could have used the alternative term *unborn child,* you might infer that he or she supports reproductive freedom. In choosing one term over the other, the author would probably be revealing something about his or her stance on abortion. In reading for interpretation, you should always ask yourself questions such as "In what other way(s) could the author have said this?" or "What *didn't* the author say here that he or she could have?" When reading interpretively, you are looking for clues to what the author has implied rather than stated overtly.

Reading Critically

Finally, you want to read beyond the literal and interpretive meanings to evaluate the worth of the writing and the validity of the au-thor's ideas or argument. In this mode, you should be even more de-tached, resistant, and analytical than you were in the interpretive mode. Critical evaluation should be done on two levels, internal and external. With *internal evaluation,* you restrict your attention, as before, to the text itself. This time, though, you focus on the overall logic of the text. Does it hang together? Does it make sense? If the author is making an argument, does it have enough supporting evidence? Does it consider alternative views? Is it appealing mainly to logic, to authority, or to emotion? Does it have any fallacies? With *external evaluation,* you go a step further. Here you evaluate the text against other texts and against your own experience. These other texts could include other writings by the same author—to get a sense of his or her general views or inter-ests—or other writings on the same topic by other authors. Engaging in this kind of comparative analysis allows you to see the text in a larger perspective. This in turn enables you to make an informed guess as to any agenda the author might have, and should give you insight into the author's purpose in writing the text. A comparative analysis will also make it easier for you to guess what's been *left out* of the text. Most writ-ers who are trying to persuade readers to a particular point of view will tend to avoid mentioning facts that might damage their cause. As a critical reader, it is important that you not allow yourself to be manipulated in this way. By looking at other texts and considering your own life experience, you can often make an educated guess as to what's been left unsaid in a particular text.

Using *external evaluation,* try to consider the text against other texts and against your own experience. Normally a good starting point for this aspect of critical reading is to note the company it keeps, that is, other texts with which it is grouped.

Authors who consistently follow one philosophy—of any kind— tend to downplay or overlook ideas or facts that are not compatible with that philosophy. Thus, to broaden your horizons as a critical reader, it is important that you not restrict yourself to that one author's view but consult a range of opinions. The burden is on you, the reader, to educate yourself on the issue, which can best be done by reading widely and critically and then weighing others' ideas against your own experience. You have a right to reject an argument that you judge to be weak or faulty. Reading a work critically, once again, is the hallmark of a critical reader.

CHECKLIST FOR CRITICAL READING

INTERNAL EVALUATION

1. Is the text coherent? Does its logic hang together and make sense?
2. If it constitutes an argument, is it appealing mainly to logic, to authority, or to emotion?
3. Does it have enough supporting evidence?
4. Are there any fallacies in the author's reasoning?
5. Does the author consider alternative views?

EXTERNAL EVALUATION

6. Where was this particular piece of writing published? Does this suggest an ideological slant of any kind?
7. Judging from the author's other writings, what are his or her general views or interests?
8. What purpose or "agenda" might the author have had in writing about this topic?
9. What do other writers have to say about this topic?
10. What might the author have *left out* of the text? Why?
11. How well does the author's representation of the world fit with your own experience?

Structuring Your Reading Process

Reading thoroughly on all three levels is crucial to understanding a text well enough to discuss it intelligently and write about it knowledgeably. If you structure your reading process according to the three steps of previewing, reading, and reviewing, you will understand what you read.

Previewing

Begin any reading session by previewing the material as a whole. By looking ahead, you gain a general sense of what is to come. This sense will help you to predict what to expect from the text as you read and to understand what you are reading. Jot down in a journal or a notebook any questions that occur to you during previewing.

As you approach a book for the first time, look closely at the table of contents to preview the book's main topics. You can also learn the relative importance of topics by scanning the table of contents. Next, preview one chapter. Page through the chapter, reading all chapter headings and subheadings in order to gain a sense of the chapter's organizational structure. Look also at any words that are in bold or italic print. These words are highlighted because the author considered them to be especially important. Finally, preview any graphs, charts, or illustrations. These visuals are included to reinforce or illustrate key ideas or concepts in the chapter. You will want to remember these key ideas.

You should also preview shorter works, such as magazine or journal articles, prior to reading them. An article may include subheadings, which provide an idea of the article's structure. Again, look for highlighted words or graphics in the article, since these can provide clues about key ideas. You should read any biographical information about the author, both to note his or her credentials and to determine whether he or she might have a particular bias on the subject. For example, an author who is a prominent spokesperson for the National Rifle Association will probably express a particular bias about gun control. As a final step in previewing an article, read the opening and closing paragraphs to get an idea of the author's thesis and conclusion.

Reading

After you preview the text, read it carefully and closely. Pace your reading based on the difficulty of the material—the more difficult the material, the more slowly you should read it. You may find that you need to take frequent breaks if the writing is especially dense or contains a lot of new information. You may also find that you need to reread some passages several times in order to understand their meaning.

Material assigned for college classes often is packed with information and therefore requires not only slow reading but also rereading. As you read, pay attention to the three levels of meaning. Do not be surprised if you find yourself having to go back several times—that, too, is an essential part of the reading process.

Reviewing

Once you have read the text thoroughly, go back and review. Pay particular attention to those portions of the text that you previewed. Have the questions you thought of when previewing been answered? If not, reread the relevant passages. It may also help to review with a classmate or a study group; discuss the text with your peers to be sure that your understanding conforms with theirs. Talking about the text with others will also help you communicate your understanding in a meaningful way. If your class has a computer bulletin board or online discussion group, post any questions that you still have about the reading. Like discussing the text, writing about it in such forums will help you articulate your ideas, which will serve you well when you are asked to write about the material more formally, in an essay or for an exam. To gain a thorough understanding of what you have read, plan to review the material several times.

Annotating the Text While Reading

One way to ensure that you are reading actively is to annotate the text as you read. Annotating means making summary notes in the margins of the text as well as underlining or highlighting important words and passages. It is usually best to preview the material before annotating. It is during the actual reading process that annotating is very important. Your annotations should restate concisely the key ideas you have just read. Take care, however, not to overannotate. You need to be selective so that you don't end up highlighting everything in the text. The excerpt below illustrates a student's annotation of a passage on public opinion polls from a government textbook.

Public opinion polls were first developed by Gallup in 1932

Public opinion polling is a relatively new science. It was first developed by a young man named George Gallup, who initially did some polling for his mother-in-law, a long-shot candidate for secretary of state in Iowa in 1932. With the Democratic land-slide of that year, she won a stunning victory, thereby further stimulating Gallup's interest in politics. The mighty oak of public opinion polling has grown from that little acorn. The firm that Gallup founded spread throughout the democratic world, and in some languages, *Gallup* is actually the word used for an opinion poll.

Polls use representative samples of populations

It would be prohibitively expensive and time consuming to ask every citizen his or her opinion on a whole range of issues. Instead, polls rely on a sample of the population—a relatively small proportion of people who are chosen to represent the whole. Herbert Asher draws an analogy to a blood test to illustrate the principle of sampling. Your doctor does not need to drain a gallon of blood from you to determine whether you have mononucleosis, AIDS, or any other disease. Rather, a small sample of blood will reveal its properties.

An important technique called random sampling is used in polls

In public opinion polling, a sample of about 1,000 to 1,500 people can accurately represent the "universe" of potential voters. The key to the accuracy of opinion polls is the technique of random sampling, which operates on the principle that everyone should have an equal probability of being selected as part of the sample. Your chance of being asked to be in the poll should therefore be as good as that of anyone else—rich or poor, African American or White, young or old, male or female. If the sample is randomly drawn, about 12 percent of those interviewed will be African American, slightly over 50 percent female, and so forth, matching the population as a whole.

Excerpt from *Government in America*, 6th ed., by George C. Edwards III, Martin P. Wattenberg, and Robert L. Lineberry (2002). Longman Publishers. Reprinted by permission.

EXERCISE

Several more paragraphs from the government textbook appear below. Annotate these paragraphs, underlining important ideas and noting key points in the margins.

Remember that the science of polling involves estimation; a sample can represent the population with only a certain degree of confidence. The level of confidence is known as the sampling error, which depends on the size of the sample. The more people interviewed in a poll, the more confident one can be of the results. A typical poll of about 1,500 to 2,000 respondents has a sampling error of 95 percent. What this means is that 95 percent of the time the poll results are within 3 percent of what the entire population thinks. If 60 percent of the sample say they approve of the job the president is doing, one can be pretty certain that the true figure is between 57 and 63 percent.

In order to obtain results that will usually be within sampling error, researchers must follow proper sampling techniques. In perhaps the most infamous survey ever, a 1936 *Literary Digest* poll underestimated the vote for President Franklin Roosevelt by 19 percent, erroneously predicting a big victory for Republican Alf Landon. The well-established magazine suddenly became a laughingstock and soon went out of business. Although the number of responses the magazine obtained for its poll was a staggering 2,376,000, its polling methods were badly flawed. In trying to reach as many people as possible, the magazine drew names from the biggest lists they could find: telephone books and motor vehicle records. In the midst of the Great Depression, the people on these lists were above the average income level (only 40 percent of the public had telephones then; fewer still owned cars) and were more likely to vote Republican. The moral of the story is this: Accurate representation, not the number of responses, is the most important feature of a public opinion survey. Indeed, as polling techniques have advanced over the last 50 years, typical sample sizes have been getting smaller, not larger.

Excerpt from *Government in America*, 6th ed., by George C. Edwards III, Martin P. Wattenberg, and Robert L. Lineberry (2002). Longman Publishers. Reprinted by permission.

USING SOURCES RESPONSIBLY AND AVOIDING PLAGIARISM

Writers gain credibility through the use of information from experts. It is the responsibility of research authors to be certain that any information from another author, whether paraphrased, summarized, or quoted, is accurately relayed and clearly acknowledged. Integrating source information into your own writing is a skill that takes practice. Being careless about your sources can lead to a serious academic offense called plagiarism—with serious consequences such as a failing grade for the course or even expulsion from school. *Plagiarism* is defined as the unauthorized or misleading use of the language and text of another author. Whenever you use exact words form a source, this must be indicated clearly through the use of a signal phrase, quotation marks, and an in-text citation at the point where the source information is quoted. When you paraphrase or summarize ideas, similarly you need to give proper attribution to the source (see Chapters 6–9 for information about in-text citations). It is not enough to list the authors in footnotes or bibliographies. Readers must be able to tell as they are reading your paper exactly what information came from which source and what information is your own contribution to the paper.

When writing a research paper, you must acknowledge any original information, ideas, and illustrations that you find in another author's work, whether it is in print or on the Internet. Acknowledging the work of other authors is called documenting sources. (The appropriate forms for documentation are discussed in Chapters 6–9.) When incorporating information form other authors into a research paper, you can present the source information in the form of a direct quotation; a paraphrase, in which you restate the ideas in your own words; or a summary, in which you condense the information. By incorporating source information appropriately, you will avoid plagiarism. (See also page 70, Working with Sources.)

NOTES

1. Adaptation of excerpt from "The Four Stages of Inquiry," in Richard E. Young, Alton L. Becker, and Kenneth L. Pike, *Rhetoric: Discovery and Change* (New York: Harcourt Brace Jovanovich, Inc., 1970). Reprinted by permission of the publisher. This four-step problem-solving process (preparation, incubation, illumination, verification) was first outlined by Wallas in 1926 (*The Art of Thought*, New York: Harcourt, Brace).

2. Charles Nicolle, "The Mechanism and Transmission of Typhus," in Rene Taton, *Reason and Chance in Scientific Discovery* (New York: Philosophical Library, 1957), pp. 76–78. Reprinted by permission of Philosophical Library, Inc.

2

Finding Library and Internet Resources

INTRODUCTION

In their experience with researching, students range from experts to novices. Your own level of experience will fall somewhere along that continuum. But even if you have used libraries and the Internet for research projects before, there is always more to learn. College libraries are large, complex entities that often seem to have a life of their own. They are constantly changing as new information, and methods to access information, are incorporated by librarians. Similarly, the Internet is an enormous, complex "web" of information that refuses to sit still. To be a researcher today means to be familiar with both library and Internet resources.

Your library contains many important general research tools that you must become familiar with in order to conduct any research project. Your library also contains specific resources that are important for research in particular disciplines. Furthermore, many of today's important research tools and resources are now available on the Internet as well as in the library. This chapter covers information on general library and Internet resources; for specific library and Internet resources used in the humanities, the sciences and technology, the social sciences, and business, turn to the chapters on these disciplines in Part Two. You may find that some of this chapter is review, but you will certainly also encounter sources and information of which you were not previously aware.

LIBRARIES AND GENERAL LIBRARY RESOURCES

The Library Reference Area

Most library research begins in the library reference area. Reference librarians are excellent resources when you need help finding information in the library. However, you need to know enough about libraries to ask the librarian to help you, just as you need to know enough about your car to suggest to a mechanic where to begin when your car needs repair. It is not productive to walk up to a mechanic and simply ask for help. You need to explain the specifics of your particular problem and describe the make, model, age, and condition of your car. Similarly, you need to tell a librarian what kind of project you are working on, what information you need, and in what form that information is likely to be stored. So that you can ask the right questions, you must first take the time to learn your way around the library. Working your way through this chapter is a good place to begin.

Librarians use terminology that you should become familiar with. Particular terms are defined throughout this chapter. We will start by looking at some major library sources and what distinguishes them.

In the heading of this section of the chapter you saw the word *reference.* As you might suspect, a reference is something that *refers* to something else. In your library there is an area designated as the reference area and a person called the reference librarian. The reference area may be a separate room or simply a section of the library. In the reference area you will find books containing brief factual answers to such questions as, What is the meaning of a particular word? What is the population density of a particular state? What is the birthplace of a certain famous person? Also in the reference area are books that refer you to other sources. These library tools—bibliographies and indexes—will help you find particular articles written about particular subjects. The reference area of the library is usually the place to begin any research project. Reference sources include the following general types of works:

Abstracts: Short summaries of larger works; may be included in an index

Almanacs: Compendia of useful and interesting facts on specific subjects

Atlases: Bound volumes of maps, charts, or tables illustrating a specific subject

Bibliographies: Lists of books or articles about particular related subjects

Biographies: Works that provide information on the lives and writings of famous people, living and dead

Dictionaries: Works that provide information about words, such as meaning, spelling, usage, pronunciation

Encyclopedias: Works that provide concise overviews of topics, including people, places, ideas, subject areas

Handbooks: Books of instruction, guidance, or information of a general nature

Indexes: Books or parts of books that point to where information can be found, such as in journals, magazines, newspapers, or books

Reviews: Works that analyze and comment on other works, such as films, novels, plays, or even research

Serials: Periodicals (magazines) that are published at specific intervals and professional (scholarly) journals that contain articles and research reports in a specific field

General Reference Works

For most research projects, you need to discover general information relevant to your research. The most commonly used general reference works are dictionaries, encyclopedias, and biographies. Depending on your project, you may also need to consult atlases, almanacs, and handbooks.

Dictionaries

Dictionaries provide information about words: definitions, pronunciations, usage, origin, and changes of meaning. It is essential that you have a good desk dictionary to consult for all your writing. Some good ones include:

American Heritage College Dictionary. 4th ed. Boston: Houghton, 2002.

Random House Unabridged Dictionary. 2nd ed. New York: Random, 1993.

Webster's Collegiate Dictionary. 11th ed. Springfield, MA: Merriam, 2003.

Webster's Dictionary and *Roget's Thesaurus*, Searchable through *refdesk.com* <http://www.refdesk.com>.

Encyclopedias

Encyclopedias provide concise information on people, places, subjects, events, and ideas. Encyclopedias are particularly useful for general background information on a specific subject or person. Look in the encyclopedia's index for references to related subtopics and articles within the encyclopedia. Both general and specialized encyclopedias exist. The specialized encyclopedias, for example, the *Encyclopedia of American History,* cover information in particular disciplines or fields. These encyclopedias often contain bibliographies that can lead you to other sources in your research. (For specialized encyclopedias, see "Discipline-Specific Resources," in each chapter of Part Two.) Some general encyclopedias include the following:

> *Encyclopaedia Britannica.* Chicago: Encyclopaedia Britannica, 1997.
> *Encyclopedia Americana.* Rev. ed. New York: Grolier, 2003.
> *Academic American Encyclopedia.* Rev. ed. Danbury, CT: Grolier, 1998.
> *Encyberpedia: The Living Encyclopedia from Cyberspace* <http://www.encyberpedia.com>.

Biographies

Biographies provide information on the lives and work of famous people. As with encyclopedias, there are both general and specialized biographies. (Specialized biographies are listed in "Discipline-Specific Resources," in each chapter of Part Two.) General biographies include the following:

> *Biography and Genealogy Master Index.* Detroit: Gale, 1985, with updates. Combines into one listing access to biographical sketches found in biographical dictionaries, subject encyclopedias, volumes of literary criticism, and other indexes. Covers both current and retrospective biographies, mostly of notable Americans from all fields.
> *Current Biography.* New York: Wilson, 1940 to present. Covers important living people from all fields, including popular figures. Published monthly with bound annual cumulation (yearbook).
> *Dictionary of American Biography.* 17 vols. plus supplements. New York: Scribners', 1943 to present. Covers famous Americans who are no longer living. Includes biographies of noteworthy figures from America's colonization on.

Bibliographies

Bibliographies are lists of books or articles about particular subjects. Some bibliographies are found at the end of articles or books; others are entire books in themselves.

Bibliographic Index. New York: Wilson, 1938 to present. Lists bibliographies found in other sources, including bibliographies in books, journals, and single volumes.

Guide to Reference Books, 11th ed. Robert Balay, et al., Chicago: American Library Association. Lists and describes reference works that can provide access to other works.

Reviews

Reviews are brief critical discussions of important works in a particular field. The following are some indexes that provide access to these reviews:

Book Review Digest. 1905 to present. (Annual). New York: Wilson. Provides excerpts of and citations to reviews of current books in English. Books on science for the general reader are included, but textbooks and technical books are not. The *BRD* is searchable by author, title, and subject.

Book Review Index. 1965 to present. (Annual). Detroit: Gale. Provides access to reviews of books and periodicals. *BRI* is a comprehensive listing of reviews that appear in more than 460 publications, representing a wide range of popular, academic, and professional interests. *BRI* is searchable by author and title only.

Abstracts

Abstracts are similar to indexes in that they provide access to sources by subject and often by author. They provide additional information through a brief summary (abstract) of each source cited. Abstracts are often compiled in two volumes, one for the abstract (with summaries) and one for the subject index. You look first in the subject index, which provides you with an abstract number. Then, using that abstract number, you can look up the abstract itself in the abstract volume.

Abstracts reflect a specific area or field of interest. For example, *Sociological Abstracts* indexes journals in the field of sociology (Fig. 2-1).

Cultural Identity
  academic performance, minorities, contemporary industrial urban societies;
    9405254
  African Americans, contemporary cultural politics; 9405131
  Australian intellectual/cultural identity; 2-book review essay; 9404980
  black history education, cultural empowerment functions; classroom observations;
    Maryland suburb; 9405167
  cultural distinctiveness, Caribbean countries; 9405098
  cultural identity development, deaf people; scale data; 9405063
  cultural identity-liberation interdependence, Latin American philosophy; 9405255
  cultural identity; Latin America; 9405239
  cyberpunk, bodily devaluation, cultural identity implications; 9405827
  ethnic group dispersion/ethnocultural orientations, Leningrad, USSR,
    1970s–1980s; questionnaire data; Armenians/Estonians/Tatars; 9405152
  ethnicity-crime relationship, methodological problems; 9406479
  freedom/rationality/justice definitions, monoculture's worldwide domination,
    global discourse; 9405252
  gay clone lifestyle, political/economic construction, profit logic, 1971–1982;
    9406209
  gender relations-nationalism relationship, citizenship/culture/origin issues;
    9406751
  homosexuality, social construction, gay culture development barriers, Nicaragua,
    1980s; 9406195
  intercultural communication/assistance; 9405516
  Irish language, historical/sociolinguistic aspects; book review esssay; 9405803
  Jewish identity/generation/space concepts, diaspora meanings, Western discourse,
    Pauline sources; 9405105
  Latvian cultural/sociopolitical history, 17th–19th centuries; 9405816

FIGURE 2-1   *Sociological Abstracts, Subject Listing*

Several abstracts are listed in the sections on "Discipline-Specific Re-sources," found in each chapter of Part Two.

One abstract of a general nature is *DAI: Dissertation Abstracts International.* Published in Ann Arbor, Michigan, by University Microfilms International, *DAI* provides a monthly compilation of abstracts of dissertations submitted to University Microfilms for publication. *DAI* is published in two sections: section A on Humanities and Social Sciences and section B on Science and Engineering. Complete copies of texts may be purchased in microfilm or photocopy from University Microfilms. The *DAI* is searchable by author, subject, and key word title.

The example of a subject listing in Figure 2-1 is from *Sociological Abstracts,* which indexes journals in the field of sociology.

Note the abstract numbers. You use them to locate the abstract (or brief summary) in the abstract volume (Fig. 2-2).

9405131
> **Gray, Herman** (Dept Sociology U California, Santa Cruz 95064), **African-American Political Desire and the Seductions of Contemporary Cultural Politics,** *Cultural Studies,* 1993, 7, 3, Oct, 364–373.
>
> ¶ Remarks on contemporary cultural politics as it pertains to African Americans, with consideration also given to the discourse & debates surrounding essentialism, postmodernism, & multiple subject positions. The localities & relationships of critical black intellectual engagements with postmodernism & essentialism are specified, & a case is made for intensifying the application of postmodern insights to the material conditions & social locations of people's lives. Comments on rap music as black self-representation are offered, & it is argued that essentialist discourses, expressed in totalizing forms of nationalism, have intervened in those public arenas, especially popular culture, where blacks do not enjoy the material privilege or the social space to construct themselves differently. 27 References. W. Howard (Copyright 1994, Sociological Abstracts, Inc., all rights reserved.)

FIGURE 2-2   *Sociological Abstracts, Abstract Listing*

Locating Library Books and Resources: Computer Cataloging Systems

In an age of exploding information, many libraries have determined that their mission is no longer to attempt to physically house all of the information sources of potential use to their patrons. Rather than simply being book repositories, today's libraries provide "access" to information, often through computers. If a library does not have a particular item in its collection, for example, the librarian may be able to tell you quickly, by a computer search, which nearby library does have a copy. Most libraries today have converted their card catalogs into computerized catalog access systems to provide their patrons with the most up-to-date information in the most timely fashion.

Online Computer Catalogs

One of the most visible computer tools in libraries today is the online catalog. Such a system, which supplements or replaces the traditional card catalog, is designed to provide library materials service, such as circulation, cataloging, and location of materials within the library collection. Most online catalogs are searchable by author, title, and subject (as are card catalogs), but many are also searchable by keyword or by combinations of subjects or keywords.

You should become familiar with your library's online catalog as soon as possible. (Note: Some online catalogs cover only the most recent additions to the library's collection, in which case older books still may be found by looking in the card catalog.) Check with your librarian to find out exactly what materials (e.g., books, magazines, journals, government documents) are cataloged in your library's online catalog.

Subject Headings

When using online catalogs, it is important to become familiar with the *Library of Congress Subject Headings (LCSH)*, a listing of specific subject headings officially used by the Library of Congress. Sometimes it is difficult to predict which terms a catalog will use, and the *LCSH* is your key or guide to the subjects recognized by the online catalog. It lists the subject headings that are assigned to books and materials in the library's collection. As there is often more than one way to describe a topic, the *LCSH* gives the exact format (wording and punctuation) for subject headings as they will appear in the database.

The *LCSH* is a large, three-volume work, usually kept near the computer terminals or somewhere in the reference area of your library. Look in the *LCSH* for as many variations on a subject as you can think of, starting with the most specific expression of your subject. For example, if your subject is the influence of classical Greece on ancient civilizations, you might begin first with "Civilization, Classical" since this is the heading listed in boldface type in the *LCSH*. The heading is followed by a scope note, describing those works listed under this particular heading. Note also the way the *LCSH* leads you to both broader (BT) and narrower (NT) subject headings, as well as telling you which entries are *not* subject headings (USE and UF "Used For") (Fig. 2-3).

The subject headings assigned to a particular book are listed by the computer as part of the entry for that book, known as the "tracings" because they trace, or keep track of, the various subjects under which a work is cataloged. Multiple headings are assigned to a book to provide alternative access points by subject. You can often discover new terms to examine for information on a topic by checking the subject tracings, in addition to using the *LCSH*.

On the other hand, if you have the wrong heading or the wrong terminology for your subject, the computer may not recognize your request and you may not discover anything in your online subject search. For example, if you are interested in classical Greek civilization, and you type into the computer *classical civilization*, you might get the response that there are no holdings in your library on that subject. When checking the *LCSH*, you discover that the appropriate subject heading is "Civilization, Classical." (The heading "Classical civilization" is accompanied by the notation "UF," which means "Used For." This notation tells you that "Civilization, Classical" is *used for* "Classical civilization" in the catalog.) To get the computer to respond

Civilization, Classical
Here are entered works on both ancient Greek and Roman civilization. Works on the combined civilizations of Greece and Rome following the conquest of Greece in 146 B.C. are entered under Civilization, Greco-Roman. Works on the spread of Greek civilization and influence throughout the ancient world following the conquests of Alexander the Great are entered under Hellenism.

UF   Classical civilization
BT   Civilization, Ancient
RT   Classicism
NT   Aggada—Classical influences
  Art, Italian—Classical influences
  Art, Renaissance—Classical influences
  Arts, Modern—Classical influences
  Balkan Peninsula—Civilization—
   Classical influences
  Byzantine Empire—Civilization—
   Classical influences
  Catalonia (Spain)—Civilization—
   Classical influences
  Central Europe—Civilization—
   Classical influences
  Civilization, Greco-Roman
  Civilization, Western—Classical
   influences
  English literature—Classical
   influences
  Europe—Civilization—Classical
   influences
  Greece—Civilization—To 146 B.C.
  Greece—Civilization—Classical
   influences
  Greece—Intellectual life—Classical
   influences
  Mexico—Civilization—Classical
   influences
  Opera—Classical influences
  Public architecture—Classical
   influences
  Rome—Civilization
  Serbia—Civilization—Classical
   influences
  United States—Civilization—Classical
   influences
Civilization, Comparative
 USE Comparative civilization

FIGURE 2-3   The *LCSH*

appropriately, you need to use the correct terminology, in this case, "Civilization, Classical."

Before beginning to search the online catalog, first check the *LCSH* to become familiar with all the possible subject terms related to your topic. Keep a comprehensive list of all the subject headings that you are using in your search of the library's holdings. These subject headings will be useful not only when searching the library's book collection but also when you begin searching for articles in magazines and journals.

How to Search the Online Catalog

When you log on to your library's computerized catalog, you will typically see a menu listing the various databases available for searching. You need to know how the information in your library is organized in order to select the appropriate databases from the computer menu. Many libraries offer instruction in the use of their computerized catalog. If yours does, take advantage of such instruction, and spend the time you need to become a confident user of your library's computer system.

Typically, libraries divide their computerized catalogs into two major parts: (1) a general database that indexes books, government documents, and audiovisual materials, often called the online catalog, and (2) specialized databases of indexes to journals, organized by discipline (Fig. 2-4). The following are some of the specialized databases found in many computerized library catalogs:

> *Wilson Guide to Business Periodicals* lists articles found in business journals.
>
> *Education Index* lists articles related to education found in education journals.
>
> *Social Sciences Index* lists articles from social science journals.
>
> *Wilson Guide to Art Index* lists articles from art magazines and journals.
>
> *Humanities Index* lists articles from journals in the humanities.
>
> *Wilson Guide to Applied Science and Technology Index* lists articles from journals related to the sciences and technology.
>
> *Biological and Agricultural Sciences Index* lists articles from biology and agriculture journals.
>
> *General Sciences Index* lists articles found in journals related to science.

The articles that you will find listed in a computerized catalog search may or may not be available through your own library. Most libraries can afford to subscribe to only a limited number of magazines,

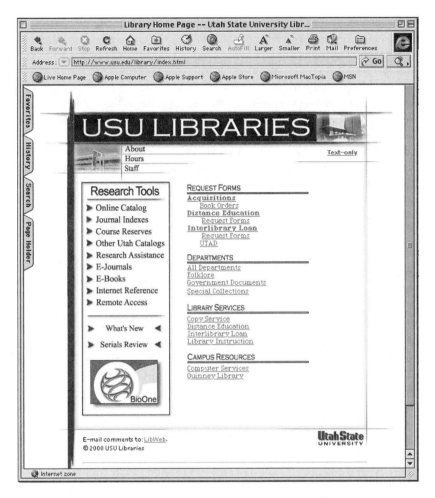

FIGURE 2-4   Main Menu of Utah State University Libraries

newspapers, and journals. Check with your librarian for a listing of which periodicals your library subscribes to. (Sometimes you will find this information in the computer record when you locate the reference from the Index.) If your library does not own a particular magazine, newspaper, or journal, don't despair. Through interlibrary loan and the Internet, often you can obtain an article from another library. Check with your librarian to find out about such reciprocal services.

Title and Author Searches.   The computer can search quickly through its database when you provide it with a correct title or an author's name. If there is more than one work by an author, the computer lists them all, and then allows you to select the one you are looking for.

You may need to request an expanded screen with more details about the specific work you have selected. The computer should also let you know whether the book has been checked out of the library and provide you with a call number to help you locate the book. In some libraries, it is possible to place a "hold" on a work through the computer, with a provision that you will be notified as soon as the book is back in circulation.

Subject Searches.   To search by subject, once again be certain to use an exact *LCSH* subject heading, as found in the *LCSH* volumes. Tell the computer that you intend to search by subject by entering the appropriate command along with the exact subject heading. The computer then tells you how many items in its database are cataloged under that subject heading (called the number of "hits") and provides you with a list of titles.

If the computer tells you that there are several hundred books with your subject heading, you may need to narrow your subject search. The *LCSH* will provide you with narrower terms (labeled "NT"). Or you can narrow your search by combining key words (see Keyword Searching section in this chapter). On the other hand, if the computer tells you there are only one or two titles with your subject heading, you may need to broaden your subject search. Again, the *LCSH* will suggest related terms (labeled "RT") or broader terms ("BT") that you can try.

Call Number Searches.   This is an excellent way to locate materials similar to works for which you currently have a call number. By typing in the exact call number of a known work, you can ask the computer to list all of the call numbers that come before and after that work in the computer's memory. This means that it is possible to read titles on the computer screen by call number, just as you would browse a shelf in the library and retrieve other books found on surrounding shelves.

Keyword Searches.   Keyword searching allows you to search for the most important term or terms for your research project. The computer locates items in its database that use a particular keyword anywhere in a work's record. However, if a record doesn't happen to include that particular keyword or term, the computer typically will not be able to supply the synonym. Therefore, you still need to try as many keywords and subject headings as you can think of in a database search. For example, if you are searching for items about UFOs, you might use *UFO* as a keyword. But you might also want to try other keywords, such as *flying saucers* or *paranormal events*.

Advanced Keyword Searches. Using keywords, it is possible to perform combined searches of two or more terms. Combining keywords helps to limit an otherwise broad topic. For example, if you were interested in teenage pregnancy but only for the state of California, you could combine the terms *teenage pregnancy* and *California* to narrow your search, thus searching the collection only for those sources that include both keywords. This kind of focused searching offers distinct advantages over using a card catalog. If your library offers instruction in advanced database searching, you would be wise to take the opportunity to learn the "tricks of the trade."

Recording Bibliographic Information

Once you have a listing of books from the online catalog, you need to note each book's specific call number so that you can locate it in your library's collection. It may be possible to instruct the online catalog to print out your search results. If not, you will need to be certain you write down the titles, along with their complete bibliographic information, on your working bibliography in your research notebook. Complete bibliographic information includes:

Author(s) full name, including initials

Title of the book, including subtitles and editions

Place (city and state) where the book was published

Name of the book's publisher

Date of publication and total number of pages (for CBE style)

Microforms

A few libraries organize their holdings on microforms rather than in computer databases or card catalogs. Microforms are either microfilm or microfiche; both make use of methods to condense information in a very compact form. Machines called microform readers are necessary to read either form. Information stored on microform is similar to that found on traditional cards. If your library uses this system, check with the reference librarian for instructions about using the microform readers.

Locating Articles in Serials: Popular Periodicals

Periodicals are popular magazines and newspapers printed at regular intervals, such as daily, weekly, monthly, or quarterly. It is possible to search for magazines and journals through both online computer databases and print indexes. The reference section of your library contains several print indexes to articles found in periodicals. The following are two important indexes of general-interest periodicals:

> *Magazine Index.* Los Altos, CA: Information Access, 1978 to present.
> *Readers' Guide to Periodical Literature.* New York: Wilson, 1901 to present.

Both sources index articles in popular magazines. The *Readers' Guide* is available in chronologically bound volumes; each contains an alphabetical listing of articles from a particular year. (The current issues are paperbound.) The *Magazine Index* is available on microform. This index is extremely useful for very current topics, because it indexes about twice as many articles as the *Readers' Guide.* In both sources, entries are arranged both by subject and by author. These indexes may also be available in your library in a computer database.

Newspapers

Your library probably stores back issues of newspapers on microform. To gain access to articles in the *New York Times,* use the *New York Times Index,* which lists all major articles from the *Times* from 1913 to the present. The *Newspaper Index* lists articles from the *Chicago Tribune, Los Angeles Times, New Orleans Times-Picayune,* and *Washington Post.* Both indexes are arranged by subject. For business news, use the *Wall Street Journal Index.*

Newspaper indexes are available in both print and computerized formats. Many search engines now offer a feature to help patrons keep track of the news headlines. Such "news tracker" services can also be customized to search for news stories related to particular subjects or topics. One of the best news tracker services is available from the *Google* search engine.

Finding Periodicals

Indexes such as the *Magazine Index* or the *Readers' Guide* may lead you to titles of articles related to your particular research topic. However, it is important to note that these indexes catalog general-interest periodicals that may not be appropriate for some academic research projects. To find discipline-specific journals, you must use discipline-specific indexes (see the section in this chapter on Locating Articles in Serials: Professional Journals).

When researching your topic, write down or print out the *complete* citation of any relevant article. The citation includes:

Author's name (if given)
Title of the article
Name of the magazine
Volume number
Issue number
Date published
Inclusive pages of the article

Your library has a particular system for listing magazine and newspaper holdings. This serials listing may appear in the online catalog, in a separate catalog, in the main card catalog, on computer printouts, or on microform. Consult your librarian to determine which system your library uses. The serials listing tells you which periodicals your library subscribes to, where they are located in the library, the inclusive dates of the issues your library has, and whether the issues are in bound or unbound volumes or on microform.

Once you have obtained the call number of the magazine containing your article from the serials listing, you will be able to find the magazine itself, whether it is in a bound volume, in the current-periodicals section of the library, on microform, or in a full-text database. Once you have the article in hand, be sure to copy down the complete publication information, which is often only abbreviated in the index. Writing everything down at this point will prevent your having to return to the library later for information you neglected to note originally.

Evaluating Periodicals

If you find the title of a magazine but are unsure of its nature or scope, a useful evaluative tool is *Magazines for Libraries,* 12th ed. (New Providence, NJ: Bowker, 2003). This work describes and explains magazines and can give you some insight into the magazine's purpose, reputation, and scope.

Locating Articles in Serials: Professional Journals

When you are researching a technical subject, you want to refer to articles written on the subject by professionals in the field. Professional journal articles, sometimes called *serials* because they are printed in series, are indexed in much the same way as the general periodicals previously discussed. However, numerous specialized indexes and databases exist for professional articles, and each index or database covers a particular discipline or subject area. ("Discipline-Specific Resources," in

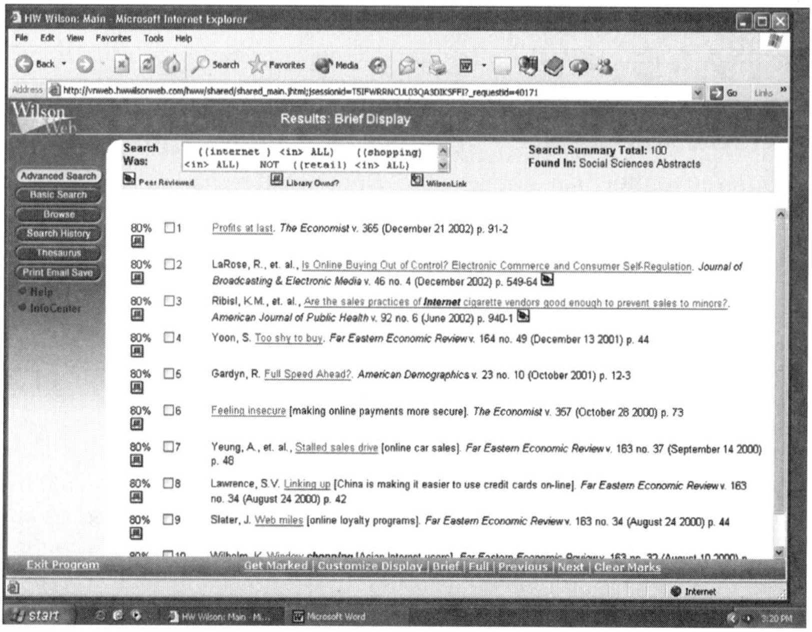

FIGURE 2-5   Excerpt from *Social Sciences Abstracts*

each chapter in Part Two, lists discipline-appropriate indexes for sciences and technology, social sciences, humanities, and business.)

Professional journal articles are indexed in much the same way as magazine and newspaper articles. However, you will need to find a specialized index or database for professional articles in the particular discipline or subject area. For example, *Social Sciences Abstracts* lists articles from science journals. Figure 2-5 shows the beginning of the "Internet + shopping" entry in the *Social Sciences Abstracts*. Discipline-specific indexes are available in most libraries, both in print and on computer.

Locating Government Documents

The U.S. government is one of the largest publishers of information and is a rich source of materials in almost every field, from aeronautics to zoology. Government documents are sometimes listed in a separate database or catalog from the main online or card catalog. Check with your reference librarian to discern how your library catalogs its documents.

The *Monthly Catalog of United States Government Publications* is the comprehensive bibliography that lists all publications received by the Government Printing Office for printing and distribution. The *Monthly Catalog,* established in 1895, is the best overall guide to finding government sources. At the back of each monthly register are indexes that provide access to the documents by authors, subjects, and series/report numbers. The monthly indexes are cumulated (that is, brought together into one volume) both semiannually and annually for ease of access.

Other ways to find government documents include the following indexes:

Index to U.S. Government Periodicals

Public Affairs Information Services (PAIS)

Resources in Education (RIE)

U.S. Government Reports, Announcements and Index

(*NTIS*—National Technical Information Service)

The *Index to U.S. Government Periodicals* provides access by author and subject to 180 government periodicals. The *PAIS* lists by subject current books, pamphlets, periodical articles, and government publications in the field of economics and public affairs. *RIE* lists government-sponsored reports related to the field of education. The *U.S. Government Reports, Announcements and Index (NTIS)* lists government-sponsored research in the technical sciences by subject fields: aeronautics; agriculture; astronomy and astrophysics; atmospheric sciences; behavioral and social sciences; biological and medical sciences; chemistry; earth science and oceanography; electronic and electrical engineering; energy conversion; materials; mathematical sciences; mechanical, industrial, civil, and marine engineering; methods and equipment; military science; navigation, communications, detection; nuclear science and technology; physics; and propulsion and fuels.

Other Technologies

CD-ROMs and Other Electronic Databases

Many libraries are now providing patrons with the opportunity to search databases themselves, using microcomputers connected to compact disk units (CD-ROMs). With compact disk technology, large databases can be made accessible and easy to use. For example, the education index ERIC (Education Research Information Clearinghouse) is now available in this format, as is the business index ABI-INFORM. Check your library reference area to see whether such tools are available to you. These databases are subject-specific, so you need to find out just which journals or subjects they index. But they often can provide a quick alternative to searching the print indexes on your subject. Another bonus of using CD-ROMs is that the information found in your search can usually be sent to a printer or downloaded onto your own computer disk.

As with any computerized search, it is important to know your subject headings and terminology. Many of the computer databases use their own "controlled vocabulary," which may vary slightly from the subject headings listed in the *LCSH*. Check with your librarian to discern whether there is a "thesaurus" or listing of subject headings for the particular database you are using. ERIC on-disk, for example, uses the "ERIC Descriptors" as its method of cataloging by subject.

The section titled Discipline-Specific Resources in each chapter of Part Two indicates which indexes may be available through computerized databases.

Electronic Full-text Databases

It is clearly impossible for libraries to own all magazines and journals in a world of rapidly exploding information. Many libraries subscribe to full-text database services that provide library patrons with Internet access to copies of the actual articles from magazines, newspapers, and professional journals. Your library has to pay for such services, and subscriptions may be expensive—but not as expensive as trying to purchase every publication that's produced! Check with your librarian to find out if your library subscribes to an online database service such as *LexisNexis* or *EBSCOHost*. If it does, you may be able to search the database via the Internet by subject or keyword to find not just a listing of the article's title and source but a reproduction of the full text of the article itself.

Accessing Information from Other Libraries

If, in your search, you discover that some item you need is not located in your library, it is still possible to find the item in another library. An online computer database called the OCLC (Online Computer Library Center) provides thousands of libraries with connections to each other's catalogs. By searching the OCLC database (by author or title), you can quickly ascertain if a nearby library contains the needed item; then you may request it through interlibrary loan or secure it yourself. It is also possible to access other library collections via the Internet. For more information, see pp. 41–48, Internet Resources.

INTERNET RESOURCES

One of the primary benefits of the Internet is that it connects computer users to information on computer networks around the world. In addition to being useful in your personal life, the Internet also has many educational uses. Much information published by educational institutions, libraries and service organizations, commercial and corporate providers, the press, and the government can be located through an Internet search.

Using Search Tools to Locate Information on Your Topic

How do you go about finding specific information on a particular topic? The most reliable way is to use one of various Internet search tools. Search tools use different methods of sorting Web pages. Some search tools, called *search engines,* use an automated system to sort pages based primarily on the use and placement of keywords. *Google, AltaVista* and *Excite* are examples of search engines. Search engines automatically find and catalog new sites as they are added to the Web, indexing information by title and keywords. Other search tools, like *Yahoo!,* are actually search directories with a system of categories in a hierarchy. Real people (not computer programs) screen sites and sort them into *Yahoo!* categories. There are also meta search tools available, which search multiple databases at the same time. *Ixquick, Zworks,* and *ProFusion* are all examples of meta search tools. You might wish to begin with a meta search tool and then choose one or two search engines or Web directories as you fine-tune your search. Some of the biggest Internet databases are found at *Google, Excite, HotBot, Yahoo!, AltaVista,* and *Lycos,* which index a large number of Web pages (see Search Tools on page 42).

Searching via Subject Directories

A search directory is basically an organized index of topics and subtopics. The *Yahoo!* subject directory on the World Wide Web, for example, lists the following subject areas on its opening screen: Arts & Entertainment, Business & Finance, Computers & Internet, Education, Government & Politics, Health & Medicine, Living, News, and Reference. Using this subject directory, you can narrow the scope of your search to only those Web pages related to your topic. For example, if you were interested in finding out more about Brazil's government but not about its entertainment or climate, you could select the "government and politics" subject list. Then, once you were in that subtopic,

SEARCH TOOLS

Name and Address	Description
AltaVista <http://altavista.com>	Large, comprehensive database. Keyword searching only. Supports Boolean searching (see Tips on Boolean Operators and Phrases for Internet Searching).
Excite <http://excite.com>	Subject directory and keyword searching available. Supports Boolean searching.
Google <http://google.com>	Subject directory and keyword searching available.
HotBot <http://hotbot.com>	Subject directory and keyword searching. Includes newsgroups and email. Supports Boolean searching.
Ixquick <http://ixquick.com>	Fast and comprehensive meta search tool; searches 14 other tools simultaneously.
Lycos <http://lycos.com>	Subject directory and keyword searching available. Supports Boolean searching.
ProFusion <http://profusion.com>	Searches multiple tools simultaneously, using keywords (includes most search tools in this table). Supports Boolean searching.
Yahoo! <http://yahoo.com>	Subject directory and keyword searching available. Includes news, chat, and email. Does not support Boolean searching.
Zworks <http://zworks.com>	One of the best meta search tools. Ranks the results of searches for relevancy by search tool.

you could type in the keyword *Brazil.* Many people like using the *Yahoo!* search directory because it is both fast and comprehensive, including listings from news groups in addition to links to thousands of Web pages. Other search directories that offer both subject directories and keyword searching include *Lycos* and *HotBot.*

Searching with Keywords

Once you have identified a search tool to use and perhaps narrowed your way down a subject directory, you need to determine what search terms to try. First, enter a single keyword that identifies your topic and search for "hits" for that keyword (Web pages on which the word appears). You may already have identified subject headings and keywords that you can use as you searched your library's collection. Many search tools also allow you to perform more sophisticated, customized searches, but these differ from one search tool to another. Check the search tool's Help screen to discover ways to customize your search, particularly if you are getting hundreds or even thousands of hits for your search term.

Using Boolean Operators

One of the ways that search tools allow you to focus is by means of Boolean operators (for example, using "AND" or "NOT" to limit your search). The same principles for searching by keyword in your library database also apply to searching on the Internet. For example, if you type *childcare in Utah*, you may get all of the hits for "childcare" in addition to all of the hits for "Utah," yielding thousands of sources. But

---

TIPS ON BOOLEAN OPERATORS AND PHRASES FOR INTERNET SEARCHING

Boolean keywords include **AND (&)**, **OR (|)**, **NOT (!)**, and **NEAR (~)**.

   AND limits your search, because both keywords joined by AND must be found in the search (e.g., **pets AND felines**).

   OR expands your search, because either keyword joined by OR will be included in the search results (e.g., **pets OR dogs OR felines**).

   NOT limits your search by excluding the keyword after the operator (e.g., **pets NOT dogs**).

   NEAR expands the search, finding keywords near the keyword you have chosen (e.g., **pets NEAR dogs**).

(Boolean operators must be typed as UPPERCASE letters (unless you are using symbols).

You must leave a white space before and after each Boolean operator.

Use parentheses if your phrase is complex, with several Boolean operators:

(Pets AND felines) AND (NOT dogs).
The same search can be indicated using symbols: **(Pets & felines) & (!dogs)**

With some search engines you can select an option that allows you to search for an entire phrase. In such a case, you do not need to include the phrase in quotation marks. If the search engine does not have a phrase option, put the phrase in quotation marks prior to searching.

---

if you combine the terms using the "AND" Boolean operator, *childcare* AND *Utah,* you have effectively asked the search engine to find only those sources that include both of these terms in the same sources (the "AND" limits the search). If you want to limit your search even more, you could add the "NOT" Boolean operator: *childcare* AND *Utah* NOT *preschool.*

Another way you can focus the search is by the use of quotation marks, which indicate that the words must appear in a particular order in the text. So "global warming" would need to occur exactly as written inside the quotation marks in order for it to be included in your search. In other words, you are in effect telling the search tool that you are not interested in *global* or *warming* by itself, but only the two words in combination. In a model search on global warming conducted by a student, for example, *Go* yielded approximately 500 hits for global warming (without quotation marks) and 17 hits for "global warming" (in quotation marks, indicating the two words must appear together). The only way to see if your search is yielding the results you are seeking is to browse through the listing of Web sites found by the search tool. Most search tools provide you with a brief description of the sites they locate so you can quickly ascertain whether the search is finding relevant sources. If not, try again with new search terms, subject areas, or delimiters. Make use of the search tool's Help screen if you are not achieving the results you desire.

Using Internet Library and Periodicals Collections

If you are working in a particular academic subject area, you may find it more efficient to use virtual library collections instead of (or in addition to) search tools. Virtual libraries are often organized in much the same way as traditional libraries—with separate listings for periodicals, dictionaries, government documents, and so on. But they are generally more limited than regular libraries, so you do not want to rely on them exclusively. Rather, use a virtual library search as a supplement to a traditional library search.

Searching Virtual Libraries

Many libraries make some of the information from their collections available via the Internet. You can also use *LibCat,* which links you to hundreds of libraries with Web access, or *LibWeb,* which provides links to online documents and image collections available from libraries around the world. Once you locate these sources, you will need to browse through an index much like the online catalog in your own library, using keyword and subject searches to find specific information.

Some libraries have set up special online directories that link researchers to resources in specific subject areas. For example, the University of California at Riverside sponsors the *Infomine Scholarly Internet Resources Collections*. It is divided topically into resources in major subject disciplines, such as scientific and medical sources, government sources, and social sciences and humanities sources.

INTERNET LIBRARIES AND COLLECTIONS

Name and Address	Description
Academic Info <http://academicinfo.net>	Gateway to quality educational resources categorized by discipline
Educator's Reference Desk <http://www.eduref.org>	Includes the ERIC database with over one million abstracts on education topics.
Internet Public Library <http://www.ipl.org>	Reference site built by the University of Michigan
LibCat <http:// www.metronet.lib.mn.us/ lc>	Links to hundreds of online libraries
Library of Congress <http://lcweb.loc.gov>	Centralized guide to information services provided by the Library of Congress
Librarians' Index to the Internet <http://lii.org>	About 6,500 links compiled by public librarians; highest-quality sites included with annotations
Purdue University Libraries <http://www. lib.purdue.edu/ eresources/readyret>	Lists many online journals by academic subject
University of California– Berkeley LibWeb <http:// sunsite.berkeley.edu>	Links to online documents and image collections around the world
University of California– Riverside Infomine <http://infomine.ucr.edu>	Lists many online sources by academic subject
Virtual Information Center <http://lib.berkeley.edu/ Collections>	Links to reference sites in many academic subjects

INTERNET SITES FOR GOVERNMENT DOCUMENTS

Name and Address	Description
Bureau of the Census <http://www.census.gov>	Alphabetical index of social, demographic, economic information; searchable by place, location, word
Bureau of Justice Statistics <http://www.ojp.usdoj.gov/bjs>	Statistics on all criminal justice topics (law enforcement, drugs, crime, etc.)
Bureau of Labor Statistics <http://stats.bls.gov>	Allows keyword search for statistics by region, economy at a glance, etc.
Department of Education <http://www.ed.gov>	Lists educational initiatives, news, publications, programs
Library of Congress <http://lcweb.loc.gov>	Centralized guide to information services provided by the Library of Congress
National Institutes of Health <http://www.nih.gov>	Provides health information, grant information, health news; database searchable by keywords
National Library of Medicine <http://www.nlm.nih.gov>	Allows free Medline searches, plus access to other medical databases
NASA <http://www.nasa.gov>	Tracks current space flights and missions, including Pathfinder on Mars
Statistical Abstract of the United States <http://www.census.gov/statab/www>	Collection of statistics on social, economic, and international subjects
Thomas (congressional legislation) <http://thomas.loc.gov>	Access to full text of current bills under consideration by U.S. House and Senate
U.S. Fish & Wildlife Service <http://www.fws.gov>	Access to information related to fish and wildlife
White House <http://www.whitehouse.gov>	Access to information on the federal government: initiatives, tours, help desk, President, Vice President, and First Lady

Searching Government Documents

The federal government also maintains numerous sites that you may want to use for research. The White House Web site offers an online photographic tour of the White House and links you to information about the federal government, including pending legislation, recently produced government documents, and Cabinet activities and reports. Another government site is maintained by NASA. Here you can find information on space flights, space research, and aeronautics. In addition, you can locate specific information on hundreds of other government Web sites, including local city and state sites, by using the search tools described earlier.

Searching Online Periodicals

Journals and magazines that are published on the Web can also be sources for your research paper. Several publishers are now offering online versions of their publications. Often you can access the full text of articles that appear in the print version. For example, the *New York Times* is available online, as is *Time* magazine. Once again, there is no single quick and easy way to locate online periodicals. If you know the

---

INTERNET SITES FOR ONLINE PERIODICALS

Name and Address	Description
CNN Interactive <http://www.cnn.com>	CNN news from around the world; includes audio and video clips
Electronic Library <http://www.elibrary.com>	Keyword searching of online magazines and newspapers (includes subject tree)
Lycos News <http://www.Lycos.com/news>	News headlines from Lycos News Service (includes CNN, ABC, Reuters)
New York Times <http://www.nytimes.com>	Access to daily contents of the *New York Times*
News Directory <http://www.newsdirectory.com>	Links to U.S. and world newspapers, magazines; searchable by subject
Yahoo Today's News <http://dailynews.yahoo.com>	News headlines from Yahoo News Service (includes CNN, ABC, Reuters)

name of the publication you need, you can search for it by name, using one of the search tools described above. In addition, some Web sites link you to major journals, newspapers, and magazines. For example, *The News Directory* provides links to thousands of magazines and newspapers from around the world, catalogued by region and organized by topic area (e.g., business, health, religion, sports, travel, social issues). Finally, you can use a search tool such as *Excite!* to search for news in magazines and newspapers by selecting "Newstracker" from the subject index.

Bookmarking Important Sites

When you find a Web site that you will return to frequently, use your browser's "Bookmark" or "Favorites" feature to mark the site so that you can get to it easily next time. If you typically work in a computer lab, it may be necessary to save your bookmarks or favorites on your own disk.

Use Internet sources in combination with indexes in other media: print, CD, or online. Note that URLs change rapidly. If a URL listed in this book doesn't work, try shortening the address or searching by title.

EXERCISES

1. In the reference section of your library, find a major biographical work. To become familiar with major biographical sources, look up information on a famous person who is or was important in your major field or in the field of your specific research project. (Be sure to look in an appropriate biography depending on whether the person is living or dead, American or British, and so on.) Take notes on that person's life and work. Write a one-page report on some aspect of the person that seems interesting to you. You may wish to consult more than one biography and compare the entries.

2. In your library's online or card catalog, look up a subject area that interests you as a possible research topic. (For ideas, browse through the *Library of Congress Subject Headings* list.) Write down the author, title, and call number of any book that seems interesting. Using the call number, find the book in the library stacks. Write a complete citation for the book, including the author's full name, the title and edition of the book, and the publication data. Then write a one-paragraph annotation describing the book. (An annotation is a short critical or explanatory note.)

3. Using one of the indexes to periodicals (either online or in print), look up the subject you looked up in question 2. Again, note one article listed in the index that sounds interesting. Find the article itself in the library by using your library's serials listing of magazine holdings and their locations. Make a photocopy of the article. On your copy, underline key ideas in the article. Turn in your underlined copy.

4. Look up the magazine you used in question 3 in *Katz's Magazines for Libraries*. Write down the information you find about the magazine. (Note: If your library does not have Katz's work, find out if it carries a similar work, such as *Farber's Classified List of Periodicals for the College Library*.)

5. Using the *Social Sciences Index*, or another index appropriate for your field, look up a current issue or social problem (for example, alcoholism, child abuse, or prison reform). Find the title of one current article in a scholarly journal. Write down or print out the citation from the index, find the complete journal name in the front of the index, and using that information, find the journal article in your library. (Remember, you will need to look up the journal name in the serials listing just as you did for a popular magazine.) Make a photocopy of the article. On your copy, underline key ideas. Then construct an outline of the article. Turn in the photocopy with your outline.

6. Find any information your library has about online computer searches and discuss computer searching in your particular field with the reference librarian.

7. Find out whether your library has any databases on videodisk or CD-ROM that you can search using a microcomputer. Try out any such tools, using appropriate subject headings and key words for your topic, and turn in the printout generated from your search.

8. Interview one of your professors about library research in his or her field. How does that professor gather information needed for his or her work? How has the research process changed over the years? How much does the professor rely on computer searching? Write a short paragraph summarizing the interview.

9. Interview a reference librarian at your campus library. How has information access changed? How many new information sources has the library acquired in the past year or so? What does the librarian foresee in the libraries of the future? Write a short paragraph summarizing the interview.

3

Using Library and Internet Sources

INTRODUCTION

Successful research depends on knowing what library and Internet resources are available, but it also depends on knowing how to find and use those resources. Developing a search strategy will help you to find materials on your research topic and to use library and Internet resources efficiently. First, you need to use search tools to locate source materials; then you must evaluate those sources and interpret them so that they will be useful to your particular research project.

PREPARATION AND INCUBATION

As a college student, you are uniquely prepared to conduct a research project. Your experiences and prior schooling have given you a wealth of information to draw from. You may begin a research project because you have been assigned to do one in a particular college class or because you have discovered an interesting question or problem on your own that you want to investigate. Although the former impetus, a course assignment, might seem artificial or contrived at first, in reality it may give you the opportunity to investigate something that has always intrigued you.

Finding a Topic

When you are choosing a research topic, it is important to find one that you are interested in, can develop an interest in, are somewhat familiar with, or have questions about. You will write much better if your interest level is high. You do not need to wait until you are well into your research to turn to the Internet. In fact, you can use the Internet to explore possible topic choices. Because Internet search tools are often organized by topic and subtopic in subject directories, you can use them to explore topic options. For example, use your Internet browser to access a search directory such as *Yahoo!* that has hierarchical subject categories. In the subject directory, look for categories that interest you or that are related to your research paper assignment. Within each category, search for possible topics (e.g., under "society" you might find the topic "environment and nature" interesting). Each time you go one level deeper in the subject directory, jot down other categories that might provide possible topics to write about.

Another good place to begin looking for a research topic is in the books you are currently using for the courses you are taking. Scan the table of contents with an eye toward a topic that you'd enjoy investigating. Or if you have no idea at all, begin by browsing through a specialized encyclopedia, such as the *Encyclopedia of Psychology* or the *Encyclopedia of Education*. (Other specialized encyclopedias are listed by discipline in the chapters of Part Two.) A library resource for finding topics is *Editorial Research Reports* (*ERR*). If your library subscribes to *ERR*, it receives a weekly description of reports on a wide variety of contemporary events, problems, and issues, such as acid rain, homelessness, or women in business. A bibliography listing several recent articles, books, and reports on each topic covered by *ERR* is also included. Skimming these reports may spark an interest in a particular topic, as well as get you started on finding relevant materials and information.

Once you have an idea for a topic, you might discuss your idea with a reference librarian, your teacher, and other students in your class. They may have ideas or suggestions related to your topic or may be able to direct you to aspects of the topic you may not have considered. Your goal is to focus your topic by asking pertinent starting questions that your research will attempt to answer. So, if your general topic is "acid rain," your specific starting question might be "What have been the effects of acid rain on the forests of New York?" Or, "What is the EPA currently doing to control pollutants that cause acid rain?" Such questions, which should be neither too trivial nor too broad, will help you to sort through information in search of an answer and may prevent you from aimlessly reading on a topic area that is too general.

SELECTING A SPECIFIC TOPIC

Kaycee Sorensen, a student in a composition class, was given the assignment of writing a research paper on a technological subject. She was not sure what technological issue she wanted to write about, so she decided to surf the Net as a way of generating some specific topics. After browsing in the *Yahoo!* search directory, Kaycee noticed the topic of "shopping and services" listed under the category "Business and Economy." She was curious about the prevalence of online shopping in our culture. Was the number of cybershoppers increasing? Was shopping via the Net a viable alternative for consumers? Was it safe to use a credit card for online shopping? These questions served as a starting place for Kaycee's research. Posing these questions allowed Kaycee to begin her background reading in search of answer, rather than reading aimlessly in an unfocused way.

NARROWING AND FOCUSING THE TOPIC

Search tools are useful not only for getting topic ideas but also for narrowing a general topic area or dividing a subject into several component parts, much as the subject directories on the Internet do. For example, under the broad topic of business and the economy, Kaycee selected the specific topic of cybershopping, passing over other possible technological topics such as intellectual property or ethics and responsibility. She then narrowed the topic of cybershopping to exclude sites related to retail sales since she was interested in the advantages and disadvantages of cybershopping but not in sites that promoted online retail sales.

Asking Research Questions.

Once you have identified a specific topic, the next step is to focus the topic by asking pertinent research questions that you will attempt to answer—your "starting questions." For the specific topic of cybershopping, Kaycee's starting questions were as follows:

Is the number of online shoppers increasing?

Is shopping via the Internet a viable option for consumers?

Is it safe to use a credit card for online shopping?

Developing a Hypothesis

As you work through the research process, attempting to answer your starting questions, you should come up with a hypothesis—a tentative statement of what you anticipate the research will reveal. A working hypothesis specifically describes a proposition that research evidence will either prove or disprove. As you begin to gather background information on your topic, you should develop a hypothesis that will help you to focus your research. Kaycee moved from her starting questions to a working hypothesis as follows:

TOPIC

Cybershopping

RESEARCH QUESTIONS

Is the number of online shoppers increasing?

Is shopping via the Internet a viable alternative for consumers?

Is it safe to use a credit card for online shopping?

WORKING HYPOTHESIS

The number of online shoppers is increasing, which means that cybershopping is becoming a convenient, affordable, safe option for consumers.

A working hypothesis should be stated in such a way that it can be either supported or challenged by the research. Kaycee's research will either support or challenge her working hypothesis. The hypothesis is called "working" because you may find that you need to change or revise it during the course of the research.

Gathering Research Materials

The Research Notebook

To keep track of all your research, you need a notebook to serve as your "research notebook." In the notebook, you record your specific topic area and the starting questions you wish to answer, outline your plans for searching the library (your library search strategy), and begin a list of sources (a working bibliography). Your research notebook is also the place where you can begin to articulate for yourself your own understanding of the answer to your starting question as it evolves through your research. It is crucial that, as you investigate your topic, you record in the research notebook not only what others have said on the subject, but also your own impressions and comments.

Your research notebook, then, will be the place for tracing your entire research process: the starting questions, the search strategy, the sources used in your search, your notes, reactions to and comments on the sources, the tentative answers you propose to your starting question, a thesis statement articulating the main points to be covered by your paper, an informal outline or an organizational plan for your paper, and all preliminary drafts of your paper. Many students like to take notes from sources in their research notebooks instead of on note cards, in order to keep all their research information in a single convenient place. If you decide on this approach, be sure to record your notes and evaluative comments in separate parts of the notebook. I suggest to students that they leave a blank page for comments in their notebooks adjacent to each page of notes. Also, remember to reserve a place in your notebook for recording any primary research data (such as interview, survey, or questionnaire data) that you collect in connection with your research project.

A Computer Research Notebook

If you are using a word processor, you can take advantage of the storage capabilities of your computer to develop a computer research notebook. Create a document or folder on your computer and label it your research notebook file. All of the items described above for a research notebook can be gathered together in this one document or folder on your computer. For example, you could include your topic and starting questions, search strategy, working bibliography, notes and evaluative comments on sources, and so on. In this way, your research project can proceed systematically as you gather information and build your own expertise on your topic through your evolving computer folders. Using word processing, then, you can revise your research notebook, organize your information, and even write your paper based on the stored information on your computer.

For example, a student who had to write a research report for a computer science class decided to write about computer crime. In thinking about the subject, he determined that first he needed to categorize the types of computer crimes so that he could arrange the information in his research notebook in an organized way. As he read books and articles on the subject, he began to sort materials into the following subheadings: computer as object or target of crime, computer as subject or site of crime, computer as instrument used to commit crime, and computer as symbol for criminal deception or intimidation. After entering these subheadings into his document, he gradually built up the report; as he encountered information for the various sections of his report, he added it under the appropriate subheading in his document. You could use a similar method for your own research notebook.

TAKING NOTES WITH
PHOTOCOPIES AND PRINTOUTS

Photocopies and Database Printouts

With photocopy machines and computer printers now so readily available in libraries and computer labs, more researchers are making use of these tools to record source information. Making your own photocopies and printouts of sources has many advantages: first, you will have the actual wording of the authors at your fingertips, so you will not have to rely on your notes for accuracy when quoting (thereby reducing the chances for inadvertent plagiarism); second, you can highlight passages that are important to your own research for future reference; third, you can actually take notes on the photocopies or printouts (see Figure 3.1). Make certain that you record complete bibliographic information on all photocopies and printouts from books, newspapers, journal articles, or full-text library databases. You will make your life much more difficult if you have to retrace your steps because you neglected to write down the publication date from an article you photocopied, for example. Refer to Chapters 6–9 for the complete bibliographic information that needs to be listed for each type of source you use in your research.

Printing Internet Sources

When you are researching on the Internet, it will most likely be easiest for you to print out copies of relevant Web pages rather than take notes by hand. If you wish to use a specific section of a Web page as a source, highlight that section using your computer's mouse and then choose PRINT/SELECTION from the PRINT dialog box. In this way, you will print only the parts you need, not the entire Web site. As with photocopies, printouts of sources from the Internet will also need to have complete bibliographic information. In addition to the usual information for all sources (the author, title, and publication data), for Internet sources you will need to note the complete URL of the page(s) you are referring to, the date you accessed the page, and the dates when the site was posted and last updated.

Downloading Internet Sources

Another method of obtaining information is to download or save Internet pages directly into your own computer files (using FILE > SAVE AS). When downloading or copying and pasting files from the Internet, you need to be especially careful not to import information directly into your own work without citing the source appropriately. To keep from

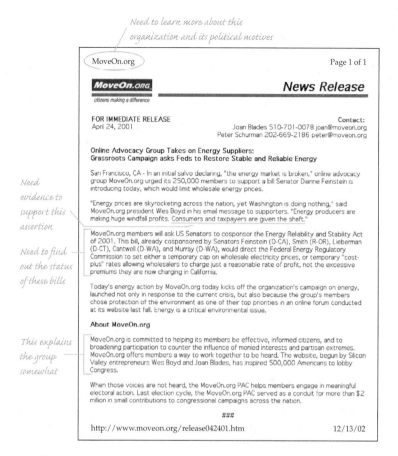

FIGURE 3-1 Example of Annotated Internet Printout

inadvertently plagiarizing form the Internet, always type into your computer notebook the complete bibliographic information from each source, and put quotation marks around any text that you COPY and PASTE from the Internet. Also, note for yourself the author of the quotation so that you can use that information in a *signal phrase* that introduces the quotation.

Saving Online Sources

If you are using sources from online databases, you may want to download them onto your own computer disk using the FILE > SAVE AS command. Be sure that complete bibliographic information appears on the pages or in the files. If it does not, make a bibliography card for the source. Include the following information: (1) author's name, if available;

(2) publication information for print and online versions; (3) the URL; (4) the date of posting or updating; (5) the date you accessed the site. If you save material from the Web, your browser may automatically include source information, but be sure to check. If you cannot find the complete address or URL, on your saved copy, record it by hand.

THE RESEARCH PROCESS

The Working Bibliography

A bibliography, as you learned in Chapter 2, is a list of books and articles on a particular subject. Your working bibliography, your preliminary list of sources, grows as your research progresses, as one source leads you to another. It is called a "working" bibliography—as opposed to the finished bibliography—because it may contain some sources that you ultimately will not use in your paper.

A working bibliography need not be in final bibliographic form, but it is important to record accurately all the information eventually needed to compose your final bibliography to keep from having to backtrack and find a book or article again. Often, a student finds a book, reads a relevant section and takes notes, but neglects to write down all of the bibliographic information, that is, the author(s), complete title, publisher, date and place of publication, and so on (see p. 34). Then, when compiling the final bibliography in which are listed all of the sources referred to in the paper, the student discovers that he or she has not written down the date of publication, for instance, or the author's first name. This means another trip to the library to find the book or journal, which may or may not still be on the shelf!

The working bibliography should be comprehensive, the place where you note down all sources that you run across—in bibliographies or databases, for example, whether your library has them and whether they turn out to be relevant to your topic. So, the working bibliography is a complete record of every possible path you encountered in your search, whether or not you ultimately followed that path. In contrast, the final bibliography lists only those sources that you actually read and used as references for your own paper.

The example below of a working bibliography comes from a student's research project on the body's immune system. The student used the CBE name/year citation style commonly used in sciences and technology.

Working Bibliography

Golub ES, Garen DR. 1991. Immunology: A synthesis.

2nd ed. Boston: Sinauer Associates. 744 p.

Bellanti JA. 1985. Immunology II. Philadelphia:

W. B. Saunders. 220 p.

Bass AB. 1985. Unlocking the secrets of immunity.

Technology Review 8:62-65.

Getzoff DE. 1987. Mechanisms of antibody binding

to a protein. Science 235:1191-1197.

Herscowitz H. 1985. Cell-mediated immune

reactions. 2nd ed. Philadelphia:

W. B. Saunders. 425 p.

Silberner J. 1986. Second T-cell receptor found.

Science News, 130:36.

Wise, H. 1987. Man bites man. Hippocratic 100:93.

Note Cards and Bibliography Cards

Many students and teachers like to record information from library sources on index cards. If you choose this method, you will develop two sets of cards: bibliography cards and note cards. The bibliography cards are used to record bibliographical information from the source (author, title, and publication data). The note cards are used to record actual notes (either paraphrased or directly quoted) from the source. See the examples of a bibliography card and a note card that a student used in his research on computer crime (Figs. 3-2 and 3-3).

Each note card contains a descriptive title and the notes themselves. Take notes on only one side of each card to allow for easy sorting and scanning of information later on. As you paraphrase material from your source, you must be careful to transcribe the meaning without using the author's wording. When you quote directly, be sure to mark words or phrases from the original with quotation marks. Provide a page reference for all notes, both quotations and paraphrases.

A number appears in the upper right-hand corner of the note card. This is the control number that allows you to match the notes with the source. On the note card in Figure 3-2, the number 3 tells you that this note was found in the third source, *Encyclopedia of Computer Science and Engineering.* The number 1 in 3-2 indicates that this note was the first one taken from source 3. Notes are numbered consecutively for each source. It is important that you number every note card in this

3.1

Crime and Computer Security
Origin

When computers began to be used for classified
government documents, the need for security was
recognized (p. 426).

FIGURE 3-2   Note Card

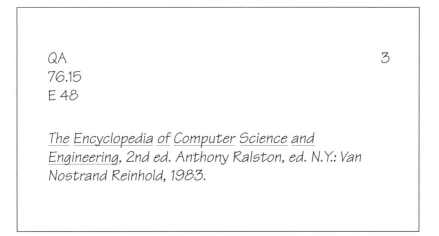

QA   3
76.15
E 48

*The Encyclopedia of Computer Science and
Engineering*, 2nd ed. Anthony Ralston, ed. N.Y.: Van
Nostrand Reinhold, 1983.

FIGURE 3-3   Bibliography Card

way, since you will be relying on this system later in documenting the
source of your information.

The Bibliography Card for a Book or Journal

On the bibliography card for a book, write down the library call
number of the book (in case you need to look up the book again) and its
complete citation: the author(s) of the book (if known), the complete

title and edition number of the book, and the publication data (place of publication, publishing company, and date). The bibliography card for a journal is similar to that for a book, except the details of the citation vary somewhat. For journals, write down the author's (or authors') complete name(s); the complete title of the article; the complete name of the journal; the volume, issue number, and date of publication; and the inclusive page numbers of the article you are citing.

Developing a Search Strategy

Once you have decided on some starting questions and have gathered the necessary research materials, you are ready to outline a preliminary search strategy. Many library research projects begin in the reference area of the library, since the library tools that refer you to other sources are kept there. Often you will begin with reference works (dictionaries, encyclopedias, and biographies), in which can be found background and contextualizing information on your topic. Then, you may proceed to more specific reference works (abstracts, indexes, and databases). To make your library search an orderly and thorough process, you should design a search strategy, beginning with general sources and working to more specific sources. In most fields, a search strategy includes the following major components:

1. Background sources—dictionaries and encyclopedias (including discipline-specific sources)
2. Biographies (on people relevant to your topic)
3. Reviews of literature and research reports (to discover how others outline or overview the subject)
4. Print and online indexes and bibliographies (for listings of source materials by subject). (Remember to use the *LCSH* for subject headings.)
5. Library online catalog and other databases (including CD-ROMs) for subject and keyword searching of books and journal articles on your topic (Use your library's serials listing to locate sources available in your library)
6. Primary research (for firsthand information such as interviews or surveys)

One student designed the following search strategy to help him begin his research on computer crime:

1. Look up "computer crime" in dictionaries and encyclopedias, including *Chambers' Dictionary of Science and Technology* and *The Encyclopedia of Computer Science and Engineering* for definitions.

2. Look up any reviews already done on computer crime, using the *Index to Scientific Reviews* and *Current Contents* for background overviews on the subject.

3. Use the *Applied Science and Technology Index* to look up current works on computer crime. Check headings to be sure that the key-word is "computer crime." (Note: This student discovered that this particular index listed articles on computer crime under the heading "Electronic Data Processing—Security Measures.") Use the *Science Citation Index* for a forward search on key sources.

4. Look up "computer crime" in the *Library of Congress Subject Headings* (*LCSH*) list to determine whether it is the subject heading used in the online catalog. Then, using the online catalog, search for sources on "computer crime" and other related headings by subject and keywords to find books and articles on computer crime.

5. Use an Internet search tool for keyword searching.

Notice that this student's search began in the reference area for background information. You would be wise to order your search strategy to begin in the reference area as well.

You may need to change or modify your search strategy as you go along; do not feel that the strategy must be rigid or inflexible. However, using a search strategy enables you to proceed in an orderly, systematic fashion with your research. On your working bibliography, write down the complete citation for each source you encounter in your search. As you read in the general and specialized encyclopedias, for example, you may find related references listed at the end of articles. Write down in your working bibliography complete citations for any references that look promising so that you can look them up later. Similarly, as you look through the reviews, the indexes, and the card catalog, write down the citations to any promising sources. In this way, you will build your working bibliography during your library search.

EXERCISES

To begin preparing for your own research project, follow these steps:

1. Select and narrow a research topic, that is, limit the topic in scope so that it is of a manageable size. Talk your topic over with others, including your classmates, your teacher, and your librarians.

2. Articulate several starting questions that you will seek to answer during your research.

3. Gather your research materials—notebook and note cards. Or create a computer document or folder for a computerized notebook.

4. Reserve space in your research notebook or computer document for both notes from sources and the evaluative comments that you will write down as you are reading.

5. Reserve space in your research notebook or computer document for your working bibliography in which you will list all of the sources you encounter during your search.

6. Outline your search strategy (refer to Chapter 2 for specific library tools to use in your search).

Outlining a Time Frame

After writing down your search strategy, you will have at least some idea of how long your research is likely to take. Now is the time to sit down with a calendar and create a time frame for your entire research project. Your teacher may have given you some deadlines, and if so, they will help you decide on a time frame. If not, you will have to set your own dates for accomplishing specific tasks so that you can proceed systematically toward the completion of the project. If you have never done a research project before, you might be overwhelmed at the thought of such a large task. However, if you break the job down into smaller parts, it will seem more manageable.

Allow yourself three to four weeks for locating, reading, and evaluating sources. As you begin to work in the library, you will see that a library search is a very time-consuming process. Just locating sources in a large library takes time; perhaps one book you need will be shelved in the third subbasement and another on the fourth floor! Sometimes a book you want will have been checked out; in such a case you will have to submit a "recall notice" to the librarian asking that the book be returned and reserved for you. You may also find that you need to obtain materials from another library through an interlibrary loan, another time-consuming process. Plan to spend two to three hours in the library each day for the first month of your research project. After that, you may find you can spend less time in the library.

Similarly, Internet research can be very time-consuming. You may find yourself going down several blind alleys, following links that seem promising but in fact turn out to be dead ends. Allow yourself sufficient computer time for trying out a variety of Internet search tools and for exploring leads that turn up in your Internet searching. There is a lot of valuable information to be found, but it may be deeply buried among a great deal of nonsense. Much of Internet searching is trial and error—and persistence.

If your research project involves primary research (see the chapters in Part Two), begin to plan for that research while you are writing your search strategy. Allow one to two weeks for conducting your primary research, depending on its nature and scope.

Schedule one to two weeks for preliminary writing. To make sense of your subject and answer your starting question, you need to spend time and effort studying and evaluating your sources, brainstorming, and writing discovery drafts. Eventually, you ought to be able to express your understanding of the subject in a thesis statement, which helps control the shape and direction of the research paper and provides your readers with a handle on your paper's main idea or argument.

Finally, give yourself enough time to plan, organize, and write the complete draft of your research paper. You need time to plan or outline your paper and to construct your argument, using your source information to reinforce or substantiate your findings in a clearly documented way. Allow yourself one to two weeks for organizing and writing rough drafts of your paper and an additional week for revising, polishing, and editing your final draft. If you intend to hire a typist or if you need to type your paper in what may turn out to be a busy computer lab, allow an extra week for the typing of the paper.

As you can see from this overview, most research projects take an entire college term to complete. Recall from Chapter 1 the stages in the research process: preparation, incubation, illumination, and verification. You need to consider all four stages as you plan your research project. Allow time for your library search, time for ideas to incubate in your subconscious, time to arrive at an understanding of your topic, and time to verify that understanding in writing.

What follows is a sample time frame to give you some idea of how you might budget your own time:

Week 1: Select preliminary research topic; articulate starting questions; gather and organize research notebook; draw up tentative search strategy; plan research time frame; read general background sources; begin to focus topic.

Week 2: Build working bibliography by using indexes, online catalogs, databases, and the Internet: begin to locate sources in the library and on the Net.

Week 3: Read and evaluate sources; take notes on relevant sources; in research notebook, comment on sources, that is, their importance to your topic and their relationship to other sources. Write down complete bibliographic information and URLs.

Week 4: Arrange and conduct any primary research; complete reading and evaluating of sources; identify gaps in research and find more sources if necessary.

Week 5:   Begin preliminary writing in research notebook—summary, synthesis, critique activities; initiate brainstorming and discovery drafting; begin to define an answer to the starting question.

Week 6:   Write a working thesis statement; sketch a tentative plan or outline of the research paper.

Week 7:   Write a rough draft of the research paper; keep careful track of sources through accurate citation (distinguish quotations from paraphrases).

Week 8:   Revise and edit the rough draft; spellcheck; check correct usage and documentation of sources.

Week 9:   Print and proofread final copy carefully; have a friend or classmate proof as well.

EXERCISES

1. Outline the time frame of your research project; refer to a current academic calendar from your school and to any deadlines provided by your teacher.

2. Plan any primary research you intend to conduct for your project. For example, if you need to contact someone for an interview, do so well ahead of time.

Locating Sources

After defining your search strategy and outlining a time frame for your project, you can begin the actual research process in the library. Refer to the relevant section of Chapter 2, "Library and Internet Resources," to begin listing possible sources for your own topic.

EXERCISE

Begin your search, writing down source citations in your working bibliography.

Evaluating Print and Electronic Sources

As a researcher in today's information-rich environment, one of your most important tasks is to evaluate what you are reading. The tendency to believe everything you read is dangerous, especially with respect to the Internet. Some, but by no means all, print sources undergo a rigorous process of peer review and evaluation before they are published. (*Peer review* refers to the practice of having written material evaluated by experts in the field before it is actually published.) Peer-reviewed sources can generally be trusted to present information accurately. In contrast, the screening process for Internet materials is usually up to each individual author. Many people who create Web sites do have a sense of personal integrity and professionalism, but others use the medium to promote themselves or their own biased viewpoints. Reading with a critical eye is always important, but even more so when Internet information is involved.

Because you will be relying on the sources you find in your research as evidence and authority for what you claim in your hypothesis, it is crucial that you choose legitimate sources. Your reputation as a researcher may in fact be at stake in this decision. To choose a legitimate source, first decide whether the source is worth reading and then decide whether the source is worth using in your own research paper.

Step One: Deciding Whether a Source Is Worth Reading

You can save yourself a great deal of time if you quickly assess the source by skimming a few key elements.

Relevance.   Is the source relevant to your research? That is, does it address the topic that you are researching? Sometimes a title may have misled you to a source that turned out, in actuality, to be on another topic or on an aspect of your topic that you are not interested in. If a source is not relevant, you can quickly move on.

Publisher or Sponsor.   Who is the sponsoring organization or publisher? Is the article in a popular magazine, such as the *Ladies' Home Journal,* or a professional journal, such as *The Journal of Behavioral Sciences?* Depending on the nature of your research project, it may or may not be appropriate to use information found in the popular press, which tends to be less scholarly than information found, for example, in a professional journal. For many college papers, however, the popular press—including major newspapers like the *New York Times* and magazines like *Newsweek*—can certainly be useful. The publishers of popular newspapers and magazines are typically commercial publishers. On the other hand, the publishers or sponsoring organizations of professional journals are usually academic societies such as the Modern Language Association or the Society for Engineering Educators. Generally you can rely on the information produced by these academic entities. But no information, regardless of the publication or its sponsoring agency, should be accepted solely at face value without critical evaluation.

Although determining the sponsoring organization or individual is no less important for an Internet site than for a print source, it may not be as easy to accomplish. One clue to the nature of the sponsoring organization for a Web site is the URL itself. Internet conventions have been established that identify a standardized suffix for Web addresses, also called a *domain type.* These domain types tell you something about the nature of the sponsoring organization. Looking at the domain type of a Web site address will help you to understand the purposes of the site—whether educational or commercial, for example. Following are some common domain types:

- Education (.edu)
- Government (.gov)
- Nonprofit organization (.org)
- Commercial (.com)
- Network (.net)
- Military (.mil)
- Other countries (for example, .ca for Canada, .uk for United Kingdom)

Author.   In addition to a sponsoring organization, is an individual author listed? Look carefully at both print and online sources to evaluate the author's credentials. Does he or she work for a government agency, a political group, a commercial industry, or an educational institution? Often the author's professional affiliation will be listed in a journal or magazine. If you are reading a Web site, it may include an "About the author" page. Of course, the sponsoring organization itself may provide the author with credibility. We assume, for example, that anyone who writes for *Time* or *Newsweek* must have appropriate credentials. A national magazine is very selective about its writers and also is extremely careful to provide authoritative information to its readers. Of course, this fact doesn't mean that sources written by authors in magazines should not be read critically.

Timeliness.   Be sure that you check the publication date of any piece you encounter. In many fields, the timeliness of the information is as important as the information itself. For example, if you are researching a medical topic, you will want to be certain that your sources are very current so that they will include the most up-to-date research. One of the many benefits of the Internet is that it allows information to be updated continually, but unfortunately not all Web sites indicate the dates on which they were first posted or last updated. With print sources, you need to be especially careful about when a piece was written and published. Often months or even years elapse between the birth of an idea or a discovery and the publication of information about it. In fields where information is changing rapidly, such as medicine, access to the most current information can be crucial.

Although the instant access to new information provided by the Internet may make it more attractive than print sources, which suffer from lag time, the down side of this instant access is that it is sometimes difficult to know what information is reliable. Many ideas presented on the Internet have not stood the test of time or endured the rigors of peer review. Much of the information that appears in print sources, in contrast, has been rigorously reviewed by peers, editors, and professional reviewers before it ever appears in print. (Of course, there are always exceptions. You need look no further than your local supermarket counter to find print sources, such as the *National Enquirer* or the *Star,* that are not appropriate sources of reliable information for a research paper!)

Cross-referencing.   Is the source cited in other works? You can sometimes make decisions about a work's credibility based on how it is cited by other sources. When you are researching a particular topic, sometimes an author's name will come up repeatedly in references or in discussions. Such an author is probably an expert on the topic, and it would be worth your while to check into sources written by that person.

There are several elements of both print and Internet sources that you should examine as you decide whether a source is worth reading. See the list of Elements to Examine.

Step Two: Deciding Whether a Source Is Worth Using in Your Paper

Once you have decided that a source is reliable, you will want to read and evaluate the source to determine whether it is something you want to use in your paper. Whatever the source, you need to exercise caution as an information "consumer." First, look at the author's rhetorical stance. Then evaluate the content of the piece itself.

Rhetorical Stance.   Who is the intended audience for the piece? Does its title help you to understand whom the piece is targeting? Is there evidence that this author has taken a particular stance in a controversy on his or her subject? Journals and magazines typically target audiences whom they assume share certain biases and opinions. If you know that bias before you read a piece, you will be able to keep the information in context. As well as thinking about audience, you will want to think about the purposes for writing and publishing the piece. What is the author or sponsoring organization trying to accomplish? Is the piece trying to sell you a product or market an idea? Is it trying to persuade you to a particular point of view? If your source is a magazine or a newspaper, turn to the opening pages and read the publication's

ELEMENTS TO EXAMINE

Print Sources	Electronic Sources
Title and Subtitle: Check both the title and the subtitle for relevance to your topic.	**Title and Subtitle:** Check the Web page title (above the browser window) and the title on the page itself for their relevance to your topic.
Copyright Page: One of the first pages of a book, it will show you who published the book and when.	**Copyright Information:** At the bottom of the homepage you should find information about who sponsors the site. Knowing the sponsor can give you clues to a site's reliability.
Table of Contents: Check the titles of parts, chapters, and sections of a book to see how useful the book will be.	**Major Links to Secondary Pages:** Check to see if the site includes links to secondary pages that elaborate on subtopics.
Abstract: Read the abstract, if there is one. It will provide you with a concise summary.	**Abstract:** Read the abstract, if there is one. It will provide you with a concise summary.
Preface: Read the preface. In it the authors will generally set out their purpose.	**Introduction:** Read any introductory material on the homepage. It should tell you about the site's purpose.
Chapter Headings and Subheadings: Check the headings and subheadings to find out what specific subtopics will be discussed.	**Headings and Subheadings:** Look closely at the major divisions on the homepage. These may tell you how detailed the site is.
Conclusion: Read the Conclusion or the Afterword. It may give you another sense of the authors' stance.	**Conclusion:** Read any concluding material on the final page of the site. This may give you another sense of the authors' stance.
Author Note: Read anything provided about the author to decide on credibility.	**Author Page:** Read any "About the author" or "About our site" information to decide on credibility. Conduct a search on the author's name, using an Internet search tool.
Index: If there is an index, check it for a listing of topics included in the book.	**Glossary:** Sometimes a Web site will include a glossary of terms. This can help you to understand the topics covered.
Bibliography: You will typically find a list of references at the end of an article or a book. It can tell you how carefully an author researched and lead you to other related sources.	**Links to References or Related Sites:** Look at the links to related sites or to sources referenced. This can tell you about the site's research and lead you to other related sources.

editorial policy; this may give you an idea of the publication's purpose. If the source is a Web site, check to see if the site includes an "About our site" page that describes a purpose or an agenda. Knowing this purpose may help you to evaluate the credibility of the information.

Content.   You may be able to decide whether to use a source by paying close attention to the content itself. Does the language seem moderate and reasonable? Or does the material include terms that might be considered inflammatory or prejudiced? Does the writer seem overly emotional? Is the tone strident or preachy? Other factors to consider as you read closely include how the piece has used source evidence itself, how logically its argument is developed, and whether it supports or contradicts what others have said on the subject.

Special Criteria for Internet Sources.   As we have discussed, some Internet sources are more reliable than others. When evaluating a Web site, look to see what other sites it links to. How useful and/or legitimate are the linked sites? If your Internet source is an online bulletin board or newsgroup, you may question its reliability. Because of the very nature of the online discussion medium, it is difficult to evaluate the credibility of the information found there. Those who enter into newsgroup discussions are ordinarily people who have some kind of interest in the topic. Occasionally a newsgroup participant will be an expert on the topic or someone with professional credentials, but usually you'll just find others like yourself with a variety of opinions to share. Newsgroup discussions can help you find out about some interesting areas for further research. But they will not help you much with the actual information you need for your research paper. When evaluating a newsgroup posting, you should be asking the questions about the author, audience, and purpose mentioned above. As a general rule, you should verify with another source any information you glean from a newsgroup posting.

Working with Sources

One of the most crucial aspects of the research process is the development of the skills needed to pull the appropriate information from the source materials you have gathered.

Reading for Meaning

The sources you locate in your library search are the raw material for your research paper. You might supplement these sources with primary data, but generally your research paper will be based on information from written secondary sources. Your job is to read carefully and actively. Reading is not a passive process by which the words float into your mind and become registered in your memory. If you read passively, you will not comprehend the author's message. You have probably had the experience of rereading a passage several times and still not understanding a word of it. In such cases, you were not reading actively. In active reading, the reader is engaged in a dialogue with the author. (See also Chapter 1, pp. 13–16.)

AVOIDING PLAGIARISM

If you use source information carefully and accurately, you will avoid any charges of plagiarism. **Plagiarism** is the unauthorized or misleading use of the language and thoughts of another author. By following the guidelines in this chapter when you paraphrase, summarize, and quote, you can avoid plagiarism.

Acknowledgment Required

Any word, phrase, or sentence that you copied directly from a source must be placed in quotation marks, and complete bibliographic information must be given, including the page reference for the quotation. Similarly, you must acknowledge paraphrases and summary restatements of ideas taken from a source, even though you have cast them in your own words. (See Chapters 6–9 for specific forms for references.)

If you find information on a Web site, it is a relatively simple matter to download it to a disk or to your computer's hard drive. However, you need to be careful to use the information fairly. When you summarize, paraphrase, or quote from a Web site, you must give proper acknowledgment to the source. It is not acceptable to CUT and PASTE text or graphics from the Internet without acknowledging the source. The same general principles about paraphrasing, summarizing, and quoting apply to other online sources found through the Internet.

Many online databases provide abstracts rather than complete works. For example, when searching the *ERIC* database on CD-ROM, you will find abstracts that tell what an article or document is about, in addition to showing its location and source. What if you use information from the abstract but do not actually read the original? You need to acknowledge the abstract when paraphrasing, summarizing, or quoting information it contains. Note in your bibliography that you are quoting the abstract rather than the source itself.

No Acknowledgment Required

You need not document "common knowledge." This term refers to information that is generally known or accepted by educated people. Information that you can find readily in general reference works such as encyclopedias or in the popular media is probably common knowledge and need not be documented, though it must be stated in your own words. Common knowledge should be verified. Be certain that several sources provide the same information before assuming that it is common knowledge. Well-proven historical facts and dates need not be documented. As a general rule, it is better to overdocument than to underdocument and be accused of plagiarizing. When in doubt, document.

Unintentional Plagiarism

Your notes should accurately record source information your own words, when possible. You should be able to tell at a glance form your notes when information is from a source and when it is your own commentary or thoughts on a source.

Students taking notes from a source sometimes commit *unintentional* plagiarism by carelessly copying words and phrases from a source into their notes and then using these words and phrases without acknowledgment in a paper. One way to avoid this problem is to read a piece carefully and then set it aside while you write your notes. If you follow the reading and notetaking procedures outlined in this chapter, paraphrasing and summarizing in your own words what you have read, you are unlikely to use the author's exact wording inappropriately in a research paper. Unintentional plagiarism can occur even if you have kept a good record of your sources because of poor paraphrases or summaries of source information.

If you record your notes by hand in a research notebook, you can divide each page into two columns, one for notes and one for your comments. If you use note cards, you can label the cards, indicating which are notes from a source and which are your own commentary. If you use a computerized research notebook, you can use the ANNOTATIONS or DOCUMENT COMMENTS feature of the word-processing program to separate source notes from your own thoughts.

Intentional Plagiarism

Sometimes plagiarism is *intentional;* that is, a writer knowingly copies the work of another without proper acknowledgment of the source. A *Newsweek* article reported on a Stanford University business school lecturer who used several pages form an article by Greg Easter-brook in his book, word for word, without acknowledging the original author (G. Easterbrook, "The sincerest flattery: Thanks, but I'd rather you not plagiarize my work," *Newsweek,* 19 July 1991, pp. 45–46). When the plagiarism came to light, the Stanford author apologized to Easter-brook but insisted that he had not plagiarized because he had included Easterbrook's name in the book's footnotes. Easterbrook's response ex-plains an important distinction; "Footnotes my foot. Footnotes mean the place a fact can be found; they do not confer the right to present someone else's words as your own work" (46).

The distinction being made here is that whenever you use words from a source, this must be indicated clearly through the use of quo-tation marks and documentation at the point in the text where the source information is used. It is not enough to list the author in the footnotes or bibliography. Readers must be able to tell as they are reading your paper exactly what information came from which source and what information is your contribution to the paper. Note that in the example we used signal phrases to indicate the informa-tion in the paragraph comes from a *Newsweek* article by Easterbrook ("A *Newsweek* article reported . . ." and "Easterbrook's response ex-plains . . ."). We also included specific documentation regarding the source itself, along with quotation marks around the exact quotation from Easterbrook. This is an example of proper attribution of source information.

Paraphrasing Appropriately

Paraphrasing may be defined as restating or rewording a passage from a text, giving the same meaning in another form. The objective of paraphrasing, then, is to present an author's ideas in your own words. When paraphrasing fails, it may be because the reader misun-derstood the passage, the reader insisted on reading his or her own ideas into the passage, or the reader partially understood but chose to guess at the meaning rather than fully understanding it. To paraphrase accurately, you must first read closely and understand completely what you are reading. Here are five suggestions that will help you as you paraphrase:

1. Place the information found in the source in a new order.
2. Break the complex ideas into smaller units of meaning.
3. Use concrete, direct vocabulary in place of technical jargon found in the original source.
4. Vary sentence patterns.
5. Use synonyms for words in the source.

Embarrassing Echoes

In both journalism and academia, plagiarism is close to mortal sin. Sometimes writers are tempted to stray, giving themselves credit for the work of another. A side-by-side comparison can be withering.

Gregg Easterbrook, Oct. 1986:
"On a very dark day in 1980, Donald Peterson, newly chosen president of Ford Motors, visited the company design studios. Ford was in the process of losing $2.2 billion, the largest single-year corporate loss in U.S. history."

Richard Pascale, March 1990:
"On a dark day in 1980, Donald Peterson, the newly chosen President of Ford Motor Company, visited the company's Detroit design studio. That year, Ford would lose $2.2 billion, the largest loss in a single year in U.S. corporate history."

Sources: *The Washington Monthly:* and *Managing on the Edge*

Michael Medved, Feb. 2, 1991:
"Apparently, some stern decree has gone out from the upper reaches of the Hollywood establishment that love between married people must never be portrayed on the screen."

H. Joachim Maitre, May 12, 1991:
"Apparently, some stern advice has come from the upper reaches of the Hollywood establishment that love between married people must never be portrayed on the screen."

Source: *The Boston Globe*

The examples below show acceptable and unacceptable paraphrasing:

ORIGINAL PASSAGE

During the last two years of my medical course and the period which I spent in the hospitals as house physician, I found time, by means of serious encroachment on my night's rest, to bring to completion a work on the history of scientific research into the thought world of St. Paul, to revise and enlarge the *Question of the Historical Jesus* for the second edition, and together with Widor to prepare an edition of Bach's preludes and fugues for the organ, giving with each piece directions for its rendering. (Albert Schweitzer, *Out of My Life and Thought*. New York: Mentor, 1963, p. 94.)

A POOR PARAPHRASE

```
     Schweitzer said that during the last two years

of his medical course and the period he spent in
```

the hospitals as house physician he found time, by

encroaching on his night's rest, to bring to

completion several works.

[Note: This paraphrase uses too many words and phrases directly from the original without putting them in quotation marks and thus is considered plagiarism. Furthermore, many of the ideas of the author have been left out, making the paraphrase incomplete. Finally, the student has neglected to acknowledge the source through a parenthetical citation.]

A GOOD PARAPHRASE

Albert Schweitzer observed that by staying up

late at night, first as a medical student and then

as a "house physician," he was able to finish

several major works, including a historical book

on the intellectual world of St. Paul, a revised

and expanded second edition of *Question of the*

Historical Jesus, and a new edition of Bach's

organ preludes and fugues complete with inter-

pretive notes, written collaboratively with Widor

(Schweitzer 94).

[Note: This paraphrase is very complete and appropriate; it does not use the author's own words, except in one instance, which is acknowledged by quotation marks. The student has included a parenthetical citation that indicates to the reader the paraphrase was taken from page 94 of the work by Schweitzer. The reader can find complete information on the work by turning to the bibliography at the end of the student's paper.]

Making Section-by-Section Summaries

As an alternative to close paraphrasing, you may wish to write brief summaries (three or four sentences) on your note cards or in your notebook. Again, use your own words when writing these summaries. If the material is particularly difficult, you may need to stop and summarize more frequently than after each section or chapter. If it is relatively simple to understand or not particularly pertinent to your topic, take fewer notes and write shorter summaries. At any rate, be certain that you are internalizing what you read—the best gauge of your understanding of the material is your ability to put it into your own words in the form of paraphrases or short section-by-section summaries. Again, as with paraphrases or quotations, note down the page numbers on which the material was found.

Reviewing

After completing your marginal notes, paraphrases, or summaries, go back and review the entire piece, taking time to think about what you read. Evaluate the significance of what you learned by relating the work to your own project and starting questions. Your research notebook is the place to record the observations and insights gained in your reading. How does the work fit in with other works you read on the same topic? What ideas seem particularly relevant to your own research? Does the work help to answer your starting question? Answering such questions in your research notebook will help you to put each work you read into the context of your own research.

Perceiving the Author's Organizational Plan

In writing, you should attempt to make your organizational plan clear to your potential readers. Similarly, while reading, you should attempt to discern the organizational plan of the author. One of the best ways to understand the author's plan is to try to reconstruct it through outlining. For an article or book that seems especially important to your research project, you may want to understand the material in a more complete and orderly way than that gained through paraphrasing or summarizing. You can accomplish this goal by constructing an outline of what you have read.

In a well-written piece, the writer will have given you clues to important or key information. Your summaries should have identified main ideas that are most likely to be the main points of the outline. However, you may still need to go back to the work to identify the author's secondary, supporting points, including examples, illustrations, and supporting arguments used to make each individual argument clearer or more persuasive. In outlining a key source, you can come to understand it more fully. Again, be sure that all the points in your outline have been stated in your own words rather than the words of the author.

ILLUMINATION AND VERIFICATION

An essential part of your research is the evolution of your understanding of the subject. As you read and evaluate your sources, you will be seeking a solution to your starting question. Several preliminary writing tasks can help you evaluate your sources and understand your topic better.

Evaluation

In your working bibliography, you record the information needed to find a source. Once you have located a source, you need to evaluate it for its usefulness to your particular research project and to your starting question. Every search will entail the systematic examination, evaluation, and possibly elimination of material. It is not unusual for an article or Web site with a promising title to turn out to be totally irrelevant. Do not be discouraged by dead ends of this sort—they are an accepted and expected part of research. You must not hesitate to eliminate irrelevant or unimportant information. (See Evaluating Print and Electronic Sources, pp. 65–70.)

EXERCISES

1. Write an evaluation of one book or article you have located in your search (or an article assigned by your teacher). Use the criteria for evaluating a source discussed on the preceding pages.

2. Read the article on pp. 80–86. First consider what you know about the author, the publication, and the organization of the piece. Does this information give you any insight into the possible coverage/approach/biases of the article?

Writing from Sources

Reading actively and taking accurate and careful notes in the form of paraphrases and summaries are the first important techniques for working with sources. Your reading notes will form the basis for all your subsequent writing about that particular source. In this section, we will discuss three important approaches to source books and articles that result in three different kinds of writing. These are (1) summarizing the main points of the source book or article in condensed form,

(2) synthesizing the information found in two or more related sources, and (3) critiquing the information found in one or more sources. These three kinds of writing differ from each other in the approach the writer takes to the source in each instance. Your purpose for writing summaries will be different from your purpose for writing syntheses or critiques. Although the source or subject may remain the same, your approach to that source or subject can change, depending on your purpose. Using different approaches to the same sources will help you to understand those sources better.

Summarizing

When summarizing, the writer takes an entirely objective approach to the subject and the source. The writer of summaries is obliged to accurately record the author's meaning. To do this, of course, the summarizer must first understand the source and identify its key ideas during active reading. Since, in general, a summary is about one-third as long as the source itself, this means that two-thirds of the information in the original is left out of the summary. So, what do you as summarizer eliminate? Typically, it is the extended examples, illustrations, and explanations of the original that are left out of a summary. The summarizer attempts to abstract only the gist of the piece, its key ideas and its line of argument. If a reader desires more information than that provided in a summary, he or she may look up the original.

To write a summary, first transcribe your short marginal reading notes onto a separate sheet of paper. Read these notes and decide what you think the author's overall point was. Write the main point in the form of a thesis statement that encapsulates the central idea of the whole article.

> *Thesis:* Cole thinks that there are close
> connections between science and art that stem
> from the creative spirit of humanity.

Be sure not to use the author's words; rather, paraphrase the author's central idea in your own words. Then, by combining the thesis sentence with the marginal notes, you will have constructed the first outline of your summary. Revise the outline for coherence and logical progression of thought.

Next, write the first draft of your summary, following your outline rather than the source. Use your own words, not the words of the author, paraphrasing and condensing his or her ideas. If you want to use the author's own words for a particular passage, use quotation marks to indicate the author's exact words and insert a page reference in parentheses:

```
Cole observes that "a tree is fertile ground

for both the poet and the botanist" (54).
```

In the first few sentences of your summary, introduce the source book or article and its author. Since you have only one source, it is acceptable to place all the publication information in the parenthetical citations rather than in a reference list at the end.

```
In the article "The Scientific Aesthetic"

(Discover, Dec. 1983, pp. 16-17), the author,

K. C. Cole, discusses the relationship of

aesthetics and science.
```

Follow this context information with the thesis statement, which reflects the author's position, and then with the summary itself. Do not insert your own ideas or opinions into the summary. Your summary should reflect the content of the original as accurately and objectively as possible.

When you have completed the first draft of your summary, review the source to be certain that your draft reflects its content completely and accurately. Then reread your draft to determine whether it is clear, coherent, and concise. Next, revise the summary for style and usage, making your sentences flow smoothly and correcting your grammar and punctuation. Finally, write and proofread the final draft. Remember, your summary will recount objectively and in your own words what someone else wrote, so you should refer often to the author by last name.

Synthesizing

When synthesizing, you will approach your material with an eye to finding the relationships among sources. Your purpose will be to discern those relationships and present them coherently and persuasively to your potential readers. Again, the process begins with the active reading of the sources. As you read, highlight and summarize key ideas from your sources in the margins. But instead of simply summarizing the information in one source, look for relationships between ideas in one source and those in another. The sources may be related in one or more of the following ways:

- They may provide examples of a general topic, or one source may serve to exemplify another.
- They may describe or define the topic you are researching.
- They may present information or ideas that can be compared or contrasted.

You must decide in what way or ways your sources are related. When you have decided on the relationships among the sources, write a thesis sentence that embodies that relationship. This thesis sentence should indicate the central idea of your synthesis.

Write an outline of your synthesis paper based on the organizational plan suggested by the thesis statement. This outline should articulate the relationship you have discerned among the sources. For example, if the passages you read all served to describe the same topic (perhaps life in colonial New England), the structure might look like this:

1. Opening paragraph with contextualizing information about the sources and the particular situation, life in colonial New England.
2. Thesis statement describing the relationship to be discussed: Life in colonial New England is described by historians and participants as rigid in its social structure.
3. Description 1 (based on source 1: a historical work about the New England colonies).
4. Description 2 (based on source 2: a diary or journal written by an early colonist).
5. Description 3 (based on source 3: a sermon written by a colonial preacher).
6. Conclusion: All the sources combined contribute to a description of the rigid social structure in colonial New England.

After outlining your synthesis, write the first draft of your paper. In the introductory section of your synthesis, just as in the summary, introduce the sources and their authors. Follow the introduction of sources with your thesis expressing the relationship among the sources. As you write your first draft, keep your thesis in mind, selecting from your sources only the information that develops and supports that thesis. You may want to discuss each source separately, as in the example above, or you may prefer to organize your paper to present major supporting points in the most logical sequence, using information from the sources to develop or support those points. Be sure that you acknowledge all ideas and information from your sources each time you use them in your synthesis.

Upon completion of your first draft, review the sources to be sure you have represented the authors' views fairly and cited source ideas and information properly. Reread your first draft to make sure it is organized logically and that it supports your thesis effectively. Be certain that you have included sufficient transitions between the various sections of your synthesis. Revise your synthesis for style and correctness. Finally, write and proofread the final draft of your synthesis. In general, a synthesis should give the reader a persuasive interpretation of the relationship you have discerned among your sources.

Critiquing

In the third kind of writing from sources, critiquing, the writer takes a critical or evaluative approach to a particular source. When writing critiques, you argue a point that seems important to you based on your own evaluation of the issues and ideas you have encountered in your sources. Critiques are necessarily more difficult to write than summaries or syntheses, because they require that you think critically and come to an independent judgment about a topic. However, critiques are also the most important kind of writing from sources to master, because in many research situations you are asked to formulate your own opinion and critical judgment (as opposed to simply reporting or presenting the information written by others).

As in the other forms of writing from sources, critiquing begins with active reading and careful notetaking from a source. You must first identify the author's main ideas and points before you can evaluate and critique them. Once you understand the source and the issues it addresses, you are in a position to appraise it critically. Analyze the source in one or more of the following ways:

> What is said, by whom, and to whom?
>
> How significant are the author's main points and how well are the points made?
>
> What assumptions does the author make that underlie his or her arguments?
>
> What issues has the author overlooked or what evidence has he or she failed to consider?
>
> Are the author's conclusions valid?
>
> How well written is the source? (Consider its clarity, organization, language.)
>
> What stylistic or rhetorical features affect the source's content?

Other questions may occur to you as you critique the source, but these will serve to get you started in your critical appraisal. To think critically about a source, look behind the arguments themselves to the basis for those arguments. What reasons does the author give for holding a certain belief? In addition, try to discern what assumptions the author is making about the subject. Do you share those assumptions? Are they valid? It is your job to evaluate fairly but with discerning judgment, since this evaluation will be the core of your critique. Formulate a thesis that states your evaluation. Do not feel that your evaluation must necessarily be negative; it is possible to make a positive critique, a negative critique, or a critique that cites both kinds of qualities.

Write an outline of your critique, including the following:

1. An introduction of the subject you wish to address and the source article you wish to critique. Be sure to include a complete citation for the source.
2. A statement of your judgment about the issue in the form of a thesis. In that thesis statement, give your own opinion, which will be supported in the critique itself.
3. The body of the critique. First, briefly summarize the source itself. Then review the issues at hand and explain the background facts and assumptions your readers must understand to share your judgment. Use the bulk of your critique (about two-thirds) to review the author's position in light of your judgment and evaluation.
4. Your conclusion, which reminds the reader of your main points and the reasons you made them.

After completing your outline, write the first draft of your critique, using your outline as a guide. Make certain that all your points are well supported with specific references to the source. Also, make certain that your main points are related to each other and to the thesis statement.

Review the source to be sure you have represented the author's ideas accurately and fairly. Reread your first draft to determine whether your thesis is clearly stated, your paper logically organized, and your thesis adequately and correctly supported. Revise your critique for content, style, and correctness. Finally, write and proofread the final draft of your critique.

Unfortunately, because critiques are subjective, it is not possible to be any more explicit in guiding your writing of them. The substance of the critique will depend entirely on the judgment you make about the source. Remember, though, that a critique needs to be well supported and your opinion well justified by evidence drawn from the source itself. In the exercises that follow, you will have the opportunity to practice writing summaries, syntheses, and critiques. It will also be valuable to write summaries, syntheses, and critiques of sources you are using in your research project as a way to better understand that topic. Do all such preliminary writing in your research notebook.

EXERCISES

1. *Summary*

   Carefully read, underline, and annotate the brief article that follows or another article you have encountered in your own research. Using the procedure described above, write a summary of the article. Be certain to turn in to your teacher both your summary and a photocopy of the article you are summarizing.

2. *Synthesis*

   A. Use two or more articles you have encountered in your research as the basis for an extended definition of an important concept. For example, perhaps you are researching the Senate hearings held prior to Clarence Thomas's confirmation for the U.S. Supreme Court. Because of the testimony of Anita Hill, an important by-product of those hearings was a heightened awareness of sexual harassment in the workplace. You could write an extended definition of sexual harassment based on the explanations you find in articles on the hearings.

   B. Use two or more articles to compare and contrast an idea presented by different authors. Again, using the sexual harassment example, perhaps two or more articles seem to disagree about whether or not a particular action was harassment. You could write a paper that contrasted their views.

   C. Use the illustrations and examples from two or more articles to describe something. For example, you could write a paper that described sexual harassment in the workplace. For such a paper, you would cite specific cases or examples of sexual harassment as reported by the authors but divide your examples into categories or types of harassment behaviors.

3. *Critique*

   Write an evaluative critique of the following article or of an article you have encountered in your own research. Remember, in a critique it is appropriate to include your opinions and experiences as well as your reactions to the article itself. Some issues you might want to focus on are (1) the fairness of the definition of sexual harassment to men in the office, (2) the fairness of making women provide proof of harassment, (3) the relationship of harassment to office politics in general, and (4) the assumption that sexual harassment happens only to women.

Innovative Steps to Take in Sexual Harassment Prevention

Rebecca A. Thacker

For organizations concerned with preventing sexual harassment in the workplace, the time to investigate prevention policies is now. Passage of the 1991 Civil Rights Act allows for punitive damages to be paid to victims of sexual harassment, an option that was not previously available. Recent information from the Equal Employment Opportunity Commission should prove alarming for organizations hoping to minimize their liability for sexual harassment claims. The EEOC reports a 50 percent increase in the number of sexual harassment complaints filed in the first three quarters of 1992. Apparently, complainants are asking the courts to judge whether they have been wronged by sexual harassment in the workplace.

The courtroom need not be the place to make such a determination. Top management of any company can set up internal prevention policies that, if implemented effectively, can provide the necessary outlet for someone who is the target of sexual harassment. Standard prevention policies, however, are not adequate for creating an environment in which targets can feel comfortable complaining about unwelcome social-sexual behavior in the workplace. This article provides guidance for top management in revising sexual harassment prevention policies and designing programs to educate and train employees.

The Problem with Most Sexual Harassment Prevention Policies

Most sexual harassment prevention policies provide for informal and formal complaint procedures. The informal route allows the harassed individual to complain to a member of management or a person designated to receive such complaints. The formal route provides for a formal, written complaint, usually accompanied by a documented investigation.

What is the problem with these policies? The problem is that individuals who are targets of the harassment are required to file a complaint. However, almost half of them do not feel comfortable complaining, either formally or informally, about the unwelcome sexual harassment. For these people, the response is likely to be passive, acquiescent, perhaps even compliant. A policy that requires passive targets to complain is similar to having no prevention policy at all.

Conversely, for those who do feel comfortable filing a complaint, the written policy is probably sufficient. For more than half the targets of sexual harassment, complaining is a natural response, along with telling the harasser to stop, or saying forcefully, "No!"

Ultimately, however, passive, acquiescent targets are harmed by a policy that requires complainant behavior. For these individuals, there is fear of retaliation, or fear that a harassing supervisor may use coercion to make the target comply ("Go out with me or lose your job"). To understand how to design prevention policies that ease the way for passive targets to complain, management must understand what is motivating them to respond in such a manner.

Targets who display passive, acquiescent responses are exhibiting learned helplessness behavior. Learned helplessness is a cognitive state in which individuals perceive that, in spite of their efforts, unpleasant outcomes cannot be averted. For targets of sexual harassment, feelings of learned helplessness may result from an organizational culture that condones sexually harassing behaviors in the workplace, particularly from supervisors and managers. In addition, learned helplessness can come from perceptions that the organization condones sexual discrimination in other forms, such as differential promotion and pay rates for males and females. Regardless of the accuracy of these perceptions, the overall effect is one that prompts targets to believe that they lack the capability of controlling their work environment and terminating unwelcome harassment.

Some passive, acquiescent targets eventually file suit, usually when a negative workplace outcome (a demotion, poor performance appraisal, or even termination) occurs. These people have already experienced retaliation and suffered the consequences of sexual harassment; as a result, they have nothing to lose by filing a suit. Management has the ability and the responsibility to prevent such devastating and costly events by providing internal mechanisms to assist passive, acquiescent targets in feeling comfortable with complaint behaviors. Not only will the organization benefit in terms of reduced litigation costs, but the target will not have to suffer emotional and physical distress as a result of the harassment.

Emphasize Commitment to Eliminating Sexual Harassment from the Workplace

All organizations should have a written sexual harassment prevention policy that includes the following:

• Confidentiality of complaint. The target should be assured that the complaint will be kept in confidence. This is a critical step in raising the comfort level of otherwise passive targets.

• Prompt, tactful investigation. This is extremely critical to providing an incentive for passive targets to file a complaint. Tactful investigation should involve speaking only to the parties involved—the target and the accused harasser. If satisfactory settlement of the complaint occurs at this step, no one else need know that the complaint was filed.

• A written guarantee that there will be no retaliation against targets for filing a complaint. Management must provide this guarantee by investigating claims of retaliation, and when necessary, disciplining supervisors and managers who retaliate against those filing sexual harassment complaints.

• Discipline proven harassers. This can follow the firm's standard disciplinary procedure. If management perceives that the problem is widespread, immediate disciplinary action, such as suspension, may be necessary. Again, for passive targets to be comfortable in filing a complaint, management must send a strong signal that sexual harassment will not be tolerated. Disciplining proven harassers can send such a signal.

• Provide visible top management support. Top management must signal that sexual harassment prevention is of top priority in the workplace. One way to accomplish this is to have a member of top management come to every training session to articulate the company's commitment to eliminating sexual harassment from the workplace.

• Carefully choose the person who will handle complaints. He or she should be tactful, kind, warm, and capable of conducting an objective investigation. If the person who might naturally receive complaints, such as the human resources manager, does not possess these characteristics, then top management should designate someone else who does. Top management should also be careful not to place into this position a person who has a hidden personal agenda (such as an individual who has previously filed a sexual harassment complaint or been the target of a complaint).

• Introduce the person who is responsible for receiving sexual harassment complaints. This should be done during each training session to help enforce top management's commitment to sexual harassment prevention. It should also increase the comfort level of passive targets, giving them an opportunity to meet and talk to the person who will receive and investigate their complaints.

Modify Your Sexual Harassment Prevention Training Programs

Because management often fails to understand the complexity of sexual harassment as a workplace phenomenon, prevention training programs are inadequate. The following are important criteria to take into account when designing these programs:

• Discuss openly both types of target response. Explain that passive, acquiescent responses are not abnormal, and that people who feel inclined to respond in this way should not feel guilty or embarrassed. A frank discussion of both types of response will make those who are passive targets feel as if they are not alone, which can remove some of the reluctance to come forward and complain.

- Discuss positive and negative aspects of both types of target response. The positive aspect of strong, forceful, complaint response is that the target gives the message that harassment is unwelcome. The potential for retaliation is also present when the target resists strongly; however, as mentioned before, the prevention policy should include a statement that retaliation for complaint behavior will not be tolerated.

There are no readily visible positive aspects to passive, acquiescent target response, but there are many negative aspects. The passive target sends a signal that the harassment is welcome, which encourages the harasser to continue. Moreover, the passive target often suffers emotional and psychological distress. Productivity may decrease and absenteeism may increase as he or she finds it increasingly difficult to deal with the harassment.

- Allow employees to role-play both the harasser and the target, and to respond both passively and forcefully in the case of the latter. Observers and participants can then discuss both types of response. Harassers can discuss the kinds of signals sent by targets displaying both types of response.

- Do not rely on sexual harassment prevention training films to do your training for you. Films are appropriate for explaining the different types of sexual harassment, providing visual examples, stimulating discussion, and illustrating target response. However, they should only be used to supplement the rest of the training.

Understand the Role of the Supervisor

Supervisors should provide the first line of defense for organizations attempting to handle sexual harassment complaints internally. However, supervisors often fail to understand their responsibilities in sexual harassment prevention as well as the concept itself. In particular, supervisors often fail to understand that hostile environment harassment (one of the two types of sexual harassment, the other being *quid pro quo* harassment, in which the harasser demands sexual favors in return for benefits of some kind) can involve almost any form of social-sexual behavior—sexual jokes, sexual comments, touching, or leering. Training programs must emphasize the definitional components of sexual harassment for supervisors.

However, in defining harassment, supervisors often fail to understand that *their* definition is not important: it is the *target's* definition that determines whether the unwelcome behavior is sexual harassment. Therefore, when supervisors observe social-sexual behavior in the workplace, the appropriate question is whether the target is bothered by it, not whether the supervisor perceives it as sexually harassing. For example, if supervisors believe that targets who passively accept the social-sexual behavior actually welcome it, they are not fulfilling their responsibility to remove sexual harassment from the workplace. Supervisors typically believe that the appropriate response to sexual harassment is to request an investigation, either internally or externally, or to file a grievance. Supervisory training must emphasize that failure to exhibit either of these responses does not mean that the target finds the social-sexual behavior to be welcome.

Even more critical is the problem of supervisors not understanding their responsibility in preventing harassment on the job. As representatives of management, supervisors must aid in providing a workplace that is free from sexual harassment by assuming the following responsibilities:

• Understand the definitions of sexual harassment as described in the EEOC guidelines. Supervisory training and sexual harassment films can take care of this responsibility.

• Be observant. Supervisors must use their understanding of the definitions of sexual harassment to "police" their work area. If they see social-sexual behavior of any sort, they should take active steps. They might approach tactfully, without being obvious, to ask those exhibiting such behavior if they realized they are engaging in potential sexual harassment. In addition, supervisors might have to ask targets if they are offended by such behavior, for it is always possible that a target is passive and acquiescent.

• Demonstrate listening skills. Listen to employees who have problems in their work area. Passive targets may be willing to articulate a personality conflict or a level of discomfort caused by working around a certain person, but they may be reluctant to mention sexual harassment. By listening, the supervisor can sometimes uncover discomfort caused by sexual harassment. Additional training in listening and communication skill development may be necessary to achieve this step. Such training, which has benefits far beyond sexual harassment prevention, is worth the training dollars spent. Improving listening and communication skills can enhance the supervisor's ability to conduct performance appraisal and disciplinary sessions, as well as enhance the supervisor's ability to motivate problem-solving teams of subordinates.

• Enforce the company's sexual harassment prevention policy. As mentioned before, someone should be designated as the recipient of sexual harassment complaints. The supervisor, as a representative of the company, is obliged to investigate such behavior. If he or she is uncomfortable conducting an investigation, then the appropriate step is to notify the company's designated complaint recipient. Once sexual harassment is observed, the company has immediate liability and must take prompt action. The supervisor then has a responsibility to follow up to ensure that the complaint has been dealt with fairly, and that the target has suffered no retaliation for complaining.

• Appraise performance objectively. Use objective criteria as much as possible to avoid a sexual harassment lawsuit. A target who is terminated, demoted, or given a poor performance appraisal may claim that the negative outcome occurred because the supervisor sexually harassed the target, who refused to go along with the harassment. An objective performance evaluation supports the company's position that the negative outcome resulted from poor performance, and is therefore job-related.

Organizations can do much to encourage targets of sexual harassment to file complaints internally. By understanding the nature of target response, management can design prevention policies that increase the likelihood that passive, acquiescent targets will use internal mechanisms to deal with unwelcome sexual harassment in the workplace. Given the incentive for courtroom litigation prompted by the monetary damages clause of the 1991 Civil Rights Act, management would do well to address these issues. Much can be done by supervisors in the workplace, whose role in sexual harassment prevention needs to be strengthened with training and education. Ultimately, organizations and employees will benefit.

References

EEOC Guidelines on Sexual Harassment, *Federal Register, 45* (1980), No. 72: 25025.

Meritor Savings Bank v. Vinson (106 S.Ct. 2399), 1986.

R. A. Thacker, "A Descriptive Study of Behavioral Responses of Sexual Harassment Targets: Implications for Control Theory," *Employee Responsibilities and Rights Journal,* 5 (1992), June: 155–171.

R. A. Thacker. "Innovative steps to take in sexual harassment prevention," *Business Horizons,* (1994), January–February: 29–32.

R. A. Thacker and G. R. Ferris, "Understanding Sexual Harassment in the Workplace: The Influence of Power and Politics Within the Dyadic Interaction of Harasser and Target," *Human Resource Management Review, 1* (1991): 23–37.

United States Merit Systems Protection Board, *Sexual Harassment in the Workplace: Is It a Problem?* (Washington, DC: Government Printing Office, 1981).

United States Merit Systems Protection Board, *Sexual Harassment in the Federal Government: An Update* (Washington, DC: Government Printing Office, 1988).

Rebecca A. Thacker is an assistant professor of management at the College of Business and Public Administration, University of Louisville, Kentucky.

4

Planning and Writing Your Research Paper

INTRODUCTION

Through the process of planning and writing your research paper you will verify for yourself, and eventually for your readers, the answer to your starting question. You need to present that answer in the best possible fashion, using an appropriate research format and correct writing style. To handle in a reasonable way the large body of material you have accrued, it helps to approach the task systematically. To illustrate one student's writing process, throughout this chapter we will refer to a paper written by Kauleen Kershisnik for a sophomore-level research writing course. Kauleen's research paper on acupuncture appears at the end of Chapter 5.

PLANNING YOUR RESEARCH PAPER

After you have completed the primary research, library research, and preliminary writing on your topic, you are ready to begin planning the actual research paper. You should consider carefully the following two important components as you begin to plan: rhetorical situation and organization.

Rhetorical Situation

The context in which you are writing an assignment is called the rhetorical situation. The term *rhetoric* refers to written or spoken communication that seeks to inform someone of something or to convince someone of a particular opinion or point of view. For any writing assignment, you need to analyze the components of the rhetorical situation: (1) the writer's purpose, (2) the writer's persona, (3) the potential readers or audience, (4) the subject matter, and (5) the appropriate language or tone.

Purpose

When preparing to write, a writer must decide on the actual purpose of the piece. What goal is the paper intended to accomplish? Many times the goal or purpose is implicit in the writing task itself. For example, for a newspaper reporter, the goal is to present the facts in an objective manner, describing events for newspaper readers. For your research paper assignment, you need to determine your purpose or goal and define it carefully. The purpose does not have to be grandiose or profound—it may simply be to convince your readers that you have a firm grasp on the topic and are making some important points, or it may be to inform your readers of the current state of knowledge in a particular field.

Take care to ascertain whether the purpose of the paper is informational or argumentative. These purposes will result in very different research processes and products. An informational paper requires you to inform your audience about a topic, without necessarily making judgments about the topic. (This kind of paper may be called a *research report*.) For example, if you are assigned to write about a historical event, you will be expected to report on the event accurately and cogently. On the other hand, you may be assigned to write a research paper that takes a position on an issue and argues for that position. For example, if you are assigned to write about a controversial issue, such as capital punishment, your audience will expect you to take a stand for or against and to argue for your position by using logical reasoning and source support. Such a research paper is argumentative. An argumentative research paper is neither better nor worse than an informational one—the two are simply different.

It is crucial in an argumentative research paper to present counterarguments, that is, arguments on the other side of the position you are taking. For example, a student writing a paper on global warming discovered that some scientists do not believe that global warming is a serious problem. She disagreed with this position and wished to argue that the problem is a serious one. In the first section of her paper, she systematically refutes the opposition by showing that there is considerable evidence that global warming is indeed happening and that its effects are likely to be quite serious. As she wrote the rest of her paper, this student was conscious throughout of the opposing viewpoint and was careful to counter that view with her own arguments.

Kauleen's purpose statement read as follows: "My purpose in this paper is to tell readers who may know nothing about acupuncture in an informative manner how this ancient Chinese remedy is evolving into many modern day uses and cures." As you can see, the purpose of Kauleen's paper is primarily informational.

Persona

You also need to decide just how to present yourself as a writer to those who will read your work. Do you want to sound objective and fair, heated and passionate, sincere and persuasive, or informative and rational? The term *persona* is used to describe the identity that the speaker or writer adopts. As you know, we all play many roles, depending on the situations in which we find ourselves: with your parents, you may be quiet and reserved; with your peers, outgoing and comical, and so on. Similarly, you can be flexible about how you portray yourself in your writing, changing your persona with your purpose and audience. First, establish your credibility by being careful and thorough in your research and by showing that you have done your homework and understand what you are writing about. Then, prepare your finished product with care and attention to detail. If you do not, your readers will assume that you are sloppy and careless and will largely discount anything you have to say. For example, many job applicants never even make it to the interview stage because their letters of application convey the subliminal message "here is a person who is careless and inconsiderate of others."

After discussions with her classmates and teacher, Kauleen decided that she wanted to adopt a persona that reflected her balanced and fair appraisal of the medical treatment known as acupuncture. She felt that the public held many negative stereotypes and preconceptions about the use of acupuncture that she wanted to dispel by sounding logical and straightforward in her presentation of the facts.

Audience

Identifying those who may be reading your writing will help you to make decisions about what to include or not include in your research paper. Those who are the most likely to read your writing make up your audience. For example, a newspaper reporter assumes a general readership made up of members of the community. But the reporter must also assume that his or her readers were not present at the event being covered; thus, he or she must take care to reconstruct details for the readers.

In the case of a college research paper, the instructor of the course may suggest an appropriate audience or may in fact be the primary audience. You will wish to discuss the paper's potential audience with your teacher. If the instructor is the intended audience, you should assume that the instructor is knowledgeable about the subject, reasonably intelligent, and particularly interested in the accuracy of the research.

In Kauleen's research writing class, the teacher discussed questions of audience with the students who decided that their target readers would be each other, their peers, rather than their instructor. The class spent time in small groups discussing their papers with each other in order to obtain a better sense of their target audience's needs as readers. Kauleen discovered that the other students in her group had heard of acupuncture ("sticking needles in people") but knew very little of the details about its background or uses in medicine today. She determined that providing explicit and detailed information for these readers would be important.

Take time before writing to consider carefully who will read your research paper. Your readers make a difference to you, both in how you approach your topic (Are my readers novices or experts in the field?) and in the tone you adopt (Are my readers likely to agree with me or must I win them over to my point of view?). If your instructor has made no stipulations about the intended audience for your research paper, you should discuss the issue of audience with him or her. If your teacher is the target audience, it is especially important for you to know whether he or she will be reading as a nonexpert (a novice in the field) or will assume the role of a knowledgeable expert. Your decisions about what to include in the paper and what level of tone and diction to adopt will depend on whether you are writing for an expert or novice audience.

Subject Matter

The most important component of the rhetorical situation, however, is the subject matter. Although no piece of writing exists in isolation (hence the need for analyzing the purpose, persona, and audience), the content that you are presenting to your audience will be the core of any piece you are writing. You must decide from the mass of material you discover in your research what to include in your written presentation. These decisions are based on your starting question, your analysis and evaluation of your sources, and your thesis statement. Knowing what your ultimate goal is, how you wish to sound, and who your readers are will help you decide what source materials to use. Kauleen had run across several source citations when using the MedLine CD-ROM database. However, as she read the abstracts, the articles seemed far too technical for the general readers she had identified as her audience, and she decided to eliminate most of them from her search.

Appropriate Language or Tone

Knowing your purpose, persona, audience, and subject matter will lead you also into appropriate decisions about language and tone. If your purpose is to inform a general audience on a technical subject, you will need to take particular care to define terms and to use general words in place of technical jargon. You might also consider providing your readers with a glossary of terms to help them through technical information. Kauleen, for example, was careful in her paper to define the medical words she was using.

If you are addressing an audience of specialists, your rhetorical decisions about language and tone will be quite different. In this case you may wish to use technical vocabulary to build your own credibility with the expert audience. You will need to take care not to bore an expert reader by providing too much background information, which such readers will not need.

Academic papers should be informative and serious, but they need not be dull or dry. It is generally not appropriate to adopt too informal a tone for an academic research paper. On the other hand, taking yourself out of the piece entirely may leave your readers with the impression that the piece is lifeless and uninteresting. Try to strike a balance in your tone to make it appropriate for your audience and purpose.

Organization

Once you have gathered and evaluated source materials on your topic, completed your preliminary writing, and analyzed the rhetorical situation, you can begin to organize your ideas. During the planning stages, you need to decide how you will give pattern and order to your research paper. The importance of planning cannot be overemphasized. Readers will use your skeletal plan, which should appear in some form in the written research paper, to reconstruct your meaning. Many recent investigations into the reading process have shown that readers reconstruct meaning in written material by using organizational plans, that is, explicit directional signals left by the writer in his or her work.

There is no one right way to make order out of the mass of material you have gathered in your research. Some people find that just beginning to write helps them to discover a direction and a pattern. Others prefer to outline and to organize or sort their notes by categories. Some writers spread their note cards in seemingly random piles across the desktop; others sort note cards neatly by topics. Eventually, regardless of the process, you want to be able to write a thesis statement that captures succinctly the main point you wish to make in your paper.

Your purpose for writing the paper and the rhetorical situation you have defined can give you some clues about how to organize your paper. If your purpose is to inform readers of something, ask yourself what organizational plan that might suggest. To be informative implies that you will need to provide background and definitions on the subject, perhaps describing how something works or how it is used. Kauleen decided to begin with a discussion of the ancient Chinese philosophy of yin and yang, upon which acupuncture is built. Next, she thought her readers would want to know about the needles, since her classmates seemed to have many questions about their uses. Finally, she planned to end the paper with some modern-day treatments based on acupuncture techniques.

Reassess Your Working Hypothesis and Write Your Thesis

Your starting questions and working hypothesis helped you to focus your research. Now is the time to reassess your working hypothesis. Does it still reflect the position you wish to take in your paper? If not, revise the hypothesis accordingly. Remember, if you are writing an argumentative paper, your hypothesis should take a side on a debatable issue.

A thesis statement for a research paper is similar to a thesis statement for an essay. That is, it states for the reader the central idea that the paper will argue. Writers often begin with a preliminary thesis statement that is subsequently revised during the writing process. Your teacher may require that your thesis (and thus your research paper) have an argumentative purpose. If so, make sure that you have taken a stand that can be supported through arguments in the research paper itself. If your research paper is not argumentative, but rather informational, your thesis should reflect the fact that you are reporting information rather than taking a stand on an issue. The examples below illustrate the two types of thesis statements.

An argumentative thesis: "Whatever the causes, males and females have different perspectives on computers and their uses."

An informational thesis: "This paper will trace the evolution of computers from the first room-sized mainframes to the current hand-held notebooks."

Your thesis statement should tell your reader very clearly what direction your paper will take. The reader should not be surprised by a position taken at the end that was never acknowledged in the introduction to your paper or in the thesis statement. Kauleen's working thesis for her informational paper follows:

```
Acupuncture is an ancient Chinese remedy which

is evolving into many modern-day uses and cures.
```

Choose an Organizational Pattern

The patterns described in the list that follows are meant only to suggest possible ways of organizing a research paper. A project may combine several of these patterns, perhaps using one main pattern as an overall guide. Or, you might find you need a totally different pattern, such as those commonly used in research reports (abstract, problem statement, methods, results, discussion). Your rhetorical situation, your intention as a writer, must be your ultimate guide. However, as human beings, we do have standard ways of making sense of our environments. The patterns described below reflect those habitual ways of organizing experience. Readers will be looking for familiar patterns in your writing, so the more explicitly you signal those patterns, the more likely it is that the readers will understand what you have to say.

1. *Cause and effect.* Many research projects and/or reports seek to link phenomena through cause-and-effect relationships. For example, from a chemical experiment: "The cause of the chemical change was the new substance introduced into the reaction mixture; the effect of the experiment was a change in the compound's chemical structure." From political science: "The cause of the failure of the incumbent's ad campaign was the negative image projected in his TV advertisements; the effect of the ad campaign was to unseat the incumbent."

Does your research topic lend itself to an organizational pattern based on causes or effects? One student, for example, writing about children's self-concept, decided that it was important to spend considerable time in her paper discussing the causes of low self-esteem in children. She also talked later in the paper about the effects of low self-esteem on a child's success in school.

2. *Compare and contrast.* Many research projects seek to compare or contrast two or more ideas, issues, or events. In comparing, we look for similarity; in contrasting, for difference. For example, from history: "The events surrounding World War I and World War II are compared and contrasted in an effort to understand how they were alike and different." From psychology: "The case histories of two psychotic individuals are studied to find common threads."

Think about your research topic; do you find yourself comparing or contrasting two very similar or very different ideas? For example, a student writing about puberty rituals found it interesting to compare and contrast the ways in which different cultures marked entry to adulthood.

3. *Classification and definition.* To make sense of our world, we classify and define ideas, issues, and events by their characteristic parts. When we define something, we describe what it is and perhaps what it is not. For example, from sociology: "A ghetto is defined as a section of an urban area heavily populated by a particular minority group. A slum is not the same as a ghetto because a slum may contain a mixture of groups, whereas a ghetto (which can be a slum) contains one predominant minority group."

Many research projects begin with definitions or classifications to help their readers understand complex topics. A student writing on computer crime, for example, began his paper by dividing up the types of computer crimes and defining the role of the computer in each of them: computer as object of crime, computer as site of crime, computer as instrument to commit a crime, and computer as symbol for criminal deception.

4. *Question and answer.* In this pattern, a specific question is raised and probable answers to the question are presented. The question-and-answer pattern can exist by itself or as a part of another pattern, perhaps cause and effect, for example, from political science: "What are the reasons for or causes behind President Johnson's decisions during the Vietnam War?"

Is there a fundamental question that your paper seeks to answer? If so, you can begin the paper by posing the question for your readers and then proceed to answer it systematically by providing details and evidence to support your position. A student writing on a literary topic framed the following question: "What are the major themes in Shakespeare's *Hamlet?*" To answer the question, she cited several examples from the text itself and reinforced her points by using expert opinions from literary criticism of *Hamlet.*

5. *Problem and solution.* In this pattern, a particular problem is identified and solutions to the problem are posed. For example, from business: "The productivity of automobile workers in the United States has fallen considerably in the past two years." The researcher looks at the problem and proposes solutions to help raise productivity levels: "Solutions might include pay incentives, improved work environment, and exercise facilities for employees."

Perhaps your research topic lends itself to a problem/solution pattern. Your readers will need to know up-front what you consider the problem to be; then, they will expect to see alternative solutions, perhaps ending with what you consider to be the best solution. A student was researching the topic of remote sensing, which she defined as the "science of deriving information about the earth's surface from images acquired at a distance." In her reading about the topic, she uncovered the problem of the "human factor" in remote sensing: as a tool, remote sensing is only as good as its human interpreter. Her solution to this problem, as posed in her paper, was to minimize human errors by field checks of data.

6. *Narration and description.* Sometimes a narrative (story) or a description of a particular thing or event is included in a research paper. For example, from astronomy: "A new star is located in our galaxy. It is described in detail with reference to its size, shape, characteristics, location, and so on." Also, a narrative may be written to account for the star's probable origin and future development (based on the description).

You may find it important to describe something in detail or to tell a story of an event as a part of your research paper. Kauleen decided to open her paper with a compelling narrative of a man undergoing major surgery using acupuncture as the only anesthetic. In this way, she hoped to grab the attention and interest of her readers immediately.

7. *Process analysis.* Often, a particular process will be important in a research paper. Analysis of the process by which nuclear fission occurs is an example from physics. An example from political science is the analysis of the election process in a democratic system.

Think about your research project; is there a process that it is important for your readers to understand? If so, you will want to spend considerable time analyzing the process. For example, a student writing about deterioration of air quality in major U.S. cities decided that he needed to analyze for his readers the chemical processes by which auto emissions become smog.

8. *General to specific.* Organizing from a general statement to specific supporting details is the most common of all patterns, and the general statement serves effectively as a topic sentence. For example, from sociology: "Every society creates an idealized image of the future—a vision that serves to direct the imagination and energy of its people." In this paper the student began with a general discussion of "every society" and then narrowed the focus to a "near-workerless society" in the specific discussion at the end of the paper.

Perhaps your research will lend itself to a general-to-specific pattern of organization. If you are discussing any general principle and then illustrating it with specific examples, you are making use of this pattern of organization.

One final note about planning: write your tentative plans in your research notebook or computer file, but be sure to keep your plans flexible. In the process of writing your first draft, you may be led to new insights and discoveries. Do not cut off the discovery function of writing by rigidly sticking to a particular plan. Rather, be open to changing your plan to accommodate any new insight you might have along the way. When an architect is planning a building, he or she makes and discards several blueprints as the planning proceeds. Use your plans as blueprints—as guides only—not finished buildings made of concrete.

EXERCISES

1. For your research paper project, brainstorm possible organizational patterns based on those previously outlined. Choose two or three patterns and freewrite several paragraphs that discuss how those patterns might be used in your paper.

2. For one of the following writing assignments, write a thesis statement, informal outline, and one-paragraph summary of contents. Pay explicit attention to rhetorical context and to organization.

   A. A brochure on making the transition from high school to college written for an audience of high-school students

   B. An editorial on academic cheating for the college newspaper

   C. A proposal for improving the food in the dorm cafeteria written to the coordinator of food services

3. Analyze the organizational patterns of the following student paragraphs. Identify the pattern that seems to dominate each paragraph and any other supporting patterns.

   A. When the rock star stepped on stage, he flashed a sexy smile at all the girls in the front row. He pranced to the music of their frantic screams, the muscles rippling on his bare torso. Slowly, excruciatingly, his left hand lifted the mike to his lips, his throat rumbling a low-pitched love phrase. He laughed as the girls fainted, exulting in his wild power over the female sex. Once again, he knew he was a god.

   B. The student who enrolls in a premedical program can look forward to a grueling four years. The primary reason for the tough course of study is that a premed student must be well versed in both sciences and liberal arts. In addition to obtaining a degree in a particular field of study, for example, psychology, the premed student must fulfill the medical school's prerequisite courses: chemistry (four semesters), physics (two semesters), biology (four semesters), and calculus (one semester). As well, the student must maintain a 3.5 grade point average to be considered by a medical school.

C. In Israel the cost of gasoline has gone to more than $3 a liter. High prices for fuel also pervade Europe and Asia. But in Ecuador, the Middle East, and the United States, prices are less than half what they are in Israel. This difference in prices is not because Israel, Europe, and Asia are incapable of marketing gasoline economically. Rather, Ecuador and the United States are capable of providing themselves with gasoline through their own transport systems while Israel, Europe, and Asia are not. The price of commodities like gasoline, which require special transport, will continue to rise as transportation costs rise.

OUTLINING AND DRAFTING YOUR RESEARCH PAPER

Constructing an Outline or Plan

As you review your notes and source materials, set aside any information that does not seem directly relevant to the main point you wish to make in the paper. Then, it might be helpful to sort your notes or note cards into related categories of information. Does the thesis you have written suggest any organizational pattern that might give you the skeleton of an outline? For example, if your thesis suggests a cause-and-effect pattern, you will probably need to discuss causes first, followed by effects. Kauleen's working thesis suggested to her that she needed to first define acupuncture and describe how it works. Then, since she wanted to show how it has evolved into today's treatments, she realized that she would need a good portion of her paper to talk about its uses and its efficacy as a treatment for certain medical problems.

Some writers like to flesh out that skeleton plan by incorporating major points and subpoints into an outline structure. Others prefer to begin writing and have the structure evolve more organically. You need not be overly concerned about formal structure at this point unless your teacher stipulates a particular outline format. An outline should be a guide for writing, not a constraint that confines and limits your thinking. You may wish to change your thesis and your organizational plan several times as you make new discoveries while writing. Here is Kauleen's informal outline:

```
          Title: Is Your Ch'i in Balance?

    Working Thesis: Acupuncture is an ancient Chinese
remedy  which is evolving into many modern day uses
and cures.
        I. Introduction
       II. How acupuncture works
              -ch'i
              -meridians
      III. Needles
              -what made of
              -how far inserted
              -where inserted
       IV. Anaesthesia
              -in China
              -in United States
        V. Treating drug addicts
              -kinds of drug addictions
              -treatment
              -how it works
```

Drafting Your Paper

Now you should be ready to begin seriously drafting the research paper itself, if you haven't yet done so. Remind yourself of your general understanding of the topic, of your starting question, and of the answer to that question as stated in your thesis. When writing your first draft, use concrete and simple language to explain in your own words your research conclusions. Ideally, you should type your draft on a computer or word processor to make revisions easier. But be certain to back up your computer files and save to a disk frequently so as not to lose any of your hard work.

Your Knowledge

Do not be overly concerned at this time about mechanics, usage, and spelling, but concentrate on communicating information and presenting that information in an orderly way. If you have prepared sufficiently, the actual writing of the paper becomes an important means of verifying for yourself the insights you have gained through your research.

As you write, it is best to put down your own understanding of your topic rather than relying heavily on your sources. Then, after you have written your draft, you can go back and add sources as support for your arguments. Your readers will want to know what *you* think about the subject. They don't want to read a string of quotes loosely joined by transitions. Studying the topic and reading the source materials should have provided you with a general understanding of your topic. Writing a preliminary thesis should have provided you with the main point you wish to make. Once you have drafted your paper, important data, illustrations, and supporting evidence can be gleaned from your sources and added to your argument to give it authority and force.

Source Knowledge

As you begin to add source information, do not be too concerned about the formal details of documentation, which can be dealt with later, but do mark in the draft any ideas or words taken from your sources. Remember to place any word, phrase, or sentence you copy directly from a source in quotation marks and to note down the author, publication date, and page reference for the quotation. Similarly, you must acknowledge ideas taken from a source even though you have paraphrased or restated them in your own words.

Common Knowledge

You need not document common knowledge, that is, knowledge that is generally known or accepted by educated people. If you can find information readily in general reference works such as encyclopedias or in the popular media (television, radio, newspapers, or magazines), that information is probably common knowledge and need not be documented.

In the model paper at the end of Chapter 5, it was not necessary for Kauleen to document the fact that acupuncture is an ancient Chinese medical procedure dating from around 2,500 BC based on a Chinese belief in a life force or energy flowing throughout the body; this information could be considered common knowledge because it is found in any general reference source. Well-proven historical facts and dates need not be documented. However, it is better to overdocument than to underdocument and be accused of plagiarizing. When in doubt, document.

Apply a Drafting Strategy

You will need to establish your own strategy for writing your first draft, one that fits comfortably with your writing style. Here are a few different ways in which writers of research papers proceed:

- *Write a draft systematically from a plan, using the building-block approach.* One approach to composing is to envision a set of building blocks that you can use to build your paper a little at a time. Many writers first compose a skeleton of their finished paper and then expand it by adding new arguments, supporting examples and evidence, or illustrative details—the "building blocks." Word processing is particularly helpful when using this approach. Many writers like to write their central paragraphs, the middle blocks of text first and add the introductory blocks and concluding paragraphs later. You can decide which blocks will be easiest to write and do those first, saving the parts that will be more difficult for last. Once you have a preliminary draft, you can amplify sections, one block at a time. You can use the new file you created from copies of your rough draft and outline files to create blocks. Use the headings in your outline to expand your text. Cut and paste text from your rough draft file to place under the headings; then rewrite and amplify the text to create blocks.
- *Write a draft from notes arranged according to the blueprint provided by your thesis.* As an alternative to composing from building blocks, you may prefer to compose from the beginning of your paper straight through to the end (thus moving from the top down). You can use your working thesis statement and its corresponding organizational plan to compose in this way. Type your working thesis statement into a new document file. As noted earlier, your thesis statement can provide you with a blueprint for composing. With the thesis statement at the top of your screen, begin writing your draft, following the blueprint suggested by the thesis. Save your draft file into the appropriate directory on your hard drive so that you can return to it later. Remember, your working thesis is just that—something to guide you while you are working. As you write, be flexible and open to new directions that may occur to you while composing.

- *Write a sketchy first draft.* You may prefer to write a sketchy, or partial, first draft without looking at your notes, instead just write down everything you remember from the research. Then, follow up by fleshing out the partial draft with a more complete version while referring to your notes.
- *Write a rough first draft and then write a revision outline that suggests how the draft should be changed.* You can write a revision outline after you have completed a first draft and perhaps received some comments on it from a peer or your teacher. In a revision outline, you update the original outline for the paper to reflect what you now see as the weaknesses of the draft. To plan for revising your draft, add comments in brackets to the revision outline, noting the items you need to change in your draft.
- *Write a draft by cutting and pasting information from an electronic research notebook.* If you have typed your notes into a computer file (an electronic research notebook), you can build your research paper by cutting and pasting information from that file into the draft of your research paper.
- *Write a draft while viewing electronic note cards in a second window.* If you have your notes on electronic note cards, you can open each note card in one window to refer to as you are composing your draft in a second window.

Write a Working Title

Because the title of a paper is the first thing a reader sees, it must make a good impression. The title also must help the reader anticipate the topic and perhaps the writer's point of view. Writing a title can help you to state very succinctly the topic of your research paper. Try out a few titles before deciding on one. It should be brief yet descriptive. Kauleen used "Is Your Ch'i in Balance?" as her title.

Write an Introduction and a Conclusion

Openings or Introductions. Writers have very little time in which to grab the reader's attention—usually only a few seconds. That is why the opening, or *lead,* is so important. But don't let concern over how you will begin become a stumbling block for you. Many writers find that it works best for them to leave the opening for the last stages of revision. When writing your lead, to grab a reader's attention, try starting with an anecdote or story, a quotation, dialogue, or descriptive scene. For example, one student began with dialogue:

> "Look at this new CD I bought!" Jane exclaims
>
> to her friend. Interested, Michael eagerly looks

```
at it. "Wow," he says. "These guys are my favorite

group! Mind if I make a copy of it?"
```

Most experienced writers don't begin a piece with their thesis or statement of purpose ("This paper will explore the pros and cons of drilling an auxiliary well in Smithfield canyon"), although some academic writing, by tradition, demands such an opening. The introduction below illustrates a traditional academic lead.

> This essay examines issues of diversity and literacy education primarily in terms of the concept of *difference* via a new term: *non-negotiable difference*. It argues that networked classrooms provide writing instructors with unique extra-linguistic cues (body language) that can help teachers and students become more responsive to racial difference.
>
> [Todd Taylor, "The Persistence of Difference in Networked
Classrooms: Non-Negotiable Difference and the African
American Student Body," Computers and Composition 14
(1997): 169–178.]

If appropriate for your writing assignment, you can try being creative or humorous as you explore a variety of approaches to writing your opening paragraph.

Closings or Conclusions.   There are two basic types of conclusions: (1) conclusions that summarize and point the reader back to the text itself, and (2) conclusions that speculate and point the reader ahead to implications or more research.

A SUMMARY CONCLUSION

Few Interneters would disagree that stealing and reselling software or credit cards is wrong. But fewer still would feel guilty about copying the latest game version of Doom, or some such, rather than forking out $39.95. Unfortunately, that often admirable ethos makes it easier for genuine crooks to perpetrate—and justify—their crimes.

> [Michael Meyer with Anne Underwood, "Crimes of the
'Net.'" Cyberreader. Ed. Victor Vitanza. New York: Simon and
Schuster, 1996. 63–65.]

A SPECULATIVE CONCLUSION

Nevertheless, in the litigations and political debates which are certain to follow, we will endeavor to assure that their electronic speech is protected as certainly as any opinions which are printed or, for that matter, screamed. We will make an effort to clarify issues surrounding the distribution of intellectual property. And we will help to create for America a future which is as blessed by the Bill of Rights as its past has been.

[John Perry Barlow, "Crime and Puzzlement." *Cyberreader*. Ed.
Victor Vitanza. New York: Simon and Schuster, 1996. 92–115.]

Don't feel obligated to write a summarizing conclusion. The second type, the speculative conclusion, sometimes works better. Speculative conclusions are most appropriate for papers that point the reader in a new direction, that reflect on the implications of the paper's content, or that suggest a need for further research.

Avoiding Writer's Block

Each writer develops his or her own writing rhythms. You need to discover what your rhythms are. If you find yourself "blocked" as a writer, set your work aside for a few days or even a few hours. At the least, get up and stretch, make yourself a cup of coffee, or grab a soft drink before returning to your draft. Coming back to it fresh may give you renewed energy. If you find the writing is flowing well, try to keep at it—writing often takes on a life of its own and provides its own momentum. Finally, don't expect perfection from a first draft. Remember that writing is essentially rewriting: everything we write needs to undergo extensive revisions in a continuous cycle of writing, revising, editing, and writing again.

SUGGESTIONS FOR OVERCOMING WRITER'S BLOCK

- **Gain some distance.** Set your writing aside for a few hours or days. Or take a coffee or snack break before coming back to your work.

- **Keep at it.** When your writing is flowing well, try to avoid being interrupted so that you can keep the momentum going.

- **Try freewriting.** Often, the act of writing itself will stimulate the creative juices.

- **Use visualization.** Picture yourself writing, or picture some aspect of the topic you are writing about. Then describe what you see.

- **Change your point of view.** Try writing from another person's point of view. Or try writing in a different genre, such as a letter or a memo.

- **Write what you know first.** Rather than beginning with the introductory paragraph, start by writing the portion of your paper that you know the most about.

- **Change your mode of writing.** If you normally compose at a computer, try using pencil and paper, or vice versa.

Collaborating

You might find it helpful as you compose to collaborate with others. In college classes, as in the business environment, writers often work on projects in writing groups or writing teams. Your teammates can serve as a sounding board for your ideas and arguments. You can compose together, with one team member acting as the scribe at the keyboard. Or you can compose separately, and then turn to each other for responses. Your peers can read early drafts and provide you with valuable feedback on your work. Take advantage of the help that can be found in such collaborative writing groups.

Working with a Group

Working with a group may be something you enjoy or something you dread, depending on whether your experience with group projects has been positive or negative. In some writing groups, one or two students may feel that they are doing all the work. In other groups, a few students may be bossy or controlling rather than cooperative. But, if group members pay attention to group dynamics and role assignments from the start of a collaborative project, they should get along just fine and together produce an outcome that none could have achieved alone.

When you first receive a collaborative assignment from your teacher, meet with your group to begin brainstorming. One member can act as the group's scribe, typing into the computer all of the ideas generated by the group. Don't cut off creative avenues; brainstorm in the spirit of both understanding and opening up the assignment for the group. Once the group has brainstormed a list of ideas, begin to classify and divide it into components, in an effort to outline a plan of action. You might want to "storyboard" the piece—that is, put the components of the overall piece onto 3 × 5 note cards and then work together to arrange the components to best advantage.

Collaborative or Team Writing

When the group has come up with an overall plan for the writing project, specific tasks or roles can be allotted to group members. For example, one writing class was assigned the task of developing a group Web site on a topic related to cyberspace. The students in each group brainstormed about the possibilities for their site, first deciding on the nature of its content. Each group member agreed to write independently a two- to three-page piece that would be incorporated as a page at the site. Then, each person in the group was assigned a specific role: *group leader* (organized group meetings, set deadlines, reported progress to the teacher), *group librarian* (recorded relevant Web sites, produced a bibliography, ensured that all links in the site were operational), *group publisher* (took responsibility for the "look" of the site by importing graphics and deciding on appropriate fonts, colors, and backgrounds), *group Webmaster* (took responsibility for placing all of the group's writing onto the server, making sure that the site was both functional and readable). Because each student in the group knew exactly what his or her contribution would be, group members were able to work together cooperatively.

Drafting with a Computer

Although some students may not have computers available and are still writing out their rough drafts by hand, other students (with computers of their own or easy access to computer labs) compose their papers directly at a computer keyboard. This section examines how computers have changed the composing process and suggest strategies for adapting to the changes.

Adapting Your Writing Habits

If you are accustomed to writing with pen and paper, you may find that your old writing habits do not translate directly when you use a computer. Old habits are difficult to break, and some writers steadfastly resist the new technology. Others stick to their old habits because they are comforting. For example, one writer reports that before each writing session, he takes a dozen pencils and sharpens them to neat points. He puts all the pencils in a pencil holder and then sits down to type at the computer, not using the pencils at all! You too may find that it helps to observe some of the rituals you have developed for writing with pen and paper. But the more familiar you become with writing at the computer, the more you will see its value to you as a writer. Once they get beyond the initial learning stages, most writers eventually find composing at the keyboard more efficient.

Changing Your Notion of Text and Draft

Changing to a new writing tool may subtly change your relationship to your own words. At first, you may find that the words on the screen seem somehow foreign and strange—unlike the words you produced with paper and pencil. A student remarked that the words on screen seemed like phantoms that could disappear at the touch of a key. However, this sense of distance that word processing creates also allows you to see your writing as more fluid and changeable. It will probably make you more willing to experiment and to abandon text that is not working so that you can start again. In fact, your notion of a "draft" will change when you compose at a computer. Each time you open a file to make changes in the text, you are in essence creating a new draft, whether or not you print it out for review. You may work through dozens of drafts as you continue to revisit your text while composing.

Using the Computer Wisely

When you begin to use a computer for composing, don't get carried away. Some writing—such as a short note to a friend—is still better done with pen and paper. If you work in a computer lab, where access is limited, you might find that it works best to write a first draft on paper and save your computer time for a later draft and for revisions. Even if you have a computer of your own, it may not be portable; keeping a notebook handy for on-the-spot composing is therefore helpful. If you are fortunate enough to own a laptop computer, it probably has a "notepad" or "scrapbook," which you can use for recording notes and organizing your ideas. Work on developing a writing system that uses the computer—and your time—to best advantage.

Working Effectively in a Lab Environment

If your only access to a computer is in a lab, then you should be as flexible as possible about your writing process. Try to schedule work at the time that best suits your own writing habits. However, if the lab is not open at 2:00 a.m., when you work best, you may need to write a draft on paper and then transfer it to the computer for revision later on. Most lab directors try to accommodate students by opening the lab some evenings or weekends, but it may be filled to capacity during those times, or some computers may not be functioning. Plan ahead and leave time to compensate for these potential problems.

You can help the lab director improve the lab environment by making suggestions and providing feedback on your lab experience. If a lab assistant is surly and unhelpful, say so. If other writers in the lab are noisy or disruptive, ask the lab assistant to quiet them down. In most cases, the lab assistants will be genuinely interested in helping you write successfully, and your suggestions can help improve the lab environment for everyone.

5

Revising and Formatting Your Research Paper

INTRODUCTION

Important work still remains on your paper once you have completed a rough draft. You must revise the paper to make the most effective possible presentation of the research. Your readers expect you to be clear and correct in your presentation so that they are not distracted by confusing language or incorrect punctuation.

To be a skillful reviser, you must put yourself in the place of your reader. When writers read their own work, however, they may have trouble seeing and evaluating what they have written. They often see what they *intended* to write rather than what they actually wrote. This chapter will offer strategies to help you shift roles from writer to reader so that you will be able to revise your work effectively.

REWRITING YOUR RESEARCH PAPER

As you begin to rewrite your research paper, read through your rough draft several times, both on the computer screen and on hard copy. Each time you read it, pay attention to a different aspect of the paper for possible revision and correction. Three rewriting skills—revising, editing, and proofreading—will be discussed in this chapter. As you think about rewriting, imagine that you are viewing your writing through the lens of a camera. Your first view is panoramic (**revising**): you look globally at the entire scene of your writing with the goal of revising its development, coherence, focus, organization, and format.

Your second view is at normal range (**editing**): you look locally at specific sentence-level features of your writing with the goal of editing for wordiness, repetition, and ineffective or awkward language. Finally, you zoom in for a close-up (**proofreading**): you proofread for any distracting errors that will interfere with your reader's understanding, including errors in punctuation and mechanics.

Rereading and Reviewing Your Draft

If possible, allow at least a day between the time you finish your draft and the time you read it to revise, edit, and proofread. You will be astonished at how much more clearly you can view your own writing after you have been away from it for awhile. If you are facing a tight deadline, even an hour or two will help. Also, try to schedule time for more than one revising session. Text that is stored electronically is much easier to revise because you don't need to retype or recopy the entire text after each change. However, rewriting, editing, and proofreading all take time. Here are a few strategies to help you read your text with a fresh eye.

1. You can gain the distance needed for revising by changing the way your text looks:
   - Change the spacing of your text from double to triple space. OR
   - Change the font from 12 point to 15 point. OR
   - Insert page breaks after each paragraph to isolate them. OR
   - Change the margins from 1 inch to 2 inches.
2. Save the reformatted text under a new name.
3. Print out the reformatted text for review.
4. Read each paragraph of the printed text carefully, using the reading questions outlined in this chapter on page 113.
5. Write revision suggestions in the margins.

Revising for Structure and Style

The first time you read your draft, pay attention to the organizational structure and overall content of the paper. At this point, decide whether you need to make any major changes in the order of the ideas or whether you should alter the tone. Use the power of your word-processing program, in particular its CUT and PASTE functions, to accomplish these global changes quickly and easily. A helpful acronym to keep in mind as you revise for such large issues is EARS: *E*liminate, *A*dd, *R*earrange, and *S*ubstitute.

Do not be afraid to eliminate irrelevant material from your paper. Your teacher will prefer a paper that is tightly focused to one padded with irrelevant details. Conversely, if you discover a section of your paper that seems thin, do not hesitate to add more information: more evidence to support an idea, more explanation to clarify an idea, and so on. Be sure that the major sections of the paper are arranged in a logical order. If there seems to be any confusion, rearrange major sections. Finally, if you find an example or a piece of evidence that does not seem persuasive in the context of the paper, substitute a new example for the one you currently have.

Remember your rough draft is exactly that—rough. It is important for you to read it critically now so that you can improve the overall presentation of your ideas. Share your draft with a friend, spouse, teacher, classmate, or coworker. Another reader can provide insights on your paper that may be very helpful to you as you revise. The following list of questions can guide both you and others as they read your draft:

1. Is my title creative and does it relate to the paper?
2. Is my introduction informative, engaging, or interesting? Does it make the reader want to read on?
3. Is my thesis clearly stated early in the paper so that the reader knows what to expect?
4. Is the organizational pattern of the paper clearly marked for the reader by subheadings or directional signals?
5. Are the various sections of the paper linked by good transitional words and phrases?
6. Have I used a variety of evidence to convey my points: examples, analyses, primary or secondary data, analogies, illustrations, narratives, descriptions?
7. Do the sections of the paper appear in a logical order, or do I need to rearrange the parts? Does the logic of the argument seem clear?
8. Is each section of the paper supported with sufficient data and evidence from the sources and from my primary research? Are sources integrated smoothly into the flow of the paper? Can the reader tell where sources stop and my own writing begins?
9. Is my conclusion adequate? Does it return to the thesis and highlight the answer to the starting question that motivated the research?
10. Have I demonstrated a depth of analysis and complexity of thought concerning the topic such that readers will feel they learned something significant from me?

Rework any troublesome aspects of the paper. If a particular section of the paper lacks sufficient evidence, go back to the library for some appropriate supporting material. If you are unsure about the tone of your paper, the clarity of the language, or the presentation of your ideas, ask for specific advice from other readers. Such outside reading of your work can sometimes provide the distance needed for an objective evaluation.

You may wish to try the technique of reverse outlining as a way of seeing any global structural problems in your draft. To reverse outline, number each paragraph in your draft. Then summarize in one sentence the essential content of each paragraph. In this way you may discover sections out of sequence or paragraphs on the same topic many pages apart. Or, if you are having difficulty summarizing a particular paragraph, you may find you have tried to cover too much information and need to divide a longer paragraph into a series of shorter, more focused paragraphs.

Improving Paragraphs

As previously suggested, you first look at the overall structure and content of your paper. Then begin to narrow the scope of your revising to individual paragraphs. Check to be sure that each paragraph has a single major focus and that the ideas within the paragraph are all related to that focus. Focusing your paragraphs in this way is a great aid to your reader. When you do this, a new paragraph indicates a change to a new idea or change in direction. Often, the first sentence of each paragraph serves as a transitional sentence, bridging the gap between the ideas in the two separate paragraphs. This is the time to check for transitions between paragraphs as well as paragraph focus. As you revise your paragraphs, ask yourself the following questions:

1. Does each paragraph relate to the overall point of my paper?
2. Does each new paragraph contain its own internal focus or coherence?
3. Does the first sentence of each paragraph offer a bridge or transition from the previous paragraph?
4. Is the language used in each paragraph concrete and clear? Are there unnecessary words or phrases that I should delete?
5. Is the tone of each paragraph objective? Do I sound interested and concerned about the subject but not overly emotional?

Improving Sentences

In continuing to narrow the scope of your revising, look at individual sentences within your paper. Revise any sentences that seem awkward or confusing. In general, the more simply and directly you state your ideas, the better. Do not use overly complex sentence structures—they will only confuse your reader. Any very long sentences may need to be broken down into shorter sentences. On the other hand, a series of short, choppy sentences may be more effective if rewritten as a single long sentence. Reading your draft aloud—to yourself or to someone else—can often help you to hear problematic sentences. Or perhaps your teacher can make additional suggestions about revising your sentence style.

As you revise your sentences, ask yourself the following questions:

1. Is each sentence a complete sentence rather than a sentence fragment?
2. Are the ends of sentences punctuated correctly with a period or question mark?
3. Have I avoided any comma splices or run-on (fused) sentences?
4. Have I used sentence structures that are parallel?
5. Do my sentences flow smoothly, or are they choppy and disjointed?
6. Have I avoided compound constructions and repetitious phrases such as "new innovation" or "repeating recurrence"?

Improving Words

Next, look at individual words in your paper with an eye toward spotting confusing vocabulary or unnecessary jargon. Define any terms that might be unfamiliar to a general reader and replace any jargon specific to a field or discipline with more common words.

The following passage from a student paper shows how the writer revised for structure and style:

> Sexual harassment not only affects the
>
> individual but also has a tremendous effect on the
>
> organization in which it occurs. [Employers are
>
> beginning to recognize ~~SH~~ this problem because it costs them
>
> ~~money and causes stressful situations in the~~
>
> ~~working environment~~ in terms of morale,
>
> productivity, and lost time.] ~~Business org. need~~
>
> ~~to admit that SH is a problem & then attempt to do~~
>
> ~~something about it.~~ If harassment keeps going on
>
> w/out anything being done about it, there will be
>
> a lack of trust between the employees and the
>
> employer.

move to end

Verbs are one part of speech that often cause writers problems. Performing these few simple editing tasks with the verbs in your research paper will vastly improve your own writing.[1]

Content Verbs versus Empty Verbs

The verb "to be"" (am, are, is, was, were) asserts a state of being, telling us only that something exists. Because "to be" in its various forms essentially has become empty of meaning, you should attempt to replace "to be" verbs with content verbs that do convey meaning.

EXAMPLES:

Original—with empty "to be" verb

> It is the custom for visitors to remove their shoes before entering a Japanese home.

Revision—with content verb

> Visitors customarily remove their shoes before entering a Japanese home.

Original—with empty "to be" verb

> Many planes are twenty years old and will have passed their life expectancy of ten to fourteen years.

Revision—with content verb

> Now twenty years old, many planes have long since passed their life expectancy of ten to fourteen years.

Action Verbs versus Nominalizations

Many writers slow down their readers by using complex nouns in their sentences instead of the more active verbs that those nouns come from. For example, *decision* is the noun form (nominalization) of the verb *to decide,* and *invasion* is the noun form of *to invade.* Somehow writers have gotten the erroneous impression that the use of nominalizations makes their writing sound more important or official. Changing your verbs into nouns, however, robs them of their power and motion, thus slowing down the reader's progress. Whenever possible, change nominalizations to action verbs.

EXAMPLES:

Original—Sentence with nominalization

> This land has the appearance of being arid.

Revision—Sentence with action verb

This land appears arid.

Original—Sentence with nominalization

He finally came to his decision. He would run for office.

Revision—Sentence with action verb

He finally decided to run for office.

Active Voice versus Passive Voice

The passive voice of a verb can be used effectively in writing when the subject is unknown or not important, or the writer does not want the subject known, as in the following:

Passive: The Vietnamese countryside was bombed. [by whom?]

Active: The U.S. Air Force bombed the Vietnamese countryside.

Passive: The boys were asked to leave. [by whom?]

Active: The neighbors asked the boys to leave.

Although passive voice has a legitimate function, it is often overworked in writing. To keep the pace of your writing moving along and to provide your readers with essential information, try to use the active voice whenever possible.

As you revise to improve your words, ask yourself the following questions:

1. Have I avoided jargon or confusing vocabulary? Have I defined any unfamiliar terms?
2. Have I used content verbs rather than empty verbs?
3. Have I used action verbs rather than nominalizations?
4. Have I used active voice rather than passive voice?
5. Have I used a single word excessively?
6. Have I repeated a single idea excessively by simply rephrasing it?

Editing for Grammar, Punctuation, and Spelling

Once you have revised the overall structure and style of your paper, you are ready to read the paper again, this time with an eye to grammar, punctuation, and spelling. It is important to present your ideas clearly, but it is equally important to present your ideas correctly.

A reader will discount you as either ignorant or careless if your work is full of grammatical errors.

As you read your paper again, ask yourself the following questions:

1. Is the grammar of each sentence correct? Does each sentence contain subjects and predicates?
2. Do subjects and verbs agree?
3. Are pronouns clear and unambiguous in their reference?
4. Is the overall punctuation correct?
5. Have I punctuated and cited quotations and paraphrases correctly?
6. Are there any words that I need to look up in the dictionary, either for meaning or for spelling?
7. Does each sentence flow smoothly without being awkward, wordy, or confusing?
8. Is the format of my paper correct, including the title page, body of the text, endnotes, or bibliography page?

It would be helpful for you to refer to a recent grammar and usage handbook for questions of English grammar, punctuation, and syntax. (For information on punctuating direct quotations, see the section below on incorporating quoted material.) Use a dictionary to check the meaning of individual words and always run SPELL CHECK with each draft. Take the time now to look carefully for all problems in your writing. Errors in grammar, punctuation, syntax, and spelling will detract from your message and make a negative impression on your reader. A paper full of grammatical or spelling errors signals to the reader that the authority of the writer, and hence the authority of the research, is questionable. The following passage from a student paper shows revising and editing to correct grammar, punctuation, and spelling:

> He also noted that ~~these~~ *sexual harassment* victi~~ons~~ *ms* often ~~felt~~ *feared that*
>
> their complaints would go unheard, and they would
>
> be blamed for w~~h~~*a*t happe*e*nd, or they would be
>
> considered unprofessional. In addition, Renick
>
> found that SHed women had many of the same
>
> feelings as ~~those~~ *women* who had been raped. These
>
> ~~feelings~~ included *feeling* humiliated, cheap, embarrassed,
>
> and angry.

Rewriting Your Paper Using Word Processing

Using a computer word-processing program to revise your research paper has many advantages. Using word processing, you can quickly and easily create a paper that is as attractive and free of distracting errors as possible. Some writers compose their research papers directly at the computer, perhaps using the research database they have already created in their computer research notebooks. Others type a rough draft into the computer for revising. Using word processing makes changing your paper easier, since it allows you to eliminate, add, rearrange, and substitute material, altering individual words, sentences, paragraphs, and even whole sections of the paper without having to recopy or retype.

Revising with Word Processing

Word processing allows you to move material in your paper from one location to another. Before doing so, however, be sure you have made a backup copy of your document so that you don't inadvertently lose part of your text. Once you have moved the material (typically using the CUT and PASTE functions), be sure to read the revised version very carefully and make any changes needed to integrate the new material smoothly into the existing text. When revising for structure and style or to improve paragraphs, sentences, and words, you will find your word-processing program's text-manipulation features to be great assets.

Editing with Word Processing

Word processing also makes editing for grammar, punctuation, and spelling easier. Most word-processing programs now offer their users a spell check feature, which is extremely helpful in identifying typographical errors. You should get in the habit of running SPELL CHECK several times as you are drafting your paper. Remember, though, that the spell check feature does not identify words that you have inadvertently misused, such as homonyms: *there* for *their*, or *its* for *it's*, and so on. You still need to proofread very carefully yourself, even after using spell check.

Another helpful tool for editing is your word processor's thesaurus. If you find you are overusing a particular word, you can use the thesaurus to supply alternatives. Or perhaps you find the verbs you have used are not as vivid and active as they could be; the thesaurus can suggest other verbs with similar meanings. Again, a note of caution: don't use a word suggested by a thesaurus that you don't know, because it might have connotations or slight variations in meaning that do not make sense in the particular context of your writing.

Grammar-Checking Software

Most word-processing programs include software that can help you edit and proofread your paper for selected stylistic or grammatical problems. Such programs will identify excessive use of inactive "to be" verbs, overuse of prepositions, vague words or jargon, and so on. However, the so-called grammar-checking programs currently available can be misleading to writers. The kinds of writing problems that such programs can check are very limited. For example, they are virtually useless at checking punctuation because they are not sophisticated enough to really analyze the underlying grammar of each sentence. Only you, the writer, can do that. So, if you use a grammar check feature, be aware of what it can and cannot do.

Bibliography and Footnote Software

Many word-processing programs currently on the market offer features to help you generate the footnotes, endnotes, or bibliography for your paper. If you are using footnotes, having the word-processing program automatically place them at the bottom of the appropriate page can be a big help. However, the documentation software is only as good as the information you give it; that is, you still need to type all of the bibliographical information into the computer. The software then manipulates the information, placing it in the proper order and formatting it appropriately. You need to know whether the documentation style built into the software is the style you need to use for your discipline. Again, you should be the final judge of what is the correct documentation format for your paper.

If you have access to a computer, you may want to investigate some of the software that is designed to help you with your writing. But do not take a computer program's advice as gospel; you cannot count on a computer to know what is best for your own writing—only you can know that.

Incorporating Reference Materials

Chapter 4 on writing the rough draft suggested that you not worry about the smooth incorporation of quoted material until you begin revising your paper. You have now reached the stage at which you should double-check all of the source material in your paper to be sure you have incorporated it smoothly and appropriately into the flow of your ideas. Your source material should be primarily in the form of paraphrases and summaries that you use to reinforce your own points.

Even though they are written in your own words, both paraphrases and summaries still require documentation (identification of the source either through in-text citations or footnotes or endnotes). Putting source material into your own words greatly improves the flow of your paper, because the paraphrase style will blend with your own writing style and thus be consistent throughout.

You should use direct quotation very sparingly. Reading strings of direct quotations is extremely distracting, because excessive quotation creates a choppy, disjointed style. Furthermore, it leaves the impression that you as a writer know nothing and are relying totally on what others have said on your topic. The better alternative is to incorporate paraphrases and summaries of source material into your own ideas both grammatically and logically. At this time, check your paper to be sure you have documented all source material accurately and fairly. By following the documentation style outlined in Part Two (Chapter 6, 7, 8, or 9), you will be able to produce a paper that is correctly and accurately documented for your chosen academic discipline. In general, remember to document both completely and consistently, staying with one particular documentation style.

Incorporating Direct Quotations

At times you may want to use direct quotations in addition to paraphrases and summaries. To incorporate direct quotations smoothly, observe the following general principles. However, it would be wise to also consult the style manual of your discipline for any minor variations in quotation style.

1. When a quotation has four or fewer lines, surround it with quotation marks and incorporate it into your text. When a quotation is longer than four lines, set it off from the rest of the text by indenting five spaces from the left and right margins and triple-spacing above and below it. You do not need to use quotation marks with such block quotes. (Note: In some disciplines, block quotations are customarily indented ten spaces from the left margin only and double-spaced throughout.) Follow the block quotation with the punctuation found in the source. Then skip two spaces before the parenthetical citation. Do not include a period after the parentheses.
2. Introduce quotations using a verb tense that is consistent with the tense of the quotation. (A woman of twenty admitted, "I really could not see how thin I was.")

3. Change a capital letter to a lowercase letter (or vice versa) within the quotations if necessary. (She pours her time and attention into her children, whining at them to "eat more, drink more, sleep more.")

4. Use brackets for explanations or interpretations not in the original quotation. ("Evidence reveals that boys are higher on conduct disorder [behavior directed toward the environment] than girls.")

5. Use ellipses (three spaced dots) within brackets to indicate that material has been omitted from the quotation. It is not necessary to use ellipses for material omitted before the quotation begins. ("Fifteen to twenty percent of anorexia victims die of direct starvation or related illnesses . . . [which] their weak immune systems cannot combat.")

6. Punctuate a direct quotation as the original was punctuated. However, change the end punctuation to fit the context. (For example, a quotation that ends with a period may require a comma instead of the period when it is integrated into your own sentence.)

7. A period, or a comma if the sentence continues after the quotation, goes inside the quotation marks. (Although Cathy tries to disguise "her innate evil nature, it reveals itself at the slightest loss of control, as when she has a little alcohol.") When the quotation is followed with a parenthetical citation, omit the punctuation before the quotation mark and follow the parentheses with a period or comma: Cal has "recognized the evil in himself, [and] is ready to act for good" (Cooperman 88).

8. If an ellipsis occurs at the end of the quoted material, add a period before the dots. (Cathy is "more than Woman, who not only succumbs to the Serpent, but becomes the serpent itself . . . as she triumphs over her victims. . . .")

9. Place question marks and exclamation points outside the quotation marks if the entire sentence is a question or an exclamation. (Has Sara read the article "Alienation in *East of Eden*"?)

10. Place question marks and exclamation points inside the quotation marks if only the quotation itself is a question or exclamation. (Mary attended the lecture entitled "Is Cathy Really Eve?")

11. Use a colon to introduce a quotation if the introductory material prior to the quotation is long or if the quotation itself is more than a sentence or two long.

```
Steinbeck puts it this way:

[long quotation indented from margin]
```

12. Use a comma to introduce a short quotation. (Steinbeck explains, "If Cathy were simply a monster, that would not bring her in the story.")

Formatting and Printing Using Computers

Besides helping you as a writer, word processing can also help you create a text that is professional in appearance. However, attention to format should be the last consideration of your writing process. Too often, writers using word processing spend excessive amounts of their time playing with the appearance of the text, varying the fonts, for example, rather than concentrating on content. Of course, in the end you must attend to both form and content if you want to communicate effectively with your readers.

Many word-processing programs offer formatting features such as underlining, boldface, italics, and so on, with which you can vary the appearance of your text and highlight important information. Be certain, however, that you check with your instructor to ascertain his or her preferences for format style before varying the style too much. Your main goal should be to make your paper professional in appearance. Thus, an English Gothic typeface that prints in scrolling capital letters, for example, would not be appropriate for a research paper. Nor are margins that are justified (even) on the right of the page typically appropriate for a formal paper. It is best to be conservative and justify left margins only.

Proofreading

Once your paper has been typed to your teacher's specifications and you have run your word-processing program's spell check and grammar check features, you will still need to proofread carefully for any errors the computer did not catch. For example, spell check cannot tell you if you have used "their" when you should have used "there." It is best to print out a clean copy of your paper after making all of your proofreading corrections.

One helpful way to proofread for typing errors is to begin at the bottom of the page and read up one line at a time. In this way, you keep yourself from reading for meaning and look only at the form of the words. You can spot errors more easily when you are not actually reading the paper. If you are proofreading on a computer screen, you can use your SEARCH command to search for periods from the bottom of the text upwards. In this way, your computer's cursor will skip to the previous sentence, thus reminding you to read it independently.

Keep your dictionary handy and refer to it whenever you have any doubt about the appropriate use of a word. Use your grammar and usage handbook to double-check any last-minute questions about grammar and punctuation. Use a thesaurus to substitute new words for any you have overused.

It is impossible to overstress the importance of careful proofreading. Even if the paper was typed and checked with a word processor, you will probably find errors when proofreading. Since you are the paper's author, any errors are your responsibility, not the computer's. It is a good idea to save early drafts of your paper even after it has been revised. Early drafts serve as a record of your thinking and your work on the paper. If you have taken care at every stage of the revision process, your paper will be one you can be justifiably proud of.

Listed below are several strategies that may help you to become a more effective proofreader.

1. Before printing your text, scroll rapidly all the way through to check for spacing, margins, indents, "widows" and "orphans" (lines left alone at the top or bottom of a page), page numbering, and so on.
2. After printing your text, wait several hours (or longer, if possible) before proofreading it.
3. When you proofread your printed text, use a pointer or ruler to force yourself to read more slowly and deliberately.
4. Proofread your text several times, both on screen and in print; each time you will pick up other errors.
5. Be sure you are not "merely reading," but have changed your approach to give yourself distance from your own words. Your normal reading process involves skimming; a typical reader only actually reads two or three words per line. In contrast, proofreading requires you to look carefully at every word and punctuation mark.
6. Ask someone else—a friend, relative, or perhaps a classmate—to proofread your printed text as well.

CONSIDERING FORMAL DETAILS

The formal details outlined in the paragraphs that follow incorporate some general principles in research writing. However, it would be wise to also consult the relevant style manual for your field to discover any minor variations from this format. The model papers in Part Two adhere to the formal conventions of their respective disciplines, so you may also use these as a resource.

Word Processing

Always use a word processor to prepare your research papers. If possible, print your final copy on a laser printer for a professional appearance and ease of reading. The paper should be a standard weight and size (8 1/2 × 11 inches).

Line Spacing

Use only one side of the paper and double space all the way through, even for long quotations that are indented in the text. (Note: Styles vary.) Double-space between major sections, between and above headings and text that follows them, and below indented, long quotations (more than four lines of text). Also, double space the endnote page (if you have one) and references page.

Margins

Use a margin 1 to 1.5 inches wide on all sides of each sheet. Your word-processing program allows you to set the margins appropriately. It will also help you to format the pages. In particular, if you are using footnotes, these can be generated automatically by most word-processing programs, which will leave the appropriate amount of space for footnotes on each page.

Title Page

Ask your instructor whether you need a title page. If the answer is yes, find out what information should appear there. Generally, title pages contain three kinds of identifying information: the title of the paper, author identification, and course identification (including date). If you do not need a separate title page, put your name, date, assignment name, and any other identifying information on the upper right-hand corner of the first page. Center the title on the first page three or four lines below the identifying information or, if you use a separate title page, 1 inch from the top of the page. The title should not be underlined, surrounded by quotation marks, or typed in capital letters. Double-space between your title and the beginning of the text.

Numbering

Number each page starting with the first page of text after the title page. (Note: Some styles omit the page number from page 1.) Place the numbers in the upper right-hand corners or centered at the bottom of the pages. Your word-processing program allows you to number your pages automatically and to suppress numbering on any pages where they are not needed. For example, you typically don't need to number the end-note page and the references page. Rather, identify them with the appropriate heading centered 1 inch from the top of the page and followed by three or four blank lines. Some styles recommend headers along with the page numbers (for example, Hult - 2). Check your word-processing manual or HELP feature for help in generating such automatic headers.

Indentation and Word Spacing

Use uniform indentation for all paragraphs (five spaces is standard). Indent long quotations (more than four lines long) five spaces from both right and left margins or ten spaces from the left margin only. Indent the second and subsequent lines of the reference-list entries five spaces. Leave either one or two spaces between each sentence and after a colon or semicolon. Divide words at the end of lines according to standard rules. Use your dictionary if you are unsure of where to divide a word.

The Abstract

An abstract is a very short summary of a paper, usually one-tenth to one-twentieth the length of the whole. The purpose of an abstract is to condense the paper into a few, succinct lines. Thus, the reader must be able to understand the essence of the paper from reading just the abstract, without actually reading the paper. Your abstract should cover the purpose of your paper as well as the major topics you discuss. To write an abstract, follow the same general procedure you use to write a summary. However, you will need to compress information into a few compact sentences. Even though the information in your abstract is necessarily densely packed, it should still be readable and understandable.

The Endnote Page

If your paper will have endnotes, type them on a separate page immediately after the text of your paper (and before the references page). Center the title, "Notes" or "Endnotes," 1 inch from the top of the page, and type it in capital and lower-case letters (not all capitals). Do not use quotation marks or underlining. Double-space between the title and the first line of your notes. Type the notes in consecutive order based on their appearance in the text. Indent the first line of the note five spaces from the left margin, type the superscript number, and leave a space before beginning the note. For any run-over lines of each note, return to the left margin. See Chapter 6 for the specific format of endnotes.

The References Page

Center the title "References," "Works Cited," or "Bibliography" and type it 1 inch from the top of the page in capital and lower-case letters (not all capitals). Do not use quotation marks or underlining. Double-space between the title and the first line of your references. The references themselves should be typed, double spaced, and listed in alphabetical order by the author's last name (or the title, if the author is not known). (Note: In the number system, references are listed consecutively as they appear in the text, see Chapter 7.) To make the alphabetical list, sort the bibliography cards (on which you have recorded the sources actually used in your research paper) into alphabetical order by authors' last names and transcribe the information in the proper form from the cards to your list. For the specific forms for references, see the appropriate chapter for your discipline (Chapter 6, 7, 8, or 9). The references page follows the last page of your paper or the endnote page (if one is included) and need not be numbered.

The Annotated Bibliography

The chapters in Part Two of this book will guide you as you construct a list of references, also called a bibliography or a works cited page. However, in some cases it is helpful to provide your readers with more information about the sources you used in your research than is typically given in a bibliography. An annotated bibliography serves this purpose. To construct an annotated bibliography, you would first compile all of your references, alphabetize them, and format them according to the documentation style for your discipline. Then, following each bibliographical entry, you would state in a sentence or two the gist of the source you had read and its relevance to your paper. An annotated bibliography can help your readers to decide which of your sources they would like to read themselves. It should not be difficult for you to annotate (that is, provide brief glosses) for sources that you have used to write your paper. For an example of an annotated bibliography, see Kauleen's paper below.

The Appendix

Material that may not be appropriate to the body of your paper may be included in an appendix. You may use the appendix for collations of raw data, descriptions of primary research instruments, detailed instructions, and so on. The appendix is located after the bibliography or references page and is clearly labeled. If there is more than one appendix, label them Appendix A, Appendix B, and so on. When referring to the appendix in the paper itself, do so in parentheses: "(For a detailed description of the questionnaire, see Appendix A.)"

NOTE

1. I am grateful to Dr. Rebecca Wheeler for these sentence-editing ideas.

Title   Is Your Ch'i in Balance?

Student
identification   Kauleen Kershisnik

Course
information   Research Paper

                        for

             Research Writing

                English 201

Date   November 19, 2003

Opening
anecdote
to gain
reader's
attention

Chen Chien was diagnosed with a severe case of tuberculosis, so severe that his left lung and one rib had to be removed. The operation took place in Hun Shan Hospital in Shanghai. Chen was lying face down on the operating table while the doctors cut through skin, bone, and muscle to get to his lung. The doctors removed the lung with care and watched as the right lung began to work harder and harder to take on the work of two lungs. While the doctors were watching, Chen spoke out that he would like something to eat. The nurses assisted him with some fruit slices. Chen remained conscious throughout the entire operation, never showing any sign of pain or discomfort. No chemical anesthesia was administered during the operation, only acupuncture. Doctors had placed a single acupuncture needle into Chen's shoulder, which blocked the pain of the entire operation.

Scenes similar to this brought acupuncture to the attention of Americans in the early 1970s when President Nixon and others visited China. Since that time many have expressed doubts that these

2

MLA
citation
style
includes
author's
last name
and page
number

operations were real. In fact, Butler

asserts that "it was all a hoax" (95).

What is the truth about acupuncture? Is it

a worthless illusion or is it an ancient

miracle cure? The truth probably lies

somewhere in between.

Some would argue that conventional

Western medicine at times may not provide

adequate medical care. Many people have

wasted time and money running from one

doctor to another just to be disappointed.

Sometimes conventional methods have

serious disadvantages, such as when a

patient becomes bed-ridden or experiences

an allergic reaction to a commonly used

drug. For some people, acupuncture may be

a good, or sometimes the only, alternative

(Marcus 18). If acupuncture is used

correctly, there seems to be little or no

risk involved, and it may even effect a

cure in a case that would not have been

cured with conventional Western medicine.

Thesis   Even though acupuncture is not completely

accepted in the United States, it is

becoming more and more acceptable.

Acupuncture is the "most frequently

recommended complementary therapy [by

3

physicians]" (Ernst and White 5), and
people should realize that they do have
the option for acupuncture in certain
cases.

Historical
background

Acupuncture has been a Chinese
medical procedure since around 2500 BC.
It is based on a Chinese belief in a
life force or energy flowing throughout
the body. This energy is called ch'i
(or qi), and is the result of "maintaining
the body's harmonious balance, both
internally and in relation to the external

Internet
source with
no page
number
available

environment" (Helms). The ch'i is divided
into two separate forces—the yin and the
yang. The yin, the female principle, is
passive and dark and is represented by the
earth; the yang, the male principle, is
active and light and is represented by the
heavens. The forces of yin and yang act in
the human body as they do throughout the
natural universe as a whole.

Disease or physical disharmony is
caused by an imbalance or undue pre-
ponderance of one of these two forces in
the body, and the goal of Chinese medicine
is to bring the yin and the yang back into
balance with each other, thus restoring

4

the person to health ("Acupuncture,"

Encyclopedia
Title
provided to
distinguish
sources

Britannica). Any imbalance of yin and yang

obstructs the flow of ch'i. Ch'i is said

to flow through twelve pathways, or

meridians, throughout the body. Acupunc-

ture is necessary to even out the yin and

yang when they get out of balance.

Acupuncturists place needles along these

meridians in over a hundred places on the

body. Each point is associated with a

certain organ within the body. The idea of

a needle being poked into the skin seems

very painful, but in actuality the pain is

no greater than a "mosquito bite and draws

no blood" (Langone 70).

   As one might suspect, there is no

scientific evidence to support the idea of

ch'i flowing through meridians. These

meridians have never been seen under any

microscope, but still, many argue, have

been effective in treating certain medical

conditions. Its proponents say that

acupuncture is based on a complete Eastern

medical system that focuses on a single

principle: man is a part of nature. Nature

is precise, therefore, man is precise.

Nature is predictable, therefore, man is

5

predictable. Any disruption results in
illness, and the work of an acupuncturist
can restore that order and cure the
illness. Western medicine tends to explain
acupuncture as a stimulation of the body's
natural pain suppressors: "Although the
mechanism of action of acupuncture is
unclear, it is thought to work by
releasing neurotransmitters, such as
endorphins" (Milton and Benjamin 21).

Doctors use many different kinds of
needles for their acupuncture procedures.
Needles have varying shapes, diameters,
and lengths and are made out of different
materials. Early needles were made out of
stone, flint, quartz, bamboo, and bones
(Nightingale 70). As a result of new
advances in technology, needles have
evolved into gold, silver, and most
commonly stainless steel. Depending on the
reason for acupuncture, the needles are
inserted 0.1-0.4 inch deep, and sometimes
they are inserted up to 10 inches deep
("Acupuncture," Britannica). Some needles
are inserted straight into the skin,
others are inserted at an angle to the
skin, and some even parallel to the skin

6

(Nightingale 74). The needle is then "twisted, twirled, or connected to a low-voltage alternating current for the duration of its use" ("Acupuncture," Britannica). Acupuncturists use all of these varying procedures to accomplish the best results for their individual patients.

The needles used in acupuncture should be sterilized after each use. Needles should be "cleansed with surgical spirit or dilute antiseptic," then autoclaved and stored in a closed container until used (Nightingale 73). Without proper sterilization, diseases such as hepatitis B and HIV can be spread. The spread of HIV is not very common, but there is at least one reported case. A boy who had never had sex, blood transfusions, or tattoos or used intravenous drugs was diagnosed with the HIV virus. He had undergone some acupuncture treatment for an earlier injury, and this was suspected as the only method of transmission. There have also been cases of hepatitis B, but only when careless doctors didn't properly sterilize their needles (Mettetal et al.

For several authors use et al., Latin for "and others."

7

250). The spread of diseases can easily be
avoided with proper sterilization. When
choosing a doctor, one should be cautious
about sanitary procedures, regardless of
what kind of doctor.

Before a doctor performs acupuncture,
he or she conducts an ordinary check-up
similar to the one a family practitioner
would use to evaluate an illness. Other
than that fact, acupuncture is handled much
differently than any other kind of
treatment. The doctor takes more time to
deal with the patient one on one. A patient
and doctor develop an actual relationship
that is rare in the United States because
of busy schedules and the mere fact that
the more patients each doctor sees, the
more money he or she can earn. According to
Langone, people should be cautious when
choosing any doctor. Some doctors realize
that you are willing to try something new
and will take advantage of it. Beware of
doctors who promise to cure everything.
Acupuncture can't cure cancer, mental
retardation, multiple sclerosis, or many
other diseases (Langone 72). These
precautions should be taken in any

8

situation, not only with acupuncture.
There are doctors in every field of
medicine who make false diagnoses and are
dangerous to the safety of their patients.
One way to find a reputable acupuncturist
is to look for a medical doctor (MD) who
is also trained and certified by the
American Academy of Medical Acupuncture
(AAMA).

Internet
sources
typically do
not have
page
numbers.

　　The story in the beginning of the
paper is an illustration of acupuncture
being used as an anesthetic. There is
considerable controversy around the use of
acupuncture for anesthesia. Western doctors
are still very skeptical about this
procedure. Their skepticism may even lead
some doctors to believe that operations
like Chen's have been staged. However, new
evidence indicates that acupuncture may
release pain-killing endorphins, which are
strong chemicals that block pain signals to
the brain (Langone 70). These endorphins
might be what enables a person to undergo
surgery without feeling any pain.
"Authorities on pain believe that
acupuncture somehow sends signals to the
brain that compete with or eliminate pain

9

signals that ordinarily would accompany surgery" ("Acupuncture," Fishbein's 42). There is not currently a consensus about the effectiveness of acupuncture as an anesthetic. A comprehensive scientific appraisal by Ernst and White concluded that "electrical stimulation of nerves via acupuncture needles is capable of producing analgesia in a variety of species of animal. . . . Experimental analgesia can also be produced in humans by acupuncture involving electrical stimulation" (87). But they remain skeptical about any probable long-term analgesic effects of acupuncture on humans.

Many Americans have accepted the use of acupuncture in curing drug addicts. In 1990, Baltimore opened Maryland's first municipally funded acupuncture treatment program whose primary function was to treat crack and cocaine abusers, but they also allow alcoholics and addicts of other drugs to participate. They have found their combined treatment of acupuncture and behavioral counseling to be very effective. The acupuncture lessens or eliminates the symptoms of withdrawal

10

and makes a patient more receptive to counseling, education, and support. Needles are placed in the ear, which is said to relieve anxiety, giving the patient a sense of well-being and relaxation ("Baltimore" 436). Especially in the case of alcoholics, acupuncture is not necessarily a cure, but it does seem to reduce the urge to drink. This at least is a step in the right direction, and, with added counseling, may even be a cure ("Acupuncture," RN 113).

Veterinary medicine has also adapted the use of acupuncture in treating animals. John Nicol is a vet who practices acupuncture on animals to relieve pain. He has saved dogs that had back problems, muscle diseases, and arthritis. Nicol has also used acupuncture treatment on cows as an anesthesia during minor surgery. The success of this treatment is impressive to people who don't believe in acupuncture, because an animal's reaction to the treatment can't be staged or misread. The animal reacts only by sensing the pain or cure, which has nothing to do with the desire to be cured (Birke 34-36).

When no author is given, use the first word of article title in quotation marks.

11

Acupuncture is used for the treatment
of many more pains, illnesses, and
diseases than mentioned so far. Milton and
Benjamin cite a consensus statement issued
in 1997 from the National Institutes
of Health:

> There is `clear evidence that
> needle acupuncture treatment is
> effective for postoperative and
> chemotherapy nausea and
> vomiting, nausea of pregnancy,
> and postoperative dental pain.'
> The 12-member expert panel also
> concluded that there are a
> number of other pain-related
> conditions for which
> acupuncture `may be effective
> as an adjunct therapy, an
> acceptable alternative, or as
> part of a comprehensive
> treatment program, but for
> which there is less convincing
> scientific data.' These
> conditions include headache,
> lower back pain, addiction,
> stroke rehabilitation,
> menstrual cramps, tennis elbow,

12

fibromyalgia, carpal tunnel
syndrome, and asthma." (Milton
and Benjamin 21)

Of course, the success of acupuncture
varies with the illness being treated, but
nonetheless acupuncture is a fairly safe
and effective treatment in many cases.

As mentioned at the outset of this
paper, acupuncture sometimes is the
most effective cure available, and it
may even be a patient's only alternative
when conventional medicine has proven
ineffective for certain conditions.
Knowing something about acupuncture,
how it works, and the risks associated
with it should give a person a better
understanding of what to expect. Being
more educated about the subject makes
people more educated about their choices.
Acupuncture is an available, alternative
choice, and patients should consider
all of their options to decide, in
consultation with their doctors, what
will be best for them.

13

Annotated Bibliography

Encyclopedia
article

"Acupuncture." <u>Fishbein's Illustrated</u>

<u>Medical and Health Encyclopedia</u>.

1983 ed.

Good source of background

information. Concentrates on an

introduction, then provides specifics

about anesthesia. Shows pictures of

acupuncture being performed.

"Acupuncture." <u>The Encyclopedia</u>

<u>Britannica</u>. 2003 ed.

Not a specialized source, but provides

some good background information.

Tells the theory of how acupuncture

works.

Journal
article

"Acupuncture Boom Punctured." <u>Nature</u> 318

(1985): 222.

A short article with some general

information about anesthesia, its

acceptance and uses.

"Acupuncture for Craniofacial Pain."

<u>Geriatrics</u> 40 (1985): 36.

From a scholarly source, this article

shows how acupuncture can be an

alternative to surgery for certain

problems.

Bibliography
entries
follow MLA
style.
Annotations
are included
to describe
the source
for the
reader.

"Acupuncture May Offer Hope for

Alcoholics. <u>RN</u> 53 (1990): 113.

Specific information on acupuncture

being used on "skid row" alcoholics.

Some statistics.

American Academy of Medical Acupuncture.

<u>General Information</u>. 2001. AAMA. 9

March 2001

<http://www.medicalacupuncture.org/

acu_info/generalinfo.html>.

A Web site provided by the American

Academy of Medical Acupuncture,

which is the accrediting agency

for physicians who wish to become

trained and certified as medical

acupuncturists. Includes lots of good

information for consumers as well as

for physicians.

"Baltimore Tries Treating Substance Abuse

with Acupuncture." <u>Public Health</u>

<u>Reports</u> 105 (1990): 436.

Scholarly source reporting on a

clinic in Baltimore that uses

acupuncture to treat people with drug

addictions.

*Internet
sources
include two
dates: date
of posting
and date of
access.*

Birke, Lynda. "An Open Mind in the
Veterinary Surgery." New Scientist
115 (1987): 34–36.

This article summarizes the use of
acupuncture on pets, some of which is
somewhat experimental. Also has some
comments on acupuncture used on
humans.

Book source

Butler, Kurt. A Consumer's Guide to
"Alternative Medicine": A Close Look
at Homeopathy, Acupuncture, Faith-
Healing, and Other Unconventional
Treatments. Amherst, NY: Prometheus,
1992.

This book provides a skeptic's view
of alternative medicine and urges a
"buyer beware" attitude for
consumers.

Ernst, Edward, and Adrian White, eds.
Acupuncture: A Scientific Appraisal.
Oxford: Butterworth/Heinemann, 1999.

This book attempts to dispel the
"romantic" mysterious view of Eastern
medicine by taking a close,
scientific look at acupuncture.

Selection from a book located on a Web site

Helms, Joseph M. "An Overview of Medical
Acupuncture." Modified from

Essentials of Complementary and
Alternative Medicine. Eds. W. B.
Jonas and J. S. Levin. Baltimore:
Williams & Wilkins, 2001. 7 March
2001.
<http://www.medicalacupuncture.org/
acu_info/articles/helmsarticle.html>.
An interesting article by an American
leader in the field of medical
acupuncture, who began the program
that certifies medical doctors as
medical acupuncturists.

Langone, John. "Acupuncture: New Respect
for an Ancient Remedy." Discover 5
(1984): 70-73.
Talks about growing acceptance of
acupuncture in the United States and
how much acupuncture has evolved.
Some specifics on certain procedures.

Mettetal, J. F., C. Rouzioux, and D.
Vittecoq. "Acute HIV Infection After
Acupuncture Treatment." The New
England Journal of Medicine 320
(1989): 250-51.
The idea of the HIV virus being
spread by acupuncture is confirmed by
a case reported in this journal.

Milton, Doris, and Samuel Benjamin.
Complementary and Alternative
Therapies: An Implementation Guide to
Integrative Health Care. Chicago:
American Hospital Association Press,
1999.
A good overview of several complemen-
tary medical procedures, including
acupuncture, by a reputable source,
the Health Forum.

Nightingale, Michael. The Healing Power of
Acupuncture. New York: Javelin Books,
1986.
Lots of general information on all
aspects of acupuncture.

6

Writing a Research Paper in the Humanities

INTRODUCTION

In many research projects in the humanities, the researcher must read a primary text carefully and interpret it. Such a research task, performed frequently by working scholars in the humanities, requires a thorough reading of the text, a systematic search for information written about the text, extensive preparation time, and a knowledge of formal conventions in the field. The same principles and skills you have learned in the earlier chapters apply when you use a primary text. These skills include:

1. The ability to read the primary text carefully and critically.
2. A familiarity with library and Internet resources relating to humanities.
3. The ability to synthesize and evaluate information and opinions from a variety of secondary sources.
4. The ability to develop a thesis consistent with the evidence found in both the primary and secondary sources.
5. The ability to organize and write a paper that effectively presents and supports your thesis.
6. The ability to employ the formal conventions of research papers in the humanities.

REPORTS AND RESEARCH PAPERS

Some of the writing you will be expected to do in the humanities is report writing, in which you report on the current consensus within the field on a particular topic or issue. In report writing, you research only in the sense of finding out what others have said on a topic. Usually, reports are written on noncontroversial subjects about which the writer can discover the facts easily and present them without the need to interpret their significance. Such a report is also sometimes called a *review of the literature.*

For example, in a history class, you might be asked to write a report on early colonial life in Plymouth, Massachusetts. As a reporter, you would look up relevant, authoritative history resources written about colonial New England and write down what those sources say about life in Plymouth.

In contrast, a research paper does more than report the facts or widely held beliefs on a particular topic. A research paper is necessarily more evaluative than a report, because it interprets the available evidence. Often, a research paper is written about a subject or topic that has sparked controversy in the field. A controversial issue is evident when scholars in the field do not agree on interpretations or when the range of known facts is great enough to allow differing opinions. A question such as "Were colonists at Plymouth significantly helped or hindered by local Native American tribes?" would allow the researcher to locate and interpret a wide range of known facts. The researcher would investigate a question that other scholars in the field had grappled with. For example, current mythology has the colonists of Plymouth sitting down to Thanksgiving dinner with benevolent Native Americans. The researcher would ask, "Is this picture based on facts? Or were the colonists really constantly on guard against attacks by Native Americans?" Some writers today portray the colonial settlers as the aggressors, indiscriminately killing tribe members to satisfy their own need for land and food. Which is the true picture? What facts do we actually have? What is a reasonable interpretation of the relationship between colonial settlers and Native American tribes based on those known facts?

The questions posed above are typical of the kinds of problems often researched in the humanities. There is room for differences of opinion, provided those opinions are supported by, and consistent with, the known facts on the subject. The researcher arrives at a thesis through lengthy preparation and investigation. Then the researcher verifies that thesis by constructing a persuasive argument woven from and supported by the known facts. Such a thesis is a reasonable answer to a research question, an answer that fits the known facts and helps to explain them.

In your work for this chapter, you will be expected to write a re-search paper, not a report paper. In other words, you need to go beyond reporting the known facts to interpretation of those facts, to formulate your own interpretation, your own thesis. The examples in this chapter are taken from a research project in an English class in which the students were asked to interpret a literary text critically. Such a research project assumes more than reporting; the student must read the primary text carefully and formulate his or her own impressions of its "meaning." The research itself mainly involves comparing those impressions to other interpretations made by scholars in the field.

THE INQUIRY PROCESS IN THE HUMANITIES

The humanities, such as classical and modern languages and literature, history, and philosophy, have as an overall goal the exploration and explanation of the human experience. Some would include the fine arts (music, art, dance, and drama) in the humanities, but others view the arts as a separate category. (We will not discuss the performance of fine arts in this book, but we will touch on the interpretation of fine arts.) In most disciplines in the humanities, written texts are extremely important, particularly in history, philosophy, and literature. Historians attempt a systematic documentation and analysis of past events experienced by a particular people in a particular country or period. Philosophers endeavor to examine coherent, logical systems of human ideas. Literary authors and artists attempt to capture for others their own lived, human experiences and their own understanding of the world. The humanities involve inquiry into consciousness, values, ideas, and ideals in an effort to describe how experience shapes our understanding of the world.

Let's take an example to show how the sciences, social sciences, and humanities all contribute to an understanding of our world. The Mississippi River has played an important role in American history. A scientist—perhaps a biologist—would study the river's wildlife, fish, surrounding vegetation, and ecology in an attempt to objectively describe the river itself. A social scientist—perhaps a sociologist—might study the river's contribution to a riverfront society and that society's dependence on the river for transportation of goods and services. A historian, who often bridges the gap between the social sciences and the humanities, might report on the importance of the Mississippi and other American waterways to westward expansion and the development of the United States. A humanist—for example, a novelist—might write about the actual experiences people had on or near the Mississippi. Mark Twain, for instance, wrote his autobiographical novel *Life on the Mississippi* to share with his readers his experiences as a youth learning the trade of riverboat pilot on a Mississippi steamboat. Without such a work of imaginative literature, we would have difficulty understanding what it was really like to be working on the river during Twain's time. Such a work of literature contributes to our understanding by putting us in a different time and place from our own, thus broadening our horizons in a manner that is somewhat different from either the natural or social sciences. The sciences attempt to give us the outside, external knowledge of a phenomenon, whereas the humanistic disciplines attempt to give us the inside, internal knowledge of a phenomenon.[1] Both make important contributions to our understanding of the world.

The Importance of Texts in the Humanities

Written texts in the humanities are generally of three types: (1) creative writing (literature, poetry, and drama), (2) interpretive writing (literary and art criticism), and (3) theoretical writing (historical and social theories of literature and art).

Creative writing produces numerous literary texts that provide us with an aesthetic experience and capture new insights into humanity. Creative writing is comparable to other creative, artistic endeavors in that it often has this twofold objective: to be aesthetically pleasing (or emotionally moving) and to be an imaginative reenactment of human experience. We ask a work of art to move us and to mean something to us, to show us a way of looking at ourselves and the world that we may not otherwise have seen.

As we experience creative art and literature as an audience, interpretive questions arise: What sort of work is it? How are we to respond to it? Much of the writing connected with the humanities is interpretive, because the audience tries to understand both the meaning and the significance of a particular creative work. Often, an interpretive critic attempts to disclose the particular intention of the artist: the novelist's attitude toward the heroine, for example, or the intended aesthetic impact of a dance. Interpretive critics research their claims by using the evidence found in the work itself to support the hypothesis, that is, the particular "reading" of the text or work of art.

The third kind of humanistic writing is theoretical. For the theorist, creative art and literature are important insofar as they exemplify more general social and historical principles. The theorist, for example, looks for connections between a particular work of art and its social and historical context or for relationships among different artistic media, such as fresco painting and architecture in medieval Europe. Theorists provide links between our understanding of art and literature and other subjects such as history, sociology, or psychology. Finally, theorists take a step back from a particular work of art or literature in an attempt to get a broader view. In looking at the entire social and historical context, they ask questions like these: How has photography affected portrait painting? What is the role of the devil in the American novel?

Research in the Humanities

The humanist ponders questions of significance, insight, imagination, and the meaning of human experience. What does it mean, then, to research in the humanities? Interpreting and critiquing art and literature is one type of research conducted by humanists. Interpreters and theorists in the humanities attempt to "talk sense" about a work of art or literature to make the audience see what the artist or author meant and to link the work with other, larger human events and experiences. A second kind of humanistic research involves reconstructing humanity's past—both the ideas (philosophical research) and the events that have occurred over time (historical research). All three types of humanistic research (literary and art criticism, philosophical research, and historical research) contribute to our understanding of the meaning of human experience.

Literary and Art Criticism

Critical researchers necessarily use their own interpretations of a work of art or literature in critiquing it. But those subjective interpretations are based on experience and reflective thought, and they are expressed in well-chosen language. Criticism in the humanities is not just a string of personal opinions. The critical researcher builds a solid argument to substantiate his or her interpretation or theory. Such an argument is based on research involving a close reading of the text itself (in literary criticism) or a close analysis of the work of art (in art criticism). The argument also takes into account social and historical factors that bear on the interpretation of the literary text or work of art. It incorporates research on other related texts or works of art by the same author or artist or secondary criticism influencing the critic's own argument. A piece of good interpretive criticism is both insightful and true to life. A piece of good literary or art criticism is complete and comprehensive; it offers the audience a sound theory that fits with the experience of audience members and that ties together related threads in their understanding. A critical researcher investigates the complex context from which a work of art or literature has come, in order to provide an understanding of how it fits into the larger realm of human experience. In this way, the critical researcher is much like a historical or social science researcher.

One example of a critical researcher who combined techniques of criticism with historical scholarship is John Livingston Lowes, who began with the question of what sources influenced the poetry of Samuel Coleridge, a nineteenth-century English poet and critic.[2] In an attempt to elucidate Coleridge's poetry, Lowes traced the sources the poet used in writing such poems as "The Rime of the Ancient Mariner" and "Kubla Khan." Richard Altick calls Lowes's book "the greatest true-detective story ever written."[3] Lowes began his research with Coleridge's *Gutch Memorandum Book,* a notebook containing suggestions for reading that Coleridge had jotted down as he looked for ideas to translate into poetry. Next, Lowes looked at the records from the Bristol Library that showed the books Coleridge had borrowed. Following these and many other leads, Lowes was able to virtually reconstruct how certain of Coleridge's greatest poems took shape in the author's mind and took form on the written page.

Philosophical Research

The philosophical researcher investigates the truths and principles of being, knowledge, and human conduct. Alfred North Whitehead, in his book *Process and Reality,* describes the process of research in speculative philosophy:

> The true method of discovery is like the flight of an aeroplane. It starts from the ground of particular observation; it makes a flight into the thin air of imaginative generalization; and it again lands for renewed observation rendered acute by rational interpretation.[4]

Here Whitehead is describing the general process of inquiry that we have been discussing. In his view, the success of any imaginative speculation is the verification of it through extended application. He sees the work of philosophical research as an attempt to frame a coherent, logical system of the general ideas of humanity. In his work, Whitehead presents a scheme that can be used to interpret or frame the "cosmology." He shows how his philosophical scheme can be used for "the interpretation of the ideas and problems which form the complex texture of civilized thought."[5] Thus, the philosophical laws are verified in their application to actual philosophical problems encountered in human experience.

Historical Research

Historical researchers proceed in much the same fashion as philosophy researchers, except that historical researchers investigate events as well as ideas. They research the events that have occurred in a person's life or at a particular time. Then they weave those events and ideas into a narrative that recounts and interprets the past. As in all the humanities, historians attempt to understand and interpret life itself. Historians also use the data gathered by social scientists—the surveys and statistical counts conducted by sociologists, economists, or political scientists. However, historians often present their understanding of the past in a story form intended to give the reader a picture of the past events, describing and recreating what those events were like for the participants. In this way, the study of history bridges the gap between the social sciences and the humanities such as literature and the arts.

The research process used by historians is much like that of the theorists. The historian investigates the facts and data available about an individual or a period of time. Through those facts, carefully verified for their accuracy, the historian recreates the past to capture the truths that reside there. The historian is not reluctant to make individual judgments about the meaning and importance of past events. As in all humanities, the historian verifies those judgments by gauging their ring of truth, their resemblance to what is known intuitively about life, and their explanatory power.

One example of a historical researcher at work is Frank Maloy Anderson.[6] Anderson was confronted with the problem of who wrote the important "Diary of a Public Man," a document by an unidentified author that first appeared in 1879 in the *North American Review*. Many historical, little-known facts about Abraham Lincoln were revealed in the diary. Anderson spent nearly thirty-five years trying to identify the document's author, using every historical clue he could find. He searched congressional records, hotel registries, business documents, and newspaper subscriptions. From this extensive search, he posited two hypotheses: (1) the diary was a fiction, or (2) it was a combination of fiction and truth. Anderson decided on the second hypothesis, because he could find nothing that was provably false in the document. He concluded that the probable author was Samuel Ward, a prominent African American orator, abolitionist, and newspaper editor, but could never prove this beyond all doubt. Nevertheless, Anderson's historical case is a good one, based as it is on intuitive speculation combined with factual evidence.

Acceptable Evidence in the Humanities

In the humanities, there is no absolute proof that leads unerringly to a particular interpretation or theory. Rather, the humanist will make a claim and argue for that claim. What is demanded in the humanities is not irrefutable proof but sensitivity and perceptiveness. The way of knowing required in the humanities can be cultivated by hard work and study.

The evidence that is acceptable in literary and art criticism or interpretation comes from the interpreter's sensibility, from the work of art or literature itself, and from the context. Some interpretations and theories may seem more insightful than others. They cast the work into a new light or integrate it into a wholeness we had not originally perceived. The claim or hypothesis made by a theorist is accepted as valid if it fits the work and helps the audience understand it. Critical and theoretical research can expand our consciousness, deepening and broadening our sensitivity to experiences. We could say, as did William James, that the performance of a piece of violin music is "the scraping of the hair of a horse over the intestines of a cat."[7] Although the description is true enough, as Meiland points out, it is not all there is to violin music; in fact, the remark leaves out just about everything that is really important in the performance of a violin piece. A valid interpretation illuminates a work in a way that makes it more meaningful to us.

The evidence that is acceptable in historical and philosophical research is that which is based either on verifiable facts or on adequate interpretations that fit known human experience. As Barzun and Graff put it, "The researcher who does historian's work can at least preserve his sense of truth by concentrating on the tangle of his own stubborn facts."[8] But in addition to those facts, the historian is also "aware of his duty to make individual judgments" regarding the meaning or significance of those facts.[9] As Whitehead states, the application of his philosophical scheme to life "at once gives meaning to the verbal phrases of the scheme by their use in the discussion, and shows the power of the scheme to put the various elements of our experience into the consistent relation to each other."[10] In both cases, these humanistic researchers insist on the role of the researcher's insight and imagination in elucidating experience and in describing and predicting what human beings are and how they think and act. Acceptable evidence in all the humanities is evidence that supports those imaginative and insightful descriptions and interpretations.

QUESTIONS FOR DISCUSSION

1. What is the general goal of inquiry in the humanities?

2. How are written texts used in the humanities? Why are they important?

3. What three kinds of research are common in the humanities? How are they alike or different?

4. What constitutes acceptable evidence in the humanities?

EXERCISES

1. Obtain a copy of a college catalog. In the catalog, find references to the academic disciplines and notice how they are classified. Are there differences between the categories you find in the catalog and those outlined in this chapter? In a paragraph, describe the major divisions of disciplines in the catalog.

2. In the college catalog, look up a discipline you are considering as a major, for example, history or mathematics. In addition to courses in that discipline, what other courses are required (for example, foreign languages, liberal arts, laboratory sciences)? In a paragraph, describe those "core" requirements and speculate on why they are included as a part of an undergraduate education.

3. In high school or college, you have probably studied sciences, social sciences, and humanities. Describe in a short essay how classes in these three areas were similar or different.

4. Obtain a copy of a textbook from a course in the sciences, the social sciences, or the humanities. Read the preface and glance through the table of contents. Does the author mention research? Is there a chapter or section discussing research? What can you infer about the discipline's approach to research from the textbook? Does it seem to differ from the approach discussed in this text? If so, in what ways? In a paragraph or two, discuss your speculations about the assumptions made about research in the textbook you are examining.

5. For each problematic situation below, propose a solution and suggest in a short report how you would go about verifying that solution.

   A. You are in charge of collecting the money for a charity or project for your dorm or for a church or other group to which you belong. You must organize the collection drive.

   B. As president of your student association, you are in charge of getting your fellow students to voluntarily comply with the no-smoking rule in the college cafeteria. Or, as the president of the union local at your place of employment, you are in charge of getting the union rank and file to voluntarily comply with a new safety regulation. Or, as the president of the PTA at your child's school, you are in charge of getting parent volunteers to help with a new school program.

   C. A newspaper has assigned you to write an article on pollution and the environment. The editor wants you to report on how students on your campus or co-workers at your place of

employment really feel about pollution and other environmental issues.

6. Interview a friend whose major is different from yours. What
    kinds of research are required of your friend in his or her
    courses? Compile your interview notes into a short report.

PRIMARY RESEARCH IN THE HUMANITIES

Researchers in the humanities employ standard research methods. There are standard methods used in the production of fine arts
(painting, sculpture, music, drama, and so on) just as there are standard
methods in the humanities for interpreting fine arts, literature, history,
and experience. Since production of fine arts is beyond the scope of this
book, we will focus here on interpretation. The goal of the humanities
is to explore and explain the human experience, so humanities researchers make extensive use of written records of experience. Such
written records are called *primary texts* and can include literary texts
(poems, stories, novels, plays), other kinds of texts (letters, diaries, journals), and historical records (court proceedings, government records).
All these texts provide the raw data with which the researcher in the
humanities works.

Using Primary Texts

Research in the humanities often begins with a primary text of
particular interest to the researcher. The researcher must read the text
very carefully as preparation, noting any significant events, themes,
characters, and so on. After finishing the close reading, much as researchers in the social sciences do, the humanities researcher posits a
hypothesis, that is, a plausible interpretation of the work and its significance. Then the researcher collects evidence from the text itself and
from other, related sources: works written by the same author, sources
used by the author, and historical works on events occurring during the
period when the work was written. These related sources are used to
help verify or refute the initial hypothesis. Ultimately, the humanities
researcher seeks to explain and interpret a primary text in such a way
that its richness of meaning is increased for its readers.

An example of an interpretation of a primary text is Eugene K.
Garber's article " 'My Kinsman, Major Molineux': Some Interpretive
and Critical Probes," about a short story by Nathaniel Hawthorne.[11]
One of the aspects of the work Garber investigates is Hawthorne's use
of myth in the story. Garber points out that the story is "a very old ar-

chetypal story—the story of the young hero whose quest for personal, religious, or cultural identity necessarily leads him down into the underworld." In tracing this myth, Garber draws parallels between Hawthorne's hero, Robin, and the archetypal hero who encounters not only "the darkness in the world" but also "the darkness in his own psyche." To a casual reader of the story, this mythical pattern may not have been immediately apparent. By reading Garber's interpretation, the complexity of the story and its rich resonances are brought to our attention. Once we grasp the parallels between mythical heros and Robin's quest for manhood, we not only understand the story better, we also understand ourselves better.

The student who wrote the excerpt below, taken from her paper titled "Jim as a Romantic," used an interpretive probe similar to that used by Garber. In this paper, Stephanie Owen uses the characteristic beliefs of the romantic age as an interpretive grid with which to better understand the underlying motivations of the character Jim in Joseph Conrad's *Lord Jim*.

Jim as a Romantic

by Stephanie J. Owen

English 201

The Romantic Age took place in Western Europe between the years of 1780 and 1850. It was an age that emphasized the importance of the individual. The use of the imagination and the emotions were considered necessary for the discovery of deep, hidden truths (Knoebel 260) in the Romantic quest for the "ideal state of being" (Miller 383). These truths were thought simple, based on the moral behavior of man (Knoebel 260).

The completion of the Romantic Age in 1850 did not end the characteristics, beliefs, and sensibilities that accompanied the age, however. Fifty years after the end of this period, Jim, the main character of Joseph Conrad's book <u>Lord Jim</u>, was described within the book as "excessively romantic" (Conrad 416). After listening to the story of his life, Stein, another character in the book, claimed, "I understand quite well. He is romantic" (212). In trying to explain how a romantic person viewed the world and what he must do to live happily within the world, Stein used a metaphor which I believe is fundamental to understanding Jim's behavior, both his failures and his successes, throughout the book. He stated,

> A man that is born falls into a dream like a man who falls into the sea. If he tries to climb out into the air . . ., he drowns. The way is to the destructive element submit yourself, and with the exertions of your hands and feet in the water make the deep, deep sea keep you up. (Conrad 214)

I believe that Jim's romantic characteristics induced his failures when he tried to escape from that which surrounded him and his successes when he submitted himself to his dream, to his ideal response to his environment.

The Romantics placed a strong emphasis on the value of imagination (Knoebel 260). Jim, too, was very imaginative. As Marlow, the main narrator of the book, stated, "He was a poor gifted devil with the faculty of a swift and forestalling vision" (Conrad 96). He often imagined himself in the positions of the heroes of books that he had read and believed that, when the necessity arose, he would be able to act in the manner that he imagined. He felt that his imagination had prepared him for any danger that might occur (6). This type of imagination ruled his life throughout the first half of the book; he lived more within his dream life than in reality. In the second part of the book, though, Jim began to realize his dreams. In Patusan, Jim acted heroically on several different occasions, often because his imagination helped him to discover the best method to approach a difficult matter. He lived very much as one of his fictional characters would live (Martin 205).

Another aspect of the Romantic Movement was the value it placed on individualism. Each person was considered to have importance, and variation was considered to be beneficial (Miller 383). Jim again proved to be romantic in the value that he placed on individuals. Throughout most of the book, however, the only individualism that he understood was his own, as Conrad expressed through the omnipotent narrator, "his thought was contemplating his own superiority" (23). In Patusan, however, Jim began to value the lives of others. He cared deeply for the lives and happiness of the Patusans, and he involved himself in their politics to help assure their freedom. Because he had learned the value of individual expression, he may have placed more value on Gentleman Brown's life than he should have. He had learned, however, that one individual should not necessarily judge another.

Jim also displayed a similarity with the Romantics in his wide range of emotions. The Romantics felt that emotions were important for true understanding of

self, and their works continually expressed a high
emotional content (Knoebel 260). Jim may not have fully
understood his emotional swings, but Marlow certainly
noticed them. He claimed, "Your imaginative people
swing further in any direction, as if given a longer
scope of cable in the uneasy anchorage of life" (Conrad
224). Immediately after having jumped off of the Patna,
Jim's unhappiness and guilt were strong enough to have
nearly driven him to suicide. However, another equally
strong emotion, his anger at the others in the boat,
prevented him (118). As Chester explained, "[He] takes
it to heart" (165). After the inquiry, his inability to
forget his extreme guilt caused Jim to continually run
away from any incident or situation that might heighten
his feelings of unhappiness. After finally having
arrived in Patusan, Jim began to succeed, and his
happiness and pride reached the same levels as his
guilt and discomfiture had previously.

The imagination, individualism, and emotionalism
already described were, for the Romantics, the basis
and means for the discovery of deep, hidden truths
(Knoebel 260). They thus rejected materialism (Miller
383) and the morals of their time period (Knoebel 260)
in deference to humanitarianism and efforts to reform
the world. They sought after "ideal states of being"
(Miller 383). I believe that Jim's feelings of
superiority and his constant search after heroism were
a result of his own desire to idealize his own "state
of being." He did have the sense of moral obligation
and correctness that was characteristic of the

Romantics, but he occasionally failed in his actions. According to Stein, the way to discover truth was to "follow the dream" (Conrad 215), and several times throughout the book, Jim did "follow the dream" to which his imagination, his individualism, and his emotions led him. In those times, he immersed himself "in the destructive element" (214), and then he succeeded. He failed only when he forgot to "follow the dream."

Jim made three major mistakes throughout his career as both a seaman and a leader of Patusan. In my opinion, each of these failures was caused, directly or indirectly, by some aspect of his romanticism that emerged when he attempted to "climb out" of the dream rather than submit himself to it. Jim's jump from the Patna, his inability to hold a job after the inquiry, and his misjudging of Brown were all actions that resulted from his uncontrolled romanticism.

[Stephanie goes on to describe each of the three mistakes Jim made.]

A reader can hardly keep from admiring Jim's giving up his life to "follow the dream" at the end of the novel, but Conrad seems almost to condemn rather than support the action. This condemnation raises the question of whether or not Jim's romantic characteristics could be considered his tragic flaw. I personally prefer to view Jim's death as a success, as a final proof that he was capable of controlling his own destiny and a final atonement for all of his mistakes, but I do recognize that his romanticism, his submission "to the destructive element," actually did destroy him. This is the question with which Marlow struggled and with which each reader must also struggle when studying Conrad and Lord Jim.

Works Cited

Conrad, Joseph. Lord Jim. 1920. New York: Oxford UP, 1989.

Epstein, Harry S. "Lord Jim as a Tragic Action." Studies in the Novel: Northern Texas State 5 (1973): 229–47.

Knoebel, Edgar E., ed. "Romantic Poetry." Classics of Western Thought: The Modern World. New York: Harcourt, 1988.

Martin, Joseph. "Conrad and the Aesthetic Movement." Conradiana 17 (1985): 199–213.

Miller, James E., Jr., et al., eds. "The Romantic Age." England in Literature. Glenview, IL: Scott-Foresman, 1976, 382–83.

Reichard, Hugo M. "The Patusan Crises: A Reevaluation of Jim and Marlow." English Studies 49 (1968): 547–52.

Stevenson, Richard C. "Stein's Prescription for 'How to End the Problem of Assessing Lord Jim's Career.'" Conradiana 7 (1975): 233–43.

QUESTIONS FOR DISCUSSION

1. What significant event, theme, or character did Stephanie identify in Conrad's work?

2. What hypothesis did Stephanie propose to help us interpret the work?

3. What parallels did Stephanie find between the main character, Jim, and the Romantics?

4. What new insights were you able to gain about Conrad's work by reading Stephanie's interpretation?

Life-History Interviewing

The methods of humanities research may at times approximate the methods in social science research even more closely than the above description suggests. Historical research, for example, may include surveys and interviews of participants in a significant historical event, and very often historical research relies on the statistics gathered by social scientists.

One example of a humanities researcher is Studs Terkel, author of the book *Hard Times: An Oral History of the Great Depression,* which chronicles life during the 1930s.[12] Terkel's primary sources for his work were people who had lived through the Depression. He interviewed people from various walks of life and parts of the country, inquiring into their own life histories. The interviews were taped and transcribed. From the transcripts, Terkel wrote his version of the life history of each individual, bringing his own interpretations and explanations to the interview data. Terkel presented these explanations to readers in story form; the pieces describe and recreate events in each informant's life and together give a composite picture of life during the Depression.

The following excerpts show how Terkel transformed the taped material from his interview with Emma Tiller into a "story." As you read these excerpts, notice the differences between the taped original and Terkel's narrative. What kinds of changes did he make? Why do you think he made the changes he did?

Emma Tiller (transcribed tape)

Studs Terkel

a white in the south is like they is i guess in most other places they will not give and help especially the ones who is turned out to be tramps and hoboes uh they come to their door for food they will drive them away white tramps they will drive them away but if a negro come they will feed him they always go and get something another and give him something to eat and they'll even give them a little do you smoke or do you you dip snuff or uh or any do you use anything like that yes ma'am yes ma'am well they would uh give him a quarter or uh fifty cents you know and give him a little sack of food and a bar of soap or something like that well uh but they own color they wouldn't do that for them then the negro woman would uh uh say you know well we've got some cold food in there we'll give you she said oh no i don't give them nothing he'll be back tomorrow you know so so they won't dispose it Terkel: Oh, you mean the Negro woman [who works] yes [for the white] yes [mistress] yes [the white- -] She would take food and put it in a bag and sometimes wrap it in newspaper and ah we would hurry out and sometimes we'd have to run down the alley because he'd be gone down the alley and holler at him hey mister and he would stop you know and say come here and he'd come back and said look you come back by after while and i'll put some food out there in a bag and i'll put it down side the can so that you don't see it if we could see soap we'd swipe a bar of soap and face rag or something or you know and stick it in there for them negroes always would feed these tramps even sometimes we would see them on the railroad track picking up stuff and we would tell them you know come to our house and give them the address and tell him to come back that we would give him a old shirt or a pair of pants or some old shoes and some food we always would give them food many times i have gone in in my house and taken my husband's old shoes and his coat and some of them he he needed them hisself but i didn't feel he needed them as bad as that man needed them because that man to me was in a worser shape than he was in regardless of whether it was negro or white i would give them to him.

Emma Tiller (pages 60–61)

When tramps and hoboes would come to their door for food, the southern white people would drive them away. But if a Negro come, they will feed him. They even give them money. They'll ask them: Do you smoke do you dip snuff Yes, ma'am, yes, ma'am. They was always nice in a nasty way to Negroes. But their own color, they wouldn't do that for 'em. They would hire Negroes for these type jobs where they wouldn't hire whites. They wouldn't hire a white woman to do housework, because they were afraid she'd take her husband.

When the Negro woman would say, 'Miz So-and-So, we got some cold food in the kitchen left from lunch. Why don't you give it to 'im?' she'll say, 'Oh, no, don't give 'im nothin'. He'll be back tomorrow with a gang of 'em. He ought to get a job and work.'

The Negro woman who worked for the white woman would take food and wrap it in newspapers. Sometimes we would hurry down the alley and holler at 'im: 'Hey, mister, come here!' And we'd say, 'Come back by after a while and I'll put some food in a bag, and I'll sit it down aside the garbage can so they won't see it.' Then he'd get food, and we'd swipe a bar of soap and a face razor or somethin', stick it in there for 'im. Negroes would always feed these tramps.

Sometimes we would see them on the railroad tracks pickin' up stuff, and we would tell 'em: 'Come to our house.' They would come by and we would give 'em an old shirt or a pair of pants or some old shoes. We would always give 'em food.

Many times I have gone in my house and taken my husband's old shoes some of 'em he needed hisself, but that other man was in worser shape than he was. Regardless of whether it was Negro or white, we would give to 'em.

From Terkel, Studs (1970). *Hard Times: An Oral History of the Great Depression.* New York: Pantheon Books. Copyright © 1970 by Studs Terkel. Reprinted by permission of Pantheon Books, a division of Random House, Inc.

QUESTIONS FOR DISCUSSION

1. What do you think Emma Tiller's job was?

2. Compare Emma's description of the treatment of hoboes by whites with that by blacks.

3. What attitude toward poor people does Emma exemplify?

4. What role do you think compassion played during the Depression?

5. How does Terkel use language to illustrate Emma Tiller's character?

6. Choose one line from the original transcript and compare it to Terkel's rendition of the same line. What changes did Terkel make? Why do you think he made those changes?

7. Which version is easier to read? Why?

8. How does Emma Tiller's story help make life during the Depression vivid and real?

9. Relate Terkel's work *Hard Times* to what you have learned about humanities research. Does Terkel's approach satisfy the goals of humanities research?

EXERCISE

In this exercise, you will use some of the tools and procedures of researchers in the humanities as you research and write an auto-biographical report. This assignment can also help you become familiar with locating and using primary sources in your library.

Procedure:

A. First, locate a primary text. In this case, locate a newspaper that was printed on the day you were born. Old newspapers are probably kept in your library on microfilm, so you will need to learn how to use the microfilm readers. If possible, choose a newspaper from a city near where you were born. For example, if you were born in the East, you could read the *New York Times* or the *Washington Post*.

B. Read the newspaper completely, looking for significant events, people, and ideas. Take notes about any important events, people, or ideas that you find in the newspaper.

C. Once you have finished reading and taking notes, formulate a hypothesis that tells something about the times in which you were born. For example, you might hypothesize that very little has changed in the kinds of news stories written then and now. Or you might find that prices are drastically different and speculate about the reasons for the change. Or you might find a significant article (on a political event or a social issue, such as the first busing for desegregation in a major city and the consequent rioting) that would provide the basis of your paper. Whatever the idea or event you choose, the task is to determine its significance and interpret it for your readers.

D. Write a short autobiographical account illustrating the times in which you were born. Or, alternatively, find something striking about the newspaper records and develop your own hypothesis. If possible, include your own experiences as a point of departure for your paper.

ORGANIZING AND WRITING THE HUMANITIES RESEARCH PAPER

We will refer to the research paper written by Maure Smith in this section of the chapter. Maure's paper appears at the end of the chapter.

A thesis statement, together with an analysis of the rhetorical situation (see Chapter 4, pp. 91–100), may suggest an organizational plan for a research paper. Maure's thesis sentence ("Viewing the novel as a comedy could cause us to misunderstand Faulkner's dark message about patriarchy and misogyny.") implies its own organizational plan. In this case, the paper will be a critical examination of the novel in order to convince readers that the message is not comedic but, rather, is darkly tragic.

Depending upon the writer's intentions and the needs of the audience, other theses might suggest other organizational plans, for example, cause and effect ("Addie's naive nature caused catastrophes in the lives of those around her"), comparison and contrast ("Addie is the

most articulate of Steinbeck's characters"), process ("Addie's life jour-
ney reveals a learning process"), and example ("Faulkner's preoccupa-
tion with the sexuality in human nature is evident in his novel *As I Lay
Dying*"). You as a writer will need to determine what approach to your
subject matter makes the most sense given what you have learned in
your research.

As you read back through your notes, it is a good idea to begin organizing your information by blocking related material together. First,
ask yourself how many blocks of related material you seem to have.
This might include a block of background material, a block of plot summary material, a block of related criticism in secondary sources on a
particular aspect of the primary text, and so on. Then, consider the
order in which the blocks of material should be presented to communicate your ideas. How will each block of material be developed, and
how much space in the paper will each require to adequately discuss
the ideas you want to present? Again, refer to your thesis statement as
an organizational guide.

Outlining

Now you are ready to outline your research paper. Do not be
overly concerned about formal outline structure. An outline should be
a guide to writing, not a constraint that confines and limits your thinking. Many writers move back and forth between a sketchy outline and
their written draft, changing both as they go along. Use your outline to
help you write, but be open to the discoveries to be made about your
topic while you are actually writing. Follow your teacher's instructions
on your final outline form, since some teachers may prefer a formal
sentence outline to a phrase outline. Maure constructed the following
outline:

Sentence Outline

Thesis: However, on further analysis, viewing
the novel as a comedy could cause us to
misunderstand Faulkner's dark messages about
patriarchy and misogyny.

    I. Lacan's language theories help us understand
       Faulkner's point about attitudes toward women
       in the south.

    A. Addie's monologue is central to the novel.

        1. Addie's monologue shows her struggle with language.

        2. She tries to account for herself with language.

    B. The birth of Addie's children is central to her understanding of life.

        1. She speaks of childbirth in anger.

        2. She transmits her feelings toward men to her own daughter.

    C. Her daughter Dewey Dell also shows a struggle with language.

        1. She cannot seem to articulate her needs.

        2. She is taken advantage of by the pharmacists.

II. Addie and Dewey's experiences reveal Faulkner's opinion concerning the controversy over women's sexuality in the South.

    A. Addie's acceptance of Anse as a husband shows her ambivalence.

        1. She accepts him as an outlet for her own sexuality.

        2. Her bleak life begins when she marries Anse.

    B. There are two types of attitudes expressed by the women.

        1. Acquiescence to their lot.

        2. Hostility toward life.

    C. Addie's death is a central event in the
       novel.

       1. It shows a symbolic rejection of the
          feminine.

       2. It shows that motherhood both controls
          and denies women's sexuality.

EXERCISE

Arrange and block your source material and notes, decide on an organizational plan, and construct an outline to guide your writing. Refer to Chapter 4 for help with organization (pp. 91–100).

Writing the First Draft

After you have completed your preliminary plan or outline, you are ready to write the first draft of your research paper. Remember, you are writing to present to your readers the answer that you have discovered to the starting question. Remind yourself of your starting question at this time. If you have prepared sufficiently, the actual writing of the paper will be an important way for you to verify the truth of your thesis. However, remain flexible as you write your first draft and be open to any fresh insights you may have along the way.

As you are writing the first draft, it is important to note which supporting material comes from which source. Do not be overly concerned at this point about the formal details of documentation, which you can deal with later, but do mark for yourself in the draft any ideas or words taken from your sources. Place any words you copy from a source, either the primary or secondary sources, in quotation marks, and follow them with the author's last name and the page number of the source in parentheses:

    "Both Addie and her daughter Dewey Dell try to
acquiesce" (Kincaid 589).

Similarly, identify paraphrases and restatements of ideas taken from a source even though you have recast them in your own words:

> Schroeder also suggests that *As I Lay Dying*
> follows this comedic pattern (35).

For general information on planning, writing, and revising your research paper, refer to Chapters 4 and 5. Use the following information on documentation in the humanities to create your citations. The sample research paper at the end of this chapter may also serve as a useful guide to you as you write.

DOCUMENTATION IN THE HUMANITIES: MLA STYLE

The MLA (Modern Language Association) documentation style, which uses in-text citation, has been generally adopted by writers of research papers in language and literature. Other disciplines in the humanities and fine arts may use the footnote/bibliography system. I will first discuss the MLA style (as detailed in the *MLA Handbook for Writers of Research Papers,* 6th ed., Joseph Gibaldi, New York: Modern Language Association, 2003) and then describe the footnote and bibliography styles commonly used in the humanities other than language and literature.

The MLA documentation style consists of parenthetical in-text citations and a list of works cited at the end of the paper. In the humanities, specific sources and page numbers are more important than the recency of the work. Thus, in-text citations show the author's name and the page number of the source rather than the author's name and the date of publication, as in the sciences and social sciences.

Internal Citation

Both the author cited and the page number of the source are important for the internal citation. Observe the following principles in the text of your research paper.

1. Generally, introduce any paraphrase or direct quotation with the name of the author. Then indicate the page number of the source in parentheses at the end of the material:

> Fatterley argues, "Women defy their years of
> academic acculturation" (424).

2. When you do not use the author's name to introduce the para-phrased or quoted material, place the author's name along with the specific page number in parentheses at the end of the material:

> However, unlike his mother, Cal has
>
> "recognized the evil in himself, and is ready to
>
> act for good" (Cooperman 88).

[Note: Do not separate author and page with a comma.]

3. Indicate every instance of borrowed material for the reader. You can indicate a paragraph taken from a single source by mention-ing the author's name at the beginning of the paragraph and giv-ing the parenthetical citation at the end:

> Schroeder also states that *As I Lay Dying*,
>
> obviously and perhaps even deliberately, follows
>
> this pattern (35).

4. When you have used two works by the same author, identify them by the author, abbreviated title, and page number of the source:

> According to Lisca, Samuel, who has been
>
> working in the field all day, "associates the
>
> buried meteorite (falling star, hence Lucifer),
>
> which wrecks his well drill with Cathy . . . (Wide
>
> World 269). After her children's birth, Cathy is
>
> once again compared with a serpent. Lisca comments
>
> that "Cathy gives birth to the twins as easily as
>
> a snake lays eggs" (Nature and Myth 168).

5. When it is apparent that your citations refer to the same work, you need not repeat the author's name. The page number will suffice:

> Steinbeck says it is "easy to say she was bad,
>
> but there is little meaning unless we know why"

(184). The question of Cathy's wicked and sinful
existence "goes forever unanswered--just as the
'reason' for the presence of evil itself goes
unanswered" (184).

6. For a primary source requiring frequent in-text citation, you can
   add a bibliographic footnote:

in-text

"irresistible, fascinating, and horrible."[1]

Footnote

[1]John Steinbeck, East of Eden (New York:
Viking, 1952) 32. Subsequent references are to
this edition of the novel and are included
parenthetically in the text.

[Note: Subsequent in-text references need only the page number.]

7. Other content footnotes may be included for the following:
   A. Blanket citations

[2]For further information on this point, see
Lisca (168), French (56), and Hayashi (29).

B. Related matters (not included in your paper)

[3]Although outside the scope of this paper,
major themes in the novel are discussed by Hayashi
and French.

C. Suggested sources (and related topics)

[4]For an additional study of Faulkner's
fictional characters, see Hayashi's Dictionary of
Fictional Characters.

D. Comparisons with another source

> ⁵On this point, see also the article by
>
> Stanley Cooperman, in which he discusses symbolism
>
> in other Faulkner novels.

[Note: If you have several content notes, you may type them on a separate endnote page, which immediately follows your text and is titled "Notes" or "Endnotes." Be sure any references listed in your footnotes or endnotes are also listed on your works cited page.]

8. When including a long quotation (more than four lines of text), indent it ten spaces from the left-hand margin. Everything still remains double-spaced throughout the indented quotation. Notice that the end punctuation for indented quotations differs from internal citations that are run into the text: the period comes before the parenthetical citation for indented quotations.

> Steinbeck explains it as follows:
>
> > If she [Cathy] were simply a monster, that
> >
> > would not bring her in [the story]. But
> >
> > since she had the most powerful impact on
> >
> > Adam and transmitted her blood to her sons
> >
> > and influenced the generations--she
> >
> > certainly belongs in this book. (<u>Journal</u> 42)

The Reference List

The reference list, at the end of the paper, contains all the sources actually cited in the paper (titled "Works Cited") or all the sources you used in writing your paper (titled "Bibliography"). The purpose of the reference list is to help readers find the materials you used in writing your paper, so you must provide complete, accurate information. The following principles should be observed in preparing your reference list.

1. Sources should be listed alphabetically by the last name of the author or (when there is no author given) by the first word of the

title (excluding *a, an, the*). Type the first word of the entry at the left margin. Indent subsequent lines of the same entry five spaces. You should double space the entire reference page both between and within entries.

2. When you have more than one work by the same author, give the name for the first entry only. For subsequent works by the same author, substitute three hyphens and a period for the author's name and arrange the titles alphabetically:

Hayashi, Tetsumaro. John Steinbeck: A Concise

   Bibliography. Metuchen, NJ: Scarecrow Press,

   1967.

- - -. John Steinbeck: A Dictionary of His

   Fictional Characters. Metuchen, NJ:

   Scarecrow Press, 1976.

3. For books and monographs, give the author's name in full form as it appears on the title page, listing the surname first followed by a comma, the given name, initial(s), and a period:

Steinbeck, John.

4. After the author's name, give the complete title of the work, underlined and followed by a period. Important words in the title should be capitalized:

Steinbeck, John. Journal of a Novel: The East of

   Eden Letters.

[Note: Do not underline a title within a title.]

5. Include the editor or translator, edition of the book, series, or number of volumes (if appropriate).

6. Indicate the city of publication (followed by a colon), publisher (followed by a comma), and date of publication (followed by a period):

Steinbeck, John. Journal of a Novel: The East of

   Eden Letters. New York: Viking, 1969.

7. For articles, follow a similar order: Author. Title of the article. Publication data. The title of the article is in quotation marks; the title of the journal is underlined. If a volume number is provided, it goes after the journal title, followed by the date in parentheses. A colon follows the parentheses. Then inclusive page numbers are provided for the entire article. For magazines that are published weekly, give only the date (not in parentheses) expressed as day/month/year. A comma precedes the date. Then inclusive page numbers are provided for the whole article:

```
Nielsen, Paul. "What Does Addie Bundren Mean,and

    How Does She Mean It?" The Southern Literary

    Journal 25 (1992): 33-9.

Greenfield, Meg. "Accepting the Unacceptable."

    Newsweek, 1 July 1985: 64-65.
```

The model references that follow are based on the MLA documentation style as described in the *MLA Handbook*. The sample paper at the end of this chapter also uses MLA documentation.

MODEL REFERENCES: LANGUAGE AND LITERATURE (MLA)

Type of Reference

BOOKS

1. One author

```
Frohock, William Merrill. The Novel of Violence in

    America. Dallas: Southern Methodist UP, 1958.
```

[Note: UP is the abbreviation for University Press.]

2. Two or more authors

```
Halliday, M. A. K., and Raquaia Hasan. Cohesion in

    English. London: Longman, 1976.
```

3. Book with editor(s)

> Kunitz, Stanley J., and Howard Haycraft, eds.
>
>   Twentieth Century Authors. New York: Wilson,
>
>   1942.

4. Book with editor and author

> Twain, Mark. Letters from the Earth. Ed. Bernard
>
>   Devoton. New York: Harper & Row, 1962.

5. Essay, chapter, or section in edited work

> Gray, James. "John Steinbeck." American Writers,
>
>   IV. Ed. Leonard Unger. New York: Scribner's,
>
>   1974. 47–65.

6. Encyclopedia entry

   (signed)

> Riddel, Joseph N. "William Faulkner." The World
>
>   Book Encyclopedia. 1983 ed.

   (unsigned)

> "William Faulkner." Encyclopedia Americana. 1992 ed.

ARTICLES

1. Journal article (one author)

> Cox, Martha Heasley. "Steinbeck's Family
>
>   Portraits: The Hamiltons." Steinbeck Quarterly
>
>   14 (1981): 23–32.

2. Journal article (two or more authors)

> Flower, Linda, and John R. Hayes. "The Cognition
>
>   of Discovery: Defining a Rhetorical Problem."

College Composition and Communication 31

(1980): 21-32.

3. Journal article that pages each issue separately (must include both volume and issue number)

Kail, Harvey, and John Trimbur. "The Politics of

Peer Tutoring." WPA: Writing Program

Administration 11.1-2 (1987): 5-12.

4. Magazine article

(signed)

Will, George F. "Machiavelli from Minnesota?"

Newsweek 16 July 1984: 88.

(unsigned)

"It Started in a Garden." Time 22 Sept. 1952:

110-11.

[Note: For a monthly magazine, give only month and year.]

5. Newspapers

Engle, Paul. "A Review of John Steinbeck's East of

Eden." Chicago Sunday Tribune 21 Sept.

1952: A3.

[Note: A3 stands for section A, page 3.]

6. An abstract from Dissertation Abstracts International

Johnson, Nancy Kay. "Cultural and Psychosocial

Determinants of Health and Illness." Diss.

U of Washington, 1980. DAI 40 (1980):

4235B.

OTHER SOURCES

1. Film or movie

   Indiana Jones and the Temple of Doom. Dir. Steven

   Spielberg. Paramount Pictures, 1984.

2. Dissertation, unpublished

   Balkema, Sandra. "The Composing Activities of

   Computer Literate Writers." Diss. U of

   Michigan, 1984.

3. Interview

   Johnson, James. Personal interview. 12 Mar. 1984.

4. Personal letter

   Reagan, Ronald. Letter to the author. 8 Sept. 1983.

5. Unpublished paper or manuscript

   Welter, William. "Word Processing in Freshman

   English: Does It Compute?" Unpublished essay,

   1985.

6. Television program

   "The Great Apes." National Geographic Special.

   Public Broadcasting Service. WGBH, Boston.

   12 July 1984.

ELECTRONIC MEDIA

   As electronic media continue to evolve, the details of citations will change to reflect new formats. However, the basic rationale for citing references will remain the same: researchers using electronic material need to provide information identifying each source, and they must give clear directions for locating it. Because electronic information can be changed easily and often, the version available to your readers may be different from the one you accessed during your research. The MLA recommends listing two dates—the date of posting or updating and the date of access (that is, the date when you viewed the source material). The MLA also recommends including the electronic address (URL) within angle brackets to distinguish it from the surrounding punctuation of the citation. Be accurate when recording URLs and other identifying information (such as the author's name or the title of a Web page) so that readers can use a search tool to find the source if the URL becomes outdated. In its guidelines for electronic citation style, the MLA acknowledges that not all of the information recommended for a citation may be available. Cite whatever information is available. It might be wise to consult your instructor before finalizing your works cited list to ensure that you are conforming to his or her requirements for electronic citations. See also the MLA's Web site at <http://www.mla.org>.

1. Entire Internet site

   Reference information on the Web varies. Include the information available at the site, in the following sequence:

   A. The title of the site or project (underlined) or, if there is no title a brief description of the site (such as homepage)
   B. The creator or author of the site (if relevant and given)
   C. The editor or compiler of the project or database (if known)
   D. The version number, the date of electronic publication or latest update, the name of the sponsoring organization or institution (if given)
   E. The date of access
   F. The electronic address (URL), within angle brackets

   Victoriana On-Line. Ed. Sylvania Dye. 1996–2002.

      12 Jan. 2002

      <http://www.victorianaonline.com>.

   Global Climate Change. 1 May 1998. Environment

      Canada. 15 May 1998 <http://www.eg.gc.ca>.

2. An information database or scholarly project

   The EServer. Ed. Geoffrey Sauer. 2000.

      University of Washington. 15 Jan. 2001

      <http://eserver.org>.

   MSNBC News. 12 July 2000. Microsoft Network. 12

      July 2000 <http://www.msnbc.msn.com>.

3. A document within an information database or scholarly project

To cite a poem, short story, article, or other work within an information database or scholarly project, begin with the author's name, if given, followed by the title of the work in quotation marks. If no author is given, begin with the title. Continue with relevant information on the database or project, including the access date and URL. Be sure to give the URL of the specific document rather than the URL of the database itself (if they are different).

> Angelou, Maya. "On the Pulse of the Morning." The
>
> Electronic Text Center. Ed. David Seaman.
>
> 2002. U of Virginia Library. 1 Jan. 2003
>
> <http://etext.lib.virginia.edu>.

4. An anonymous article from a reference database

To cite an anonymous article from a reference database, start with the title of the article (in quotation marks). Continue with the electronic publication information from the reference work. Be sure to give the unique address of the article you are citing if it is different from the URL for the database itself.

> "Feather." Britannica Online. Vers. 98.1.1. May
>
> 1998. Encyclopedia Britannica. 12 Aug. 1998
>
> <http://www.eb.com:175>.

5. Online book

The complete texts of many books are now available online as well as in print. Provide the print information first, followed by the Internet information.

> Woolf, Virginia. The Voyage Out. London: Faber,
>
> 1914. The EServer. Ed. Geoffrey Sauer. 2003.
>
> U of Washington. 15 Jan. 2003
>
> <http://eserver.org/fiction/voyage-out.txt>.

6. Online periodical

Many magazines, newspapers, and scholarly journals are now available in online formats. Generally, citations for online periodicals use the same format as citations for print periodicals, but this information is followed by the URL.

Ricks, Delthia. "Sickle Cell: New Hope." <u>Newsday</u>

12 May 1998. 13 May 1998

<http://www.newsday.com/homepage.htm>.

Reinhardt, Leslie Kaye. "British and Indian

Identities in a Picture by Benjamin West."

<u>Eighteenth Century Studies</u> 31.3 (1998). 12 July

1998 <http://muse.jhu.edu/journals/

eighteenth_century_studies>.

Dedman, Bill. "Racial Bias Seen in U.S. Housing

Loan Program." <u>New York Times on the Web</u> 13

May 1998. 13 May 1998

<http://www.nytimes.com/archives>.

Bast, Joseph L. Rev. of <u>Our Stolen Future</u>, by Theo

Colborn et al. <u>Heartland Institute</u> 18 Apr.

1996: 27 pars. 25 June 1997

<http://www.Heartland.org/stolen1.htm>.

[Note: "Pars." stands for "paragraphs."]

Reid, Joy. "Responding to ESL Students' Texts."

<u>TESOL Quarterly</u> 28 (1994): 273-92. Abstract.

12 July 2000 <http://vweb.hwwilsonweb.com/

cgi-bin/webspirs.cgi>.

7. Database published on CD-ROM

Periodicals and reference works are commonly distributed on CD-ROM, with updated CDs issued regularly. When citing such works, include the information on the printed source, plus the publication medium, the name of the vendor (if relevant), and the electronic publication date.

Arms, Valerie M. "A Dyslexic Can Compose on a

Computer." <u>Educational Technology</u> 24.1 (1984):

39-41. <u>ERIC</u>. CD-ROM. SilverPlatter. Sept. 1984.

8. Work from a personal subscription service

If you are using a personal subscription service such as AOL, provide the title and publication date, name of the service, the date of
access, and a keyword.

```
"Dr. Phil's Relationship Rescue." Online with

    Oprah. 12 July 2000. America Online. 15 Aug.

    2000. Keyword: Oprah.
```

9. Work from a Library Subscription Service

To cite online documents or articles that you derive from a service
to which your library subscribes (e.g., *Lexis-Nexis, ProQuest,* or *EB-
SCOhost*), follow the citation for the source itself with the name of
the service (underlined), the site sponsor, the library, and the date
of access. If you know the URL of the database service's homepage, provide it in angle brackets at the end of the citation. If the
library service provides only a starting page for the article's original printed version rather than numbering the pages, provide the
number followed by a hyphen, a space, and a period. *115-.*

```
Bozell III, Brent L. "Fox Hits Bottom--Or Does

    It?" Human Events 57.4 (2001): 15-. Academic

    Search Elite. EBSCO. Utah State U Lib., Logan.

    15 Oct. 2002 <http://www.epnet.com>.


King, Marsha. "Companies Here Ponder Scout

    Ruling." Seattle Times 6 July 2000: Al.

    Academic Universe. Lexis-Nexis. Utah State U

    Lib., Logan. 15 Aug. 2000 <http://web.lexis-

    nexis.com/universe>.
```

10. Electronic Communication

For an email message, provide the writer's name (or alias), the
subject (title) of the communication in quotation marks, the desig-
nation "Email to," the name of the person to whom the email is
addressed, and the date of the message.

Gillespie, Paula. "Members of the NWCA Board." E-
        mail to Michael Pemberton. 1 Aug. 1997.

For an online posting in a discussion forum, listserv, or news
group, include the description "Online posting" and the date of
the posting. Provide the name of the forum, if known. If possible,
cite an archival version of the posting so that readers can more
easily find and read the source.

White, Edward. "Texts as Scholarship: Reply to Bob
        Schwegler." Online posting. 11 Apr. 1997. WPA
        Discussion List. 12 Apr. 1997
        <http://gcinfo.gc.maricopa.edu/~wpa>.

FOOTNOTE AND BIBLIOGRAPHY STYLE

In the humanities and fine arts other than language and literature,
a two-part documentation system is common. This system uses footnotes (or endnotes) plus a bibliography. The footnotes appear at the
bottom of the page on which the source is cited; the endnotes are typed
in consecutive order on a separate page at the end of the paper. The bibliography, like the bibliography in the MLA style, is a typed list of
sources arranged alphabetically. Since the bibliography style is generally the same in the two systems, here we will cover only the format for
footnotes (and endnotes). Please refer to the earlier section on the reference list for the style of the bibliography page.

1. In the text, a note is indicated by a superscript number typed immediately after the source paraphrase or quotation:

   The New York Times called his work "a vital,
   sensitive, timely contribution which sheds light
   on mankind's spiritual heritage."[1]

2. For footnotes:

   A. Type single spaced at the bottom of the page on which they
      occur.

    B. Double space between notes if there is more than one note per page.

    C. Indent the note five spaces; use a superscript number followed by a space and the note itself.

    D. Number notes consecutively throughout the text.

    E. Separate footnotes from the text by typing a twelve-space bar line from the left margin.

3. For endnotes:

    A. Type endnotes on a separate page at the end of your paper, titled "Notes" or "Endnotes."

    B. List the notes as they occur in the text and number them consecutively, using a superscript number followed by a space.

    C. Double space the entire endnote page.

4. The format of both footnotes and endnotes is as follows:

    A. Indent the first line of the note five spaces, type the superscript note number, skip a space, and begin the note.

    B. The second line and each subsequent line of the same note should return to the left margin.

    C. Begin notes with the author's name (given name first) followed by a comma:

> [7] Thomas Merton,

    D. Then provide the title of the book or article (underlined or in quotation marks):

BOOK

> [7] Thomas Merton, <u>Mystics and Zen Masters</u>

ARTICLE

> [9] Steven Brachlow, "John Robinson and the Lure of Separatism in Pre-Revolutionary England,"

    E. Provide the publication information after the title. Include the place of publication, the publisher, the date of publication, and the page number of the source. The form differs slightly for books and articles:

BOOK

> [7] Thomas Merton, <u>Mystics and Zen Masters</u> (New York: Dell, 1967) 315.

ARTICLE

> [9] Steven Brachlow, "John Robinson and the Lure
> of Separatism in Pre-Revolutionary England,"
> Church History 50 (1983): 288-301.

5. In subsequent references to the same text, you need not repeat all
   the information of the first note; use only author's last name and
   a page number:

> [9] Brachlow, 289.

6. Where there are two or more works by the same author, you must
   include a shortened version of the work's title:

> [12] Merton, Mystics, 68.
>
> [16] Merton, Buddhism, 18

MODEL NOTES: HUMANITIES

Type of Reference

BOOKS

1. One author

> [1]Francis A. Schaeffer, How Should We Then
> Live? The Rise and Decline of Western Thought and
> Culture (Old Tappan, NJ: Revell, 1976) 39.

2. Two or more authors

> [2]William Ebenstein, C. Herman Pritchett, Henry
> A. Turner, and Dean Man, American Democracy in
> World Perspective (New York: Harper & Row, 1967)
> 365.

3. Book with editor(s)

> [3]Louis Schneider, ed., Religion, Culture, and
> Society (New York: Wiley, 1964) 127.

4. Book with editor and author

   [4]Albert Schweitzer, An Anthology, ed. Charles
   R. Joy (New York: Harper & Row, 1947) 107.

5. Essay, chapter, section in an edited work

   [5]Morris R. Cohn, "Baseball as a National
   Religion," Religion, Culture, and Society, ed.
   Louis Schneider (New York: Wiley, 1964) 74.

6. Encyclopedia entry

   (signed)

   [6]Frank E. Reynolds, "Buddhism," The World Book
   Encyclopedia, 1983 ed.

   (unsigned)

   [7]"Buddhism," Encyclopedia Americana, 1976 ed.
   [Note: No page numbers are necessary in citations
   for material from alphabetically arranged works.]

   ARTICLES

1. Magazine
   (signed) monthly

   [8]Douglas H. Lamb and Glen D. Reeder, "Reliving
   Golden Days," Psychology Today, June 1986: 22.

   (unsigned) weekly

   [9]"An Unmellowed Woman," Newsweek, 9 July
   1984: 73.

2. Scholarly journal

[10]Edward Voutiras, "Dedication of the Hebdomaiston to the Pythian Apollo," <u>American Journal of Archaeology</u> 86 (1982): 229.

3. Newspaper

[11]P. Ray Baker, "The Diagonal Walk," <u>Ann Arbor News</u>, 16 June 1928: A2.

EXERCISES AND RESEARCH PROJECT

Follow the procedures outlined in this chapter to research a primary literary text and write a humanities research paper. The exercises that follow will give you additional practice with skills related to research projects.

1. Write an extended description of one major character in the primary text you have chosen to research. Describe the person's physical appearance, mental state, actions, and the like, so that your reader will be able to picture that person. Use direct evidence from the text to illustrate and support your description.

2. Discuss one major theme from your primary text. Trace the development of that theme through the text, using evidence to support your idea of how the author develops the theme.

3. For each entry on your bibliography, write a three- or four-sentence annotation describing the contents of that source.

4. Write a three- to four-page review of the literature, summarizing the major ideas in your sources. Often a literature review, which lists and comments on the sources, is a component of a larger research project.

DISCIPLINE-SPECIFIC RESOURCES FOR HUMANITIES

Technology and the Humanities

Scholars in the humanities are beginning to use technology in their research and their writing. Students of the humanities, too, should familiarize themselves with available resources, particularly those in library databases and the Internet. Take a look at some of the Internet sources in the following list, such as the *Project Gutenberg* Web site, which contains numerous full texts of important works of literature, or the *Ancient World* Web site, which has links to sites on classical languages and literature. There are also numerous discussion groups, bulletin boards, and newsgroups related to the humanities. You can find these discussion sites through an Internet search.

Resources for the Humanities

ART AND ARCHITECTURE
Dictionaries

Dictionary of Contemporary American Artists. 5th Ed. Cumming, P. New York: St. Martin's, 1988. Concise information on living American artists.
Dictionary of Architecture. Meikleham, R. New York: Gordon, 1980. 3 vols. General information.

Indexes and Abstracts

Art Abstracts
Art Index

Web Sites

The Center for Creative Photography <http://dizzy.library.arizona.edu/branches/ccp>
The Parthenet <http://www.mtholyoke.edu/~klconner/parthenet.html>
World Wide Arts Resources <http://www.world-arts-resources.com>

ENGLISH LITERATURE AND LANGUAGE
Dictionaries and Encyclopedias

Dictionary of Literature in the English Language. Meyers, R. New York: Pergamon, 1978. 2 vols. useful background information on classic English literary works.
Princeton Encyclopedia of Poetry and Poetics. 3rd ed. Preminger, A. and T. V. Brogan, eds. Princeton: Princeton UP, 1993. Concise information on poetry

and poetics through time; covers history, theory, technique, and criticism of poetry.

Indexes and Abstracts

MLA International Bibliography
Wilson Biographies (full text)
Literary Index

Web Sites

EServer—Iowa State University <http://www.eserver.org>
Literary Resources on the Net <http://andromeda.rutgers.edu/~jlynch/Lit>
Project Bartleby <http://www.gutenberg.net/index.shtml>
Project Gutenberg <http://www.gutenberg.org/index.shtml>
Voice of the Shuttle: English Literature <http://vos.ucsb.edu>

HISTORY AND CLASSICS

Dictionaries and Encyclopedias

Encyclopedic Dictionary of American History. 4th Ed. Faragher, J. M., ed. Guilford: Dushkin, 1991. Complete background information on American history.
Encyclopedia of American History. 7th ed. Morris, R. B., and Morris, J. B., eds. New York: Harper, 1996. Valuable overview of American History; contains brief biographies of famous Americans.
Encyclopedia of World History: Ancient, Medieval, and Modern. Langer, W. L., ed. Boston: Market House, 1999. Major world events from earliest times to the 1990s. (The *New Illustrated Encyclopedia of World History* is essentially the same work with illustrations.)

Indexes and Abstracts

Historical Abstracts
America: History and Life

Web Sites

Nineteenth Century Scientific American <http://www.history.rochester.edu/Scientific_American>
Ancient World Web <http://www.julen.net/ancient>
The Perseus Digital Library <http://www.perseus.tufts.edu>

MUSIC

Dictionaries

Dictionary of Composers and Their Music. Gilder, E. New York: Random, 1993. Useful background information.

The New Grove Dictionary of Music and Musicians. 2nd ed. Sadie, S. and Tyrrell, J. eds. London: Groves Dictionaries, 1998. 20 vols. Information on musical topics from ancient to modern times.

Indexes and Abstracts
International Index to Music Periodicals
FILM Abstracts of Music Literature
Music Index

Web Sites
Music Education Links <http://www.music.indiana.edu/music_resources/mused.html>
Music Link: Music on the Internet <http://www.lib.utk.edu/~music>

PHILOSOPHY
Encyclopedias
Encyclopedia of Philosophy. Edwards, P., ed. New York: Macmillan, 1973. 4 vols. Complete reference work on both Eastern and Western philosophical thought.
Encyclopedia of Bioethics. 2nd ed. Reich, W. T., ed. New York: Macmillan, 1995. Information on philosophy and religion.

Index
Philosopher's Index

Web Sites
The American Philosophical Association <http://www.apa.udel.edu/apa.index.html>
Handilinks to Philosophy <http://www.handilinks.com>

RELIGION
Dictionaries and Encyclopedias
Dictionary of Comparative Religions. Brandon, S. G., ed. New York: Scribner's, 1978. Information on world religions.
Encyclopedia of Religion. Eliade, M., ed. New York: Macmillan, 1993. 14 vols. Concise articles on world religions.

Indexes and Abstracts
Religion One Index
Religious and Theological Abstracts

Web Site

Comparative Religion <http://www.academicinfo.net/religindex.html>

THEATER AND FILM

Indexes and Abstracts

New York Times Theater Reviews
Play Index
Film Literature Index
International Index to Film Periodicals

Web Site

The Theatre Links Page <http://www.theatre-link.com>

SAMPLE RESEARCH PAPER: HUMANITIES FORMAT (MLA)

(optional title page)

Addie's Monologue in *As I Lay Dying*

Maure Smith

English 2170

Dr. Bookman

April 16, 2001

Maure Smith

English 2170

Dr. Bookman

April 16, 2001

Addie's Monologue in *As I Lay Dying*

Faulkner's novel *As I Lay Dying* is not a funny book. Although I realize that *As I Lay Dying* has many elements of the classical comedic form, including multiple narratives that allow the readers to distance themselves from the horrifying realities of the text, this does not make it a comedy. Patricia Schroeder argues that "in its classical form, comedy is the inverse of tragedy: it celebrates community survival, applauds the status quo, and affirms life in the face of death" (35). She also states that *As I Lay Dying*, obviously and perhaps even deliberately, follows this comedic pattern (35). However, on further analysis, viewing the novel as a comedy could cause us to misunderstand Faulkner's dark messages about patriarchy and misogyny.

Lacan's theories about language and entering the Symbolic Order can help us to understand what Faulkner is trying to communicate about attitudes towards women in the rural South. Addie's monologue is full of examples of her struggle with language. At the birth of her first child, she realizes, "Words are no good; that words don't ever fit even what they are trying to say at" (1595). Quite clearly, "Words are for her what they are for all the laconic tribes of the novel, perhaps not her best medium" (Nielsen 34). She has this realization at the moment she becomes a mother, which hints at the Symbolic Order that Lacan wasn't sure women could fully grasp—however, she is the only character in the novel that tries to account for herself through language. Her monologue is at the center of the novel, insinuating that she is central to the story, as well as to the characters' lives.

Her discussion is mostly about the births of her children, as if she is trying to make meaning of her existence

Smith 4

through motherhood. However, she doesn't speak in the gushing way we might expect new mothers to talk about their children. Darl's birth is such a profound moment of anger for her that she feels tricked by Anse into having more children, and she is so unhappy with him that she refuses to have any more sex. Her other children are what she gives Anse after the affair with Whitfield to make up for Jewel, but she says that she "did not ask for them" (1597). It is no surprise then that her daughter Dewey Dell feels the same way toward her own unanticipated child.

Dewey Dell also has no control over her native language; it is clear to readers that either she has no idea what she needs, or she cannot articulate the fact that she is pregnant with an unwanted child. Her experience with the pharmacist who turns her away implies that what she is asking for is completely illegal. Ironically, Dewey Dell has no idea what she is asking for. At the second store, not only is she taken advantage of, but she also realizes that the "treatment"

will not get rid of the child she is
carrying. In effect, motherhood for both
Dewey Dell and Addie is a way of
containing and denying female sexuality.

Addie's monologue and the experience
of her daughter Dewey Dell as women in the
South reflect the controversy over birth
control and women's sexuality in the
beginning of the century (Bergman 394).
Even Addie's odd acceptance of Anse's
proposal can be accounted for if a reader
considers her sexual desire. Not only is
she bored out of her mind teaching her
mundane students, and Anse's farm provides
her an escape from her terrible job, but
he also offers her a sexual outlet. She
describes her sexual frustration and her
acceptance of Anse's proposal in this
passage:

> In the early spring it was
> worst. Sometimes I thought that
> I could not bear it, lying in
> bed at night, with the wild
> geese going north and their
> honking coming faint and high
> and wild out of the wild

Smith 6

darkness, and during the day it
would seem as though I couldn't
wait for the last one to go so
I could go down to the spring.
And so when I looked up that
day and saw Anse standing there
in his Sunday clothes, turning
his hat round and round in his
hand . . . (1595)

Addie's bleak and terrible life begins
with her description of her marriage, "So
I took Anse" (1595). But it is not solely
her marriage to Anse that ruins her life;
rather it is her experience with sexual
desire and motherhood.

Nanci Kincaid offers the drowned
mules as a strong southern symbol, and one
that reflects the two types of sexuality
available to women. In Faulkner's story
much is made of their stiff phallic legs
pointing heavenward. She sees these as
either symbols of hostility or
acquiescence—the only two options for
feminine sexuality that Faulkner offers
his characters. "Both Addie and her
daughter Dewey Dell try to acquiesce"

Smith 7

(Kincaid 589), but fail miserably. Neither one of them is capable of being the good devout women their society (and their men!) want them to be, in large part because they lack the skills to express themselves.

Addie's death, which is the central event of the novel although we tend to overlook it, can be interpreted as the symbolic rejection of the feminine that men must experience to enter the Symbolic Order and to speak with a full command of the language. Ironically, none of Addie's boys are able to enter the Symbolic Order anyway, in spite of her death. Darl goes completely mad, Jewel hardly says a word, and Vardamon can't acknowledge aloud that his mother has died, not for a long time (1556). It is extremely ironic, because "It is precisely motherhood that convinces Addie that living is terrible" (Bergman 397). And it is precisely motherhood that controls and denies the expression of female sexuality in this novel, and in the South at that time. Judith Fetterley argues, "Women defy their years of

Smith 8

academic acculturation into a patriarchal

literary canon . . . by learning to resist

as they read" (Blaine 424-25). Resisting

reading *As I Lay Dying* as a comedy allows

us to understand the misogyny that was

prevalent regarding women and their

experiences with motherhood and sexuality

in the rural South.

Works Cited

Bergman, Jill. "'This was the answer to

  it': Sexuality and Maternity in As I

  Lay Dying." The Mississippi Quarterly

  49 (1996): 393-407.

Blaine, Diana York. "The Abjection of

  Addie and Other Myths of the Maternal

  in As I Lay Dying." The Mississippi

  Quarterly 47 (1994): 419-39.

Faulkner, William. As I Lay Dying. The

  Norton Anthology of American

  Literature. Eds. Nina Bayam et al.

  New York: Norton, 1998. 1534-1630.

Fetterley, Judith. The Resisting Reader: A

  Feminist Approach to American

  Fiction. Bloomington: Indiana UP,

  1978.

Batten 9

Kincaid, Nanci. "As Me and Addie Lay
Dying." <u>The Southern Review</u> 30
(1994): 582-95.

Nielsen, Paul. "What Does Addie Bundren
Mean, and How Does She Mean It?" <u>The
Southern Literary Journal</u> 25 (1992):
33-9.

Schroeder, Patricia. "The Comic World of
<u>As I Lay Dying."</u> <u>Faulkner and Humor.</u>
Eds. Doreen Fowler and Ann J. Abadie.
Jackson: Mississippi UP, 1986. 34-46.

NOTES

1. Jack Meiland, *College Thinking: How to Get the Best out of College* (New York: Mentor, 1981) 174.

2. John Livingston Lowes, *The Road to Xanadu: A Study in the Ways of the Imagination* (1927; reprint ed., London: Pan Books, 1978).

3. Richard Altick, *The Art of Literary Research* (New York: W. W. Norton, 1963) 100.

4. Alfred North Whitehead, *Process and Reality* (New York: Free Press, 1929) 5.

5. Whitehead, xi.

6. Frank Maloy Anderson, *The Mystery of "A Public Man": A Historical Detective Story* (Minneapolis: University of Minnesota Press, 1948).

7. As found in Meiland, 186.

8. Barzun and Graff, 250.

9. Barzun and Graff, 251.

10. Whitehead, xi.

11. Eugene K. Garber, " 'My Kinsman, Major Molineux': Some Interpretive and Critical Probes," *Literature in the Classroom: Readers, Texts, and Contexts*, Ed. Ben F. Nelms (Urbana, IL: National Council of Teachers of English, 1988) 83–104.

12. Studs Terkel, *Hard Times: An Oral History of the Great Depression* (New York: Pantheon Books, 1970).

7

Writing a Review Paper in Science and Technology

INTRODUCTION

As discussed in Chapter 1, sciences in general attempt to explain phenomena in the natural and physical world. Since scientists rely on current technology as tools to help them in their work, technology itself has become a branch of science. Scientific researchers must have knowledge of the current research being conducted by others in their fields. They must also have knowledge of the technologies needed to conduct that research. Although the experimental method is at the heart of scientific research, library research is also important. It is in the scientific journals and reviews that scientists report their findings for scrutiny and replication by other researchers. You need to become familiar with the library tools used by scientists so you can gain access to the current thinking in their fields.

Two major types of papers are typically written in science and technology: the research report and the review paper. The research report is a formal report of original (primary) research. The purpose of a scientific or technological research report is to describe clearly and understandably a particular researcher's findings and conclusions. The report may be argumentative or persuasive in tone—arguing in favor of a particular research method or result, for example. Or the report may be interpretive, explaining or interpreting a particular research finding and attempting to draw conclusions or make recommendations. The review paper, on the other hand, presents a synthesis of existing work on a particular, defined scientific topic rather than presenting original findings.

In the scientific review paper, you analyze for your readers the present state of knowledge in an ongoing field of research. Your contribution, then, is in the way you interpret, organize, and present the complex information, thus making it easily accessible to the reader. In the scientific review paper, you argue a particular position with support from the literature and review the topic through paraphrase and summary as objectively as you can, but you don't introduce any new primary data. The following library research skills will be important as you investigate the topic you have chosen to review:

1. A familiarity with library research tools, including databases, bibliographies, and indexes used in science and technology.
2. The ability to understand and evaluate information and data from a variety of sources.
3. The ability to paraphrase and summarize information and data in your own words.
4. The ability to synthesize the information and data gathered into an organized presentation.
5. The ability to employ the formal conventions of scientific review papers.

THE INQUIRY PROCESS IN SCIENCE AND TECHNOLOGY

In the Western world, the sciences hold an authoritative position and are a dominant force in daily life. Scientists have been enormously successful at formulating and testing theories related to phenomena in the natural and physical world. These theories have been used to solve physical and biological problems in medicine, industry, and agriculture. Generally, the sciences have been divided into life sciences (such as biology and botany), physical sciences (such as physics and chemistry), and earth sciences (such as geology and geography). Scientific insights and methods have also been carried over to fields of applied science and technology, such as computer science and engineering.

The Importance of Observation in the Sciences

The motivation or impetus for much scientific research is an observed event or experience that challenges our existing ideas and promotes inquiry. In the context of existing theories, such an event is incongruous and thus sparks in the researcher's mind a question or problem to be investigated. The researcher must be prepared to recognize the inconsistency and to see its importance. He or she must be familiar with current theories and concepts about the natural and physical world. In general, the aim of scientific work is to improve the relationship between our ideas (theories and concepts about the world) and our actual experiences (observations of the world).

An example of a scientist using educated observation is described by Rene Taton in his book *Reason and Chance in Scientific Discovery*.[1] In 1928, Sir Alexander Fleming, an English biologist, was studying mutation in some colonies of *Staphylococcus* bacteria. He noticed that one of his cultures had been contaminated by a microorganism from the air outside. But instead of neglecting this seemingly inconsequential event, Fleming went on to observe the contaminated plate in detail and noticed a surprising phenomenon: the colonies of bacteria that had been attacked by microscopic fungi had become transparent in a large region around the contamination. From this observation, Fleming hypothesized that the effect could be due to an antibacterial substance secreted by the foreign microorganism and then spread into the culture. Fortunately for us, Fleming decided to study the phenomenon at length to discover the properties of this secretion and its effect on cultures of *Staphylococcus* bacteria. (The foreign organism in the culture turned out to be a variety of the fungus *Penicillium*, from which we now make the antibiotic penicillin.) Fleming designed experiments that tested his hypothesis concerning the effects of *Penicillium* on bacteria, and eight months later, he published his research findings in the *British Journal of Experimental Pathology*. Fleming's research is an example of the research process: first controlled observation, then a struggle with the problem and the formulation of a hypothesis, and finally the verification of that hypothesis using experiments.

The Importance of Formulating and Testing Hypotheses

On the basis of a scientist's prior knowledge and preparation, he or she formulates a hypothesis to account for the observed phenomenon that presents a problem. Arriving at a hypothesis takes much effort on the part of the researcher. Brainstorming for possible hypotheses is an important component of research, because the researcher can creatively make conjectures based on prior experience. The researcher may have to test several possible hypotheses before deciding which one seems to account for the observed phenomenon. Fleming, for example, hypothesized that the clear circle he observed around the bacteria resulted from the contaminating microorganism in the culture. In the sciences, there are systematic ways of testing a hypothesis once it is formulated. Fleming used such a procedure to verify his hypothesis: he demonstrated through scientific experiments that *Penicillium* was effective against bacteria.

The following outline describes the systematic way, or *scientific method*, by which scientists customarily proceed:

1. The scientist formulates a question and develops a hypothesis that might shed light on the question posed.
2. On the basis of the hypothesis, the scientist predicts what should be observed under specified conditions and circumstances.
3. The scientist makes the necessary observations, generally using carefully designed, controlled experiments.
4. The scientist either accepts or rejects the hypothesis depending on whether the actual observations correspond with the predicted observations.

Using the scientific method, a researcher is able to integrate new data into existing theories about the natural and physical world. In step 2 above, the researcher draws on accepted scientific ideas and theories to predict an outcome for the experiment. Fleming, for example, predicted that his experiments would show the antibacterial action of *Penicillium* when used on certain bacteria, and he confirmed his hypothesis through careful laboratory experiments.

Neither Fleming nor the scientific community of his day recognized the profound implications of his research for the field of medicine. *Penicillium* was a difficult-to-handle, impure, and unstable substance, which at the time made it seem impractical for widespread application. Subsequent discoveries and refinements of the antibiotic, however, enabled penicillin to revolutionize modern medicine.

Ordinarily, the individual researcher uses currently held scientific theories and ideas to incorporate new data into the mainstream of current scientific belief. Research advances are the cumulative result of researchers working on various problems in various parts of the world; a synthesis of existing data is used to create new ideas and theories. Taton notes that many of the immense scientific discoveries of the twentieth century were the collective work of teams of specialists from various schools working with more and more refined technical resources.[2] Although the role of the individual researcher is important, he or she is but a cog in the wheel of the scientific community in general.

Critical Scientific Research

Much of the research conducted by scientists is an attempt to incorporate new data into existing theories, but another type of scientific research, critical scientific research, attempts to challenge currently held beliefs and theories in an effort to improve them. Critical scientific research investigates the adequacy, or the sufficiency, of theories about the natural and physical world. In this context, the question asked is, "How well do current theories actually explain the natural and physical world as we know and observe it?"

A particular field of science may operate for years under certain theoretical assumptions. For example, Newtonian physics, based on the theories of Isaac Newton, dominated the scientific world for some time, and thousands of scientists conducted regular experiments based on Newton's theories. But because physicists encountered numerous phenomena that were incompatible with Newton's laws of physics, new theories became necessary. The physicist Albert Einstein challenged the agreed-upon Newtonian physics by presenting an alternative system that accounted for more of the observed data. Most physicists have now adopted Einstein's more comprehensive theories or have gone on to develop and adopt new theories.

This process of challenging and replacing scientific theories is one way scientific fields advance their knowledge and understanding of the natural or physical world. Thus, scientific thought progresses both by regular scientific observation and experimentation, using widely accepted theories and beliefs, and by critical scientific research that challenges those widely held theories and suggests new ones.

The Importance of Replicability and Scientific Debate

Scientists who have created and tested a hypothesis must then report their findings to other scientists, as Fleming did by publishing his experiments in the British journal. The goals of publishing one's findings include having other scientists accept the hypothesis as correct, communicating knowledge, and stimulating further research and discussion. A report of the research must necessarily include a careful, accurate description of the problem, the hypothesis, and the method used to test the hypothesis (the experimental design), in addition to the researcher's experimental findings and conclusions.

Other scientists then test the validity and reliability of the findings by attempting to repeat the experiment described by the researcher. A carefully designed and executed scientific experiment should be accurately described in writing so that other scientists using a similar experimental process can replicate it. The community of scientists as a whole then critiques the new research, deciding collectively whether it is good, sound research. To do this, other scientists will test the experiment's validity (Did it measure what the researcher said it would measure?), its reliability (Can it be repeated or replicated with similar results by other scientists?), and its importance (How does this experiment fit into a larger theoretical framework and what does it mean for our currently held assumptions and beliefs?). The forums of science—the professional organizations and journals, universities, scientific societies, and research laboratories—combine to resolve scientific issues to the benefit of all scientists.

QUESTIONS FOR DISCUSSION

1. What is the general goal of inquiry in the sciences?

2. What often sparks a scientist's interest and motivates research?

3. How does observation contribute to scientific inquiry?

4. What is "critical scientific research"? How do its goals differ from those of science in general?

5. What is meant by replicability and why is it important in science?

PRIMARY RESEARCH IN THE SCIENCES

Lab Experiments and Reports

Central to an understanding of research in the sciences is an understanding of the scientific method. In the sciences, the method by which an experimenter solves a problem is as important as the result the experimenter achieves. Guided by the scientific method, researchers investigate the laws of the physical universe by asking and answering questions through empirical research. As you may have discerned from the description of the scientific method on page 218, writing plays a role at every step. A researcher must describe in great detail both the method used in the experiment and the results achieved. A report of the experimental findings is based on the laboratory notes taken during the experiment. All researchers must keep written records of their work. In the natural sciences, such records generally take the form of a laboratory notebook. The researcher uses the notebook to keep a complete, well-organized record of every experiment and all experimental variables (phenomena not constant in the experiment). The researcher must record information in a clear, easy-to-understand format so that he or she (and co-workers) will have easy access to it when it is time to draw conclusions from the experiment.

In your undergraduate science courses, you are expected to conduct scientific experiments and record your methods and results in a laboratory notebook. You may also be expected to report your experiments in a systematic way. A good lab report introduces the experiment, describes the materials and methods used in collecting the data, explains the results, and draws conclusions from those results.

Your scientific experiments in your coursework will typically be connected with a laboratory. For example, many courses in the physical sciences, such as chemistry or physics, are accompanied by laboratory sections for practical lab experimentation. However, laboratory courses still involve writing. It is important to realize that the scientific method employed by laboratory researchers necessitates the careful, organized, and complete presentation of methods and results through written reports.

EXERCISE

To help you understand the scientific method, the following exercise takes you through the design and implementation of a simple experiment. Or, you may use an experiment of your own choosing, following the same method as scientists would use. You may wish to work collaboratively in groups of three to five to complete this exercise.

Television advertisers tout their particular brand of popcorn as the "biggest and fluffiest." Is there any basis in fact to their claims of superiority? Is Orville Redenbacher's gourmet popcorn *really* better than other brands?

1. Write a hypothesis related to popcorn that you can test experimentally. For example, "Orville Redenbacher's gourmet popcorn leaves fewer unpopped kernels than other brands."

2. Predict what you should observe under specified conditions and circumstances in your popcorn "laboratory." For the above hypothesis, you might specify that when comparable bags of microwavable popcorn are popped in the same microwave for the same amount of time, there will be fewer unpopped Redenbacher's kernels than unpopped kernels of the competing brands. Be certain to control for all variables, such as the weights of the unpopped bags.

3. Conduct your experiment, taking careful laboratory notes based on your experimental design and your observations during your controlled experiment.

4. Compare how your actual observations correspond to your hypothesis: Were there fewer unpopped kernels of the Redenbacher

popcorn? If so, your hypothesis is proven correct; if not, your hypothesis is disproved. Either way, you have learned something about truth in advertising (or at least about the scientific method).

Field Observations and Reports

In some scientific disciplines, empirical or experimental work is supplemented by field observations that occur outside the laboratory. For example, a biologist interested in moose behaviors might visit Yellowstone National Park and observe juvenile moose and their parents to determine whether juvenile moose imitate maternal or paternal feeding behaviors. In this section, we will discuss a field experiment and report assigned to students in a physical geography laboratory.[3] This field experiment illustrates one approach to problem solving that incorporates both scientific data and field observation.

The students in the physical geography lab at Texas Tech University study landforms. In their laboratory research assignment, students are asked to investigate the urban flood hazard in Lubbock, Texas, and to report their findings. The students work in groups of four or five to gather the necessary data. It is not unusual in the scientific community for researchers to work in teams, collaborating on both the actual research and the written report of the research. For this assignment, the teacher provides important background readings to help students identify the potential problem of urban flooding. Students must apply general knowledge obtained in the class discussions and course readings to the particular problem of urban flooding in the city where they are attending college.

In this assignment, students are using a common approach to problem solving. The instructor gives them a potential problem, and their first step is to identify and define that problem carefully. In the list below, provided by the geography professor, notice the similarity to the inquiry steps discussed in Chapter 1 (preparation, incubation, illumination, verification) and to the steps in the scientific method (p. 209).

Students must

1. Clearly identify and define the problem.
2. Define an objective or goal that might lead them to a solution to the problem.
3. Gather information from their own backgrounds and from books, printed matter, media, other people, observations, and laboratory experiments.
4. Define the constraints that might limit the solution; generate possible solutions (hypotheses).

5. Evaluate all the possible solutions to determine which is most likely to solve the problem, which satisfies the basic objective, and which is the most feasible, practical, economical, safe, legal, and so on.

6. Prepare a written report that describes the problem, the experimental and field data-collection methods, and the proposed solution to the problem. In the report, the evidence gathered is used to support the proposed solution.

What follows is an excerpt from a collaborative student report on urban flooding written for an introductory geography course. To complete the assignment, students used primary research methods—observation, experimentation, and report. They also used secondary research methods, incorporating into their report the pertinent ideas they found in books and articles they read for their course. As you read this report, notice how the students have followed the approach to problem solving outlined above. Also, notice how they have used the various sources as evidence to support their position.

```
           Geography 113 Report: Group 5

                    Leslie Bayer

                    Kim Springer

                  Charlotte Wedding

                      Pat Cates

     The main objective of this report is to present a

flood hazard reduction plan for Maxey Park in Lubbock,

Texas. Within this scope we plan to:


1. Determine the specific boundaries around the park

   that would be flooded with a heavy rain.

2. Conduct discussions with other individuals who can

   give in-depth information about Lubbock's existing

   flood-management program.
```

3. Establish satisfactory or possible solutions for
   the flooding around Maxey Park.

   To begin, a description of the location and nature
of the flood problem in Lubbock is in order. Lubbock
is located on the Texas South Plains. This area is
relatively flat with only minor changes in elevation,
which decreases the ability of water to drain easily.
Because of this, Lubbock's drainage system is designed
around what are known as playa, or man-made lakes.
These lakes receive run-off, which is channeled mainly
by streets and other man-made drainage channels.
Therefore, Lubbock's flooding is called inflooding,
because the lakes within the city fill up and overflow
the surrounding areas.

   The specific area of consideration, Maxey Park, is
located in the western central part of Lubbock. The
park and the immediate surrounding residential and
commercial areas lie in a slightly depressed area,
which increases the likelihood of flooding around this
particular park.

   [Students included drainage-basin analysis data from laboratory
   experiments.]

   Three other problems that increase flooding are
that (1) Lubbock is a semiarid region, which somewhat
reduces infiltration capacity; (2) Lubbock streets are
squared off, increasing flood peaks because run-off
has reduced time to occur; and (3) Lubbock's rainfall

is short and intense, increasing the demand on the drainage system.

The present flood problems facing Lubbock are definitely more acute than those of the past. Such a situation is caused by increased urbanization as a result of years of growth. The only time in the past during which Lubbock has had a rainfall close to the 6.4-inch rainfall of October, 1983, was in 1967, when 5.7 inches fell. An interview with Emory Potts, a Lubbock City Engineer, suggests that the flood in October, 1983, was between a 50- and 100-year flood. Regarding the amount of rainfall (6.4 inches) during a 24-hour period, the flood was closer to a 50-year flood. However, the total accumulation over the 4-day period was 9 to 10 inches, which classifies the flood as a 100-year flood.

From the facts given, it is evident that Lubbock has a serious problem regarding flooding. The city has implemented several measures to curb flooding. Its primary action has been to pass a Lakes ordinance to protect residential and commercial areas. This ordinance is designed to decrease flooding of these areas by building parks around natural playa lakes so that no homes or buildings will be constructed within the immediate area.

The city's second measure has been the construction of a storm sewer system that empties into the Canyon Lakes. Unfortunately, this system is not very extensive.

[Students went on to describe the city's current storm-sewer and flood-prevention systems.]

One possible solution to alleviate flooding around Maxey Park is to dredge the accumulation of silt in Maxey Lake. This action would probably allow the lake to hold more water and possibly increase the natural percolation. Another solution is to build the homes and buildings on a higher or elevated foundation to help protect them from the water. However, Mr. Potts (city engineer) also emphasized that very little can be done to "counteract mother nature."

Because of the potential flooding situation around Maxey Park, with few possible solutions to the problem, none of the members of our group would want to purchase a house immediately adjacent to the area. However, those who own homes in the area should acquire adequate flood insurance. Owners should also be prepared to sandbag the lawn, plan alternate routes of travel, and have a plan for safe and quick evacuation if it should become necessary.

[Students included charts and graphs illustrating the Maxey Lake area and its flood problems.]

QUESTIONS FOR DISCUSSION

1. What are the stated objectives of the report?

2. What is the nature of the flooding problem described by the report?

3. Where did the group get its information? What kinds of primary and secondary sources did the students use? Did they acknowledge those sources?

4. What possible solutions were posed for lessening the hazard? What measures should home owners take to reduce the flood problem?

EXERCISE

To help you understand the process of observation and reporting this exercise encourages you to think through a problem-solving task. You may use the same steps to problem solving outlined in the geography assignment just described as you explore possible solutions to a problem that you have identified in your community. The task that follows outlines problem solving for a traffic hazard. You may wish to find an equivalent project of your own design and follow similar steps to complete it. For this exercise, work in groups of four or five people; be sure that you divide the work evenly among the members of your group.

1. Identify a traffic hazard (or comparable problem) that you have observed in your community. Perhaps it is an intersection where accidents occur frequently or a school crossing zone that has no painted crosswalk. Describe the problem as carefully as you can, giving the location of the problem area (maps might be appropriate).

2. Define an objective or goal that might lead to the solution of the problem you have identified. For a traffic hazard, perhaps a stoplight, a painted crosswalk, or a crossing guard would eliminate the problem.

3. Gather information from your own observations and from books, printed matter, media, other people, and observations. You may want to attend a public meeting, perhaps of the local traffic commission, or you might wish to study the commission's long-range plans for the community. You may want to speak to the principal of an elementary school about a school crossing hazard.

4. While gathering data, generate possible solutions and define the constraints that might limit them. For a traffic hazard, perhaps the city budget precludes installing any more traffic lights. In such a case, you might look for alternative sources of funding that the city has not yet explored.

5. Evaluate the possible solutions you generated in step 4 to determine which is most likely to solve the problem, which satisfies the objective, which is the most feasible, practical, economical, safe, legal, and so on.

Prepare a report three to five pages long that describes the problem, the data-collection method, and the proposed solutions. In the report, use the evidence gathered to support the proposed solution.

Make an oral presentation of your report to your class, using as a reference point a one-page outline of your report (which you should prepare after the report is finished). Your group will need to meet to work out the details of the oral presentation, but all should participate.

ORGANIZING AND WRITING THE SCIENTIFIC REVIEW PAPER

A major task in writing a scientific review is organizing the material you have gathered. It is your job to make sense of the information you found in your library search. Remember, you are trying to make the information accessible to your readers as well as objective and comprehensive. In this section of the chapter, we follow the research process of a group of engineering students, led by Mark Greenwood. Their scientific review paper is included at the end of the chapter.

When the group began to narrow their topic, they decided to focus on analyzing the cleanup of a hazardous site in Montana. As they thought through the rhetorical situation, they decided that they wanted to convey to readers both the problem and its solutions. (For more information on rhetorical situation, see Chapter 4, pp. 92–95).

After completing their library research and interviewing key people, the group articulated an answer to their starting question in the form of a thesis statement: "After reviewing the techniques, we have decided on the use of air stripping for the source area and using MNA for the plume area." This thesis statement provided them with an overall focus for the paper.

In order to understand the process of MTBE in the environment, the group decided to first discuss how MTBE is produced and the mechanisms of spread; then they would discuss the objectives of their study, and finally analyze the remediation processes and select solutions. This organizational plan made the information easily available to the reader. They divided each subsection with descriptive headings to further help the reader discern the organizational plan. Scientific reviews often are subdivided in this way to allow the reader easy access to the information.

EXERCISE

Write a thesis statement and sketch a preliminary organizational plan for your research paper. Refer to Chapter 4 (pp. 91–100) for help with organization.

Arranging the Materials

Once Mark and his group had decided on the thesis statement and organizational plan, they grouped related information on a computerized research notebook, using the CUT and PASTE functions of the word processor, under the headings they had decided on in planning the paper. Because all the information was stored in the computer research notebook, it was an easy matter to move blocks of material in the notebook using the block move (CUT and PASTE) commands; furthermore, they didn't need to worry about plagiarizing any of the sources because they had already been very careful to summarize and paraphrase while taking notes. (Be sure to make a backup file of your notebook before beginning to manipulate the information in this way.)

Mark's group moved to the end of the computer file any information that did not seem to fit into the paper, such as information they had gathered on other sites. This material was not relevant to the particular thesis statement. To make a unified, coherent presentation of your research, you must discard any information that is irrelevant. With the preliminary plan set, Mark's group wrote a more detailed outline to guide them in writing the paper.

> Executive Summary
> 1.0 Introduction
>   1.1 MTBE in the Environment
>   1.2 Location and History of Site
>   1.3 Parties Involved
>   1.4 Objectives
>   1.5 Remediation Techniques
> 2.0 Monitored Natural Attenuation (MNA)
> 3.0 Air Stripping
> 4.0 Soil Removal
> 5.0 Recommendations and Conclusions

EXERCISE

Sort your note cards by their titles, number related ideas in your research notebook, or block related information together in a computer file. Write an informal outline of your research paper, using your thesis statement and organizational plan as a guide. Begin writing the first draft of your research paper. (See Chapter 4 for additional guidance.)

Writing the First Draft: Verification

After you have completed your outline, you are ready to write the first draft of your research paper. Remember, you are writing in order to review for your readers the current state of thinking on a particular scientific topic. Remind yourself at this time of the general understanding you had of your topic and of your answer to the question you posed as you began researching. When writing your first draft, use concrete and simple language to explain as objectively as you can the current thinking on your topic. Your outline will guide the writing of this first draft. Any word, phrase, or sentence you copy directly from a source must be placed in quotation marks, followed by the last name of the author and the date the source was published. Similarly, any paraphrase needs to be documented with source information as follows:

```
This attenuation of the plume was determined to be
the mineralization of the MTBE by site
microorganisms (Loustannan 2003).
```

(Note: In the number system, sources are identified by a superscript number or a number in parentheses immediately following the sources instead of the author's name and date in parentheses. See "The Number System" later in this chapter.)

For general information on planning, writing, and revising your scientific review paper, refer to Chapters 4 and 5. Use the following information on documentation in the sciences and technology to cite sources in the correct form. The sample review paper at the end of this chapter serves as a model of a scientific review conducted on an engineering topic.

DOCUMENTATION IN SCIENCE AND TECHNOLOGY

There is no uniform system of citation in the sciences and technology, but various disciplines follow either the style of a particular journal or that of a style guide, such as the guide produced by the Council of Biology Editors: *Scientific Style and Format: The CBE Manual for Authors, Edi-*

tors, and Publishers, 6th ed. (New York: Cambridge University Press, 1994). The Council of Biology Editors (CBE) became the Council of Science Editors (CSE) on January 1, 2000. The new name, which was voted on by the membership during 1999, more accurately reflects its expanding membership. Until it is revised and updated by the CSE, the CBE style will remain the preferred system for science citations and is the system we will follow in this chapter. The CBE style uses in-text citation plus a list of works at the end of the text, called references. Entire journal articles rather than specific pages may be cited, and direct quotations are seldom used.

Internal Citation

In the CBE style, authors are cited within the text itself by means of either the name/year system or the number system.

The Name/Year System

The name/year system is widely used in the sciences and has been adopted (with variations) by the social sciences and business. It is a fairly easy system for the reader to use. The following principles should be observed:

1. When an author's journal article is cited in general, the source material is followed by the last name of the author and the date of the source article in parentheses:

   ```
   Angiogenesis plays an important role in cancer
   research (Kleinsmith and Kelly 2001).
   ```

2. If the source material is paraphrased or directly quoted, the page numbers should be included:

   ```
   Analysis indicates that "binding does not change
   the structure of interacting units" (Davis 1987,
   p 134).
   ```

3. If the author's name is used in introducing the source material, only the date is necessary:

   ```
   According to Kerrigan (1999) scientists are on the
   verge of discovering the secrets of antibodies.
   ```

4. Multiple sources are cited in chronological order:

   The most common type of immune malfunction is
   caused by aberrations in lifestyle: physical
   overexertion, malnutrition, stress, alcohol,
   drugs, all of which lower your resistance and
   allow pathogens to invade your body (Miller 1986;
   Klurfeld 1993; National Cancer Institute 2001).

5. When citing a work with three or more authors, use "and others":

   Earlier work provided an illustration of the
   benefits of gene testing (Kleinsmith and others
   2001).

6. When citing a work with two authors, join them with *and*:

   Similar observations have been made in the cancer
   genome project (Greenhut and Kelly 2001).

7. Information obtained from another work cited within a work should appear as follows:

   Such a factor is apparently not present in
   unactivated sturgeon (Chulitskai 1977, cited in
   Meyerhof and Masui 1980).

8. When the same author has written two or more publications in the same year, designate them with a, b, and so on following the year:

   Some of the earliest responses of eggs to
   sperm-egg interaction are electrical (Nuccitelli
   1980a).

The Number System (or Citation-Sequence)

The number system is also used in the sciences and technology. Here a number is assigned to each source listed on the references page.

To cite the source within the text, one simply lists the number of that source as a raised superscript:

```
Temperature plays a major role in the rate of
gastric juice secretion.3
```

You can cite multiple sources easily with this system:

```
Recent studies3,5,8 show that antibodies may also
bind to microbes to prevent their attachment to
epithelial surfaces.
```

[Note: The model paper at the end of this chapter shows the number, or citation sequence, system.]

Content Notes

Some scientific papers might require notes that explain something about the text itself rather than referring to a particular source being cited. These content notes are listed either as footnotes or endnotes rather than as internal citations. For the proper form of footnotes and endnotes, see Chapter 6.

The Reference List

The reference list, found at the end of your research paper, contains all the sources actually used in the paper. The title of this page is "References," "Works Cited," or "Literature Cited." The purpose of the reference list is to help readers find the materials you used in writing your paper. Therefore, you must give complete, accurate information here. In the CBE style, the reference list can follow either the name/year or the number (citation sequence) system. The following principles are generally accepted for the reference list in the sciences and technology.

1. On the references or works cited page, references are arranged in alphabetical order. (Note: The numbering system, also called the citation-sequence system, may proceed consecutively, i.e., in the order in which the sources appear in the text.)
2. Authors are listed by surnames and initials, without periods.
3. Generally the first word only of a title is capitalized, the title of an article is not enclosed in quotation marks, and the title of a book is not underlined.

4. Names of journals are often abbreviated.
5. The volume and page number system often resembles that found in indexes (for example, 19:330–60). Some editors may place the volume number in boldface type, indicated by a wavy line in manuscript: **16**, or 16. (Other editors may choose to highlight specific bibliographic elements other than the volume number for special treatment.)
6. The year of publication for a journal article appears immediately after the author's name in the name/year system. However, in the numbering system, the date is placed at the end of the citation.

BOOK

Name/Year Golub ES, Garen DR. 1991. Immunology: A synthesis.

2nd ed. Boston: Sinauer Associates. 744 p.

Number   1. Kruuk H. The spotted hyena: a study of
C–S
predation and social behavior. Chicago: Univ

of Chicago Pr; 1972.

ARTICLE

Name/Year Milleen JK. 1986. Verifying security. ACM

Computing Surveys 16:350-4.
or

Number   1. Milleen JK. Verifying security. ACM Computing
C–S
Surveys 1986 Nov 13;16:350-4.

7. If the same author has published two or more works in the same year, indicate this with a lowercase a, b, and so on: 1984a, 1984b.
8. **Name/year system:** The first word of the entry is typed at the left margin. Generally, the entire reference list is double spaced. **Number system:** The numbers are typed at the left margin. The first line of each entry is typed two spaces after the number. Subsequent lines are even with the first line.

If you are writing a paper for a specific discipline, it is important to find out which documentation form your instructor prefers. These style guides will help you:

The ACS Style Guide: A Manual for Authors and Editors. Janet S. Dodds, ed. Washington, DC: American Chemical Society, 1986.

Scientific Style and Format: The CBE Manual for Authors, Editors, and Publishers. 6th ed. New York: Council of Biology Editors.

Geowriting: A Guide to Writing, Editing, and Printing in Earth Science. 3rd ed. Alexandria: American Geological Institute, 1979.

Style Manual: For Guidance in the Preparation of Papers for Journals Published by the American Institute of Physics. 3rd ed. New York: American Institute of Physics, 1978.

(Note: Some scientific journals follow the APA style as outlined by the *Publications Manual of the American Psychological Association.* See pp. 298–309.)

The model references that follow are based on the CBE form used in many science journals. They follow the style found in the *CBE Manual for Authors, Editors, and Publishers,* 6th ed. (CBE). For further examples, refer to one of the manuals listed above. (Note the position of the date in CBE number system style. As an alternative, many science journals place the date immediately after the author's name.)

MODEL REFERENCES:
NATURAL AND PHYSICAL SCIENCES
(NUMBER SYSTEM) (CBE)

For the number system, list the citations in the order of their appearance in the text. List authors with last names first, followed by initials. Capitalize only the first word of a title and any proper nouns. Do not enclose titles of articles in quotation marks, and do not underline titles of books. Abbreviate names of journals, where possible. Include the year of publication. Cite volume and page numbers when appropriate.

BOOKS

1. Book by one author

    1. Kruuk H. The spotted hyena: a study of predation and social behavior. Chicago: Univ of Chicago Pr; 1972.

    2. Abercrombie MLJ. The anatomy of judgment. Harmondsworth (Eng.): Penguin; 1969.

2. Book by two or more authors

    3. Hersch RH, Paolitto DP, Reimer J. Promoting moral growth. New York: Longman; 1979.

3. Book by a corporate author

> 4. Carnegie Council on Policy Studies in Higher Education. Fair practices in higher education: rights and responsibilities of students and their colleges in a period of intensified competition for enrollment. San Francisco: Jossey-Bass; 1979.

4. Book with two or more editors

> 5. Buchanan RE, Gibbons NE, editors. Bergey's manual of determinative bacteriology. 8th ed. Baltimore: Williams & Wilkins; 1974.

5. Chapter or selection from an edited work

> 6. Kleiman DG, Brady CA. Coyote behavior in the context of recent canid research: problems and perspectives. In: Bekoff M, editor. Coyotes: biology, behavior, and management. New York: Academic Pr; 1978. p 163-88.

6. Government document

> 7. Mech D. The wolves of Isle Royale. National Parks fauna series. Available from: United States GPO, Washington; 1966.

PERIODICALS

7. Journal article by one author

> 8. Schenkel R. Expression studies of wolves. Behavior 1947; 1:81-129.

8. Journal article by two or more authors

> 9. Sargeant AB, Allen SH. Observed interactions between coyotes and red foxes. J Mamm 1989; 70:631-3.

9. Article with no identified author

    10. [Anonymous]. Frustrated hamsters run on their wheels. Nat Sci 1981; 91:407.

10. Newspaper article

    11. Blackman J. Altermen grill Peoples officials on heating costs. Chicago Tribune 2001 Jan 16; Sect 1A:2(col 3).

11. Magazine article

    12. Aveni AF. Emissaries to the stars: the astronomers of ancient Maya. Mercury 1995 May: 15-8.

OTHER SOURCES

12. Unpublished Interview

    13. Quarnberg T. [Interview with Dr. Andy Anderson, Professor of Biology, Utah State University, 1988 Apr 15].

13. Dissertation

    14. Gese EM. Foraging ecology of coyotes in Yellowstone National Park [dissertation]. Madison (WI): University of Wisconsin; 1995. 124 p.

14. Unpublished Manuscript

    15. Pegg J, Russo C, Valent J. College cheating survey at Drexel University. [Unpublished manuscript, 1986].

15. Personal letter

    16. Fife A. [Letter to President Calvin Coolidge, 1930.] Located at: Archives and Special Collections, Utah State University, Logan, UT.

ELECTRONIC MEDIA IN CBE STYLE

Internet formats are covered briefly in *Scientific Style and Format: The CBE Manual for Authors, Editors, and Publishers,* 6th ed. The Vancouver style for electronic citations, a set of conventions observed by the American Medical Association, the American College of Physicians, and the World Association of Medical Editors, expands basic CBE citation conventions to encompass electronic journals and print-based Internet sources (*<http://www.nlm.nih.gov/pubs/formats/internet.pdf>*).

16. Online Professional or Personal Site

    17.   Gelt J. Home use of greywater: rainwater conserves water--and money [Internet]. 1993 [cited 2003 Nov 8]. Available from: http://www.ag.arizona.edu/ AZWATER/arroyo/ 071rain.html

17. Online Book

    18.   Bunyan J. The pilgrim's progress from this world to that which is to come [book on the Internet]. London: Kent; 1678 [cited 2001 Jan 16]. Available from http://www.bibliomania.com/0/0/frameset.html

18. Article in an online journal

    19.   Lechner DE, Bradbury SF, Bradley LA. Detecting sincerity of effort: a summary of methods   and approaches. Phys Ther J [serial on the Internet] 1998 Aug [cited 2003 Sept 15]. Available from: URL: http://www.ptjournal.org/pt_journal/Aug98/ 1997-118.cfm

19. Article in an online newspaper

    20.   Roan, S. Folic acid may mask vitamin deficiency [Internet]. Salt Lake Tribune;

```
2003 Aug 7 [cited 2003 Aug 8]. Available
from: http://www.sltrib.com/2003/aug/
08072003/thursday/81868.asp
```

20. Email message

```
21.  Shaver, A. Regarding toxicity screen [email
     on the Internet]. Message to: Jack Schmidt.
     2003 Feb 5, 4:30 pm. Accessed 2003 Feb 6.
```

21. Electronic posting to a listserv

```
22.  Kasianowicz, J. Careers in biochem. In:
     MEDLINE-L [posting on the Internet].
     Washington: Bureau of Weights and Measures;
     2003 Mar 2. Accessed 2003 Apr 23.
```

EXERCISES AND RESEARCH PROJECT

Complete the exercises outlined in this chapter as you research a scientific or technical topic and write a scientific review paper. The three exercises that follow will give you additional practice using skills needed for science research projects.

1. For each entry on your reference list, write a three- or four-sentence annotation that describes the content of that source.

2. Write a review of the literature that summarizes in three to four pages the major ideas found in your sources. In your review, try to avoid using direct quotes or copying words used in the articles. Often, a literature review, which lists and comments on the work to date in a particular area of scientific investigation, is a component of a larger scientific paper. A review of the literature often proceeds in chronological order based on the publication date of the source and thus may differ from a scientific review paper, which is typically organized around concepts or other categories.

3. When you have finished writing your paper, write an abstract (approximately one hundred words) of your paper in which you summarize the major points in your review (see Chapter 5 for a discussion of how to write abstracts).

DISCIPLINE-SPECIFIC RESOURCES FOR SCIENCE AND TECHNOLOGY

Scientists were quick to see that technology could help them with their research and their writing. As a student of the natural sciences, you too should familiarize yourself with the available resources, particularly those in library databases and on the Internet. An extended listing of useful Internet sites for the natural sciences follows. Take a look, for example, at the *Discovery Channel* site, which has many links to general science information on the Internet. There are also numerous discussion groups, bulletin boards, and newsgroups related to the natural sciences. You can find these discussion sites through an Internet search.

Resources for the Sciences and Technology

BIOLOGY AND ANIMAL SCIENCE

Dictionaries and Encyclopedias

Dictionary of Biology. 4th ed. Martin, E., ed. New York: Oxford UP, 2000.
The Encyclopedia of Bioethics. 2nd ed. Reich, W., ed. New York: Macmillan, 1995.

Indexes and Abstracts

Biological and Agricultural Index
Biological Abstracts

Web Sites

Biozone <http://www.biozone.co.nz/links.html>
American Society of Animal Science <http://www.asas.org>

BOTANY AND PLANT GENETICS

Indexes and Abstracts

Botanical Abstracts
Genetics Abstracts
Plant Breeding Abstracts

Web Sites

Genetics <http://www.biology.arizona.edu/mendelian_genetics/
    mendelian_ genetics.html>
Bio Online <http://bio.com/resedu>

CHEMISTRY

Dictionaries, Encyclopedias, and Handbooks

Dictionary of Chemistry. Daintith, J., ed. New York: Oxford UP, 1996.

Handbook of Chemistry and Physics. 69th ed. Weast, R. C., ed. Cleveland: Chemical, 1990. Facts and data on chemistry and physics.

Indexes and Abstracts

Chemical Abstracts
Analytical Abstracts

Web Sites

American Chemical Society <http://www.chemistry.org>
The Learning Matters of Chemistry <http://www.knowledgebydesign. comtlmc/ tlmc.html>

COMPUTERS

Dictionaries adn Encyclopedias

Dictionary of Computing. 4th ed. Illingworth, V., ed. New York: Oxford UP, 1997.
Encyclopedia of Computer Science. 4th ed. Ralston, A., ed. New York: Groves, 2000. Concise information in the fields of computer science and engineering.
Encyclopedia of Computer Science and Technology. Belzer, J., ed. New York: Dekker, 1997. 37 vols. Short articles on subjects in computer science.

Indexes and Abstracts

Computer Abstracts
Computer and Control Abstracts
Computing Reviews

Web Sites

Electronic Frontier Foundation <http://www.eff.org>
Internet Society <http://www.isoc.org>

ENGINEERING

Encyclopedias

McGraw-Hill Encyclopedia of Engineering. 2nd ed. New York: McGraw-Hill, 1993. Short articles on all fields of engineering.

Indexes

Engineering Index (Eicomendex)
Electrical and Electronics Abstracts

Web Sites

Cornell's Engineering Library <http://www.englib.cornell.edu>
ICARIS for Civil Engineering <http://itc.fgg.uni-lj.si/ICARIS>

ENVIRONMENT AND ECOLOGY

Encyclopedias

McGraw-Hill Encyclopedia of Environmental Science. 3rd ed. Parker, S. P., ed. new York: McGraw-Hill, 1993. Information on the earth's resources and how they have been used.

Indexes

Environment Index
Environment Abstracts

Web Sites

ATSDR Science Page (Agency for Toxic Substances and Disease Registry) <http://www.atsdr.cdc.gov/science>
International Institute for Sustainable Development <http://iisd1.iisd.ca>

GEOGRAPHY AND GEOLOGY

Dictionaries

Dictionary of Geology and Geophysics. Lapidus. D. F., ed. New York: Facts on File, 1988. Definitions of many terms in the context of modern geological theories.
Dictionary of Earth Science. New York: McGraw Hill, 1996.

Indexes

Bibliography and Index of Geology
Geographical Abstracts

Web Sites

American Geological Institute <http://www.agiweb.org>
Geological Surveys and Natural Resources <http://www.lib.berkeley.edu/EART/surveys.html>

HEALTH SCIENCES

Handbooks

Medical and Health Information Directory. 8th ed. Detroit: Gale 1999. 3 vols. Comprehensive guidebook.
Physician's Handbook. 22nd ed. Krupp, M. A., et al., eds. E. Norwalk: Appleton and Lange, 2000. Useful, quick reference book for all medical questions.

Indexes

Cumulated Index Medicus
Medline Clinical Collection

Web Sites

National Institutes of Health <http://www.nih.gov>
World Health Organization <http://www.who.int/en>

MATHEMATICS AND STATISTICS

Dictionaries and Encyclopedias

Dictionary of Mathematics. Lincolnwood: NTC, 1996.
CRC Concise Encyclopedia of Mathematics. Weisstein, E. W., ed. Boca Raton,
   C-R-C, 1999. Short articles on all areas of mathematics.

Indexes

MathSci
American Statistics Index

Web Sites

American Mathematical Society <http://www.ams.org>
The University of Tennessee Math Archives <http://archives. math.utk.edu>
National Council of Teachers of Mathematics <http://www.nctm.org>

PHYSICS AND ASTRONOMY

Dictionaries and Encyclopedias

Dictionary of Physics. New York: McGraw-Hill, 1996. Comprehensive dictionary
   of terms.
The Encyclopedia of Physics. Lerner, R. G., and Trigg, G. L., eds. Reading: Addi-
   son, 1990. Background information on major principles and problems in
   physics.

Indexes

Physics Abstracts
SPIN

Web Sites

American Institute of Physics <http://www.aip.org>
American Physical Society <http://www.aps.org>

WILDLIFE AND FISHERIES

Indexes

Wildlife Worldwide
Fish and Fisheries Worldwide

Web Sites

National Audubon Society <http://www.audubon.org>
National Fish and Wildlife Foundation <http://www.nfwf.org>
U. S. Fish and Wildlife Service <http://www.fws.gov>

[NOTE: This paper uses the CBE Number, or citation sequence, system]

SAMPLE ENGINEERING PAPER: SCIENCE FORMAT (CBE)

Greenwood Engineering Services

Group 4

12-08-2003

MTBE Remediation Techniques

at the Ronan, Montana Site

Team Leader: Mark Greenwood

Information Manager: Jacob Young

Oral Presentation Organizer: W. Rick Mayer

Log Book Manager: Chad Brown

Visual Effects Specialist: Lisa Kent

Executive Summary

In 1994 the gasoline station, George's British Petroleum, removed a leaking underground storage tank that released 3300 lbs of BTEX, the toxic components of gasoline, and approximately 1500 lbs of methyl *tert*-butyl ether (MTBE), a fuel oxygenate added to reduce knocking and improve car emissions. Remediation techniques were carried out to contain the spill soon after the tank was removed[1].

The station is located in Ronan, Montana in the Flathead Indian Reservation, 60 miles north of Missoula, Montana. Three hundred and fifty yards west of the station is Spring Creek, which is a source of water for the multiple farming communities in the reservation. In 1996, the MTBE contaminant plume was detected near this creek. In the soil next to the creek and in the creek itself, there was no MTBE found. This attenuation of the plume was determined to be due to the mineralization of the MTBE by site microorganisms[2].

3

Natural attenuation at the site can currently prevent the MTBE from entering the creek, but if the concentrations or ground water flow were to increase, the mineralization of MTBE might not be fast enough. For this reason and others, it has been decided that the site should be cleaned of the contaminants. The remediation techniques evaluated to solve this problem were Monitored Natural Attenuation (MNA), Air Stripping, and Soil Removal. After reviewing the techniques, we have decided on the use of air stripping for the source area and using MNA for the plume area. This will allow for a low impact and highly effective clean up with a low budget.

1.0 Introduction

For more than twenty years, fuel additives, such as Methyl *tert*-butyl Ether (MTBE) have been used to substitute for lead to increase the combustion efficiency and decrease knocking in internal combustions engines[3]. This ability can be seen in the molecular structure of MTBE with the presence of an oxygen atom

4

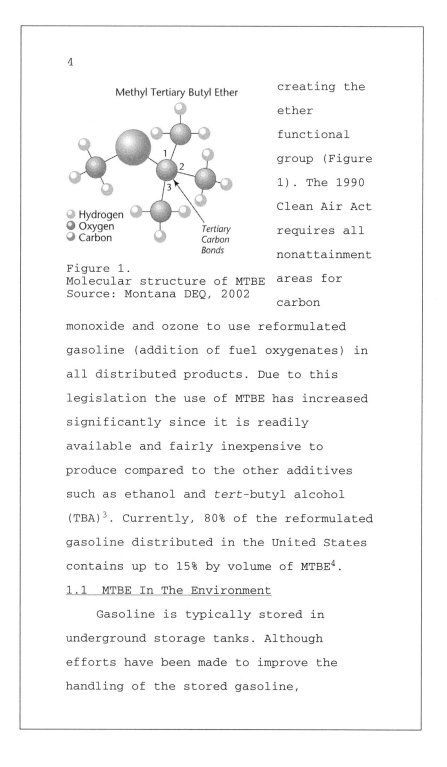

Methyl Tertiary Butyl Ether

Hydrogen
Oxygen
Carbon

Tertiary
Carbon
Bonds

Figure 1.
Molecular structure of MTBE
Source: Montana DEQ, 2002

creating the ether functional group (Figure 1). The 1990 Clean Air Act requires all nonattainment areas for carbon monoxide and ozone to use reformulated gasoline (addition of fuel oxygenates) in all distributed products. Due to this legislation the use of MTBE has increased significantly since it is readily available and fairly inexpensive to produce compared to the other additives such as ethanol and *tert*-butyl alcohol (TBA)[3]. Currently, 80% of the reformulated gasoline distributed in the United States contains up to 15% by volume of MTBE[4].

1.1 MTBE In The Environment

Gasoline is typically stored in underground storage tanks. Although efforts have been made to improve the handling of the stored gasoline,

5

Table 1. Comparison of Gasoline Contaminants
Source: Daubert 1985

Chemical	Vapor Pressure (mm Hg)	K_{ow} part. coeff.
tert-butyl Alcohol (TBA)	31.00	0.35
Methyl *tert*-butyl Ether (MTBE)	249.00	1.06
Ethanol	59.26	1.24
BTEX:		
Benzene	95.00	2.13
Ethylene	52130.00	1.13
Toluene	28.40	2.73
Xylene	6.61	3.12

historical leaks and spills have resulted
in groundwater and surface water
contamination[3]. MTBE has a short half life
in surface water due to its high
volatility[5]. Table 1 shows a comparison of
vapor pressure for gasoline components.
Notice that the only substance more
volatile is ethanol.

MTBE, however, does not have a short
half life in groundwater systems. Due to

6

its high water solubility, a low octanol-
water partitioning coefficient, K_{ow} is a
ratio of the concentration of a chemical
in octanol to water at equilibrium in a
specified temperature, and resistance to
biodegradation, it is very persistent in
groundwater systems[6]. MTBE behavior in
groundwater is relatively conservative
under normal environmental conditions,
which makes it difficult to remediate.

MTBE's wide spread use and persistent
nature makes it the second most commonly
found volatile organic compound in shallow
groundwater systems[6]. Research performed
by the EPA[7] shows that MTBE can have
negative effects on human health and is
also a suspected human carcinogen.
Therefore MTBE contaminated sites pose a
potential health risk to those who consume
impacted groundwater.

The State of California has recently
seen the damaging affects of MTBE in its
groundwater supply. There are currently
sites located in South Lake Tahoe, Santa
Monica and Temecula Valley, and it is
estimated that up to $900,000 is spent per

7

year on each of these sites. Because of
this, California has started to phase out
the use of MTBE in place of other
oxygenates such as ethanol and possibly
TBA[8] .

1.2 Location and History of Site

Ronan, Montana, is located 60 miles
north of Missoula, Montana in the Flathead
Indian Reservation as illustrated in

Figure 2. The
Former Conoco
George's
British
Petroleum
Station is
located at the
south end of

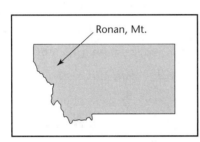

Figure 2.
Ronan location.

town on the east side of Highway 93. The
station had an underground storage tank
that leaked petroleum contaminants into
the surrounding environment. The leak was
suspected in 1993 and detected in 1994
when the 16,000 gallon tank was removed.
The spill was estimated to have displaced
3300 lbs of BTEX, the toxic components of
gasoline, and approximately 1500 lbs of

8

Methyl *tert*-Butyl Ether (MTBE), a fuel
oxygenate. Remediation activities began
soon after the tank removal in 1995 to
help contain the spread of the
contaminant[1]. According to Jeff Kuhn, the
most noticeable and effective activity was
the sparging trench placed just to the
west of the contaminant area (Jeff Kuhn,
Remediation Technologies Head for Montana
Department of Environmental Quality,
Personal Communication 2003). The
contaminants have formed a free product
plume on the water table and have then
moved underneath Highway 93 into the
groundwater flow heading west, creating a
larger dissolved and diluted plume. The
BTEX is contained in the source area by
the sparging trench due to its low
solubility. The MTBE, however, is
spreading past the sparging trench and
throughout the groundwater system. The
plume has spread underneath a privately
owned alfalfa field and is close to
discharging directly into Spring Creek.
This public creek is located approximately
350 yards west of the station and is also

9

the source of water for multiple farm lands in the area[1]. At the current concentrations, the MTBE appears to be decreasing from 1200 µg/L down to a no detection level at or next to the stream bed. Complete mineralization of MTBE to CO_2 by in situ bioremediation has been demonstrated[2].

1.3 Parties Involved

The Ronan site has multiple parties who all have an interest in preventing the further spread of MTBE throughout the groundwater system. The leading group is the State of Montana since they are currently funding the clean up of the site. The State has a minimum requirement for MTBE concentrations set at 30 µg/L. The concentrations at the site range from 9000 µg/L down to 3.7 µg/L[1]. Since the former owner of the station has gone bankrupt, the State carries the responsibility for cleaning the site.

The Flathead Indian Tribe is also very concerned with the further spread of the contaminant into its limited water supply. The past years of drought have

10

limited the use of all water supplies. Since the main source of income in the reservation is agriculture, the quality of water is an important issue (Jeff Kuhn, Remediation Technologies Head for Montana Department of Environmental Quality, Personal Communication 2003).

Another party involved is the American Petroleum Institute (API). They have a vested interest in the site because of the bioremediation activities occurring next to Spring Creek. All MTBE producers and distributors have recently experienced several large lawsuits against them for the use of MTBE with the knowledge of its recalcitrance in the environment[9]. According to Bruce Bowman, the presence of MTBE degrading organisms might aid the company in present and future lawsuits (Bruce Bowman, Personal Communication, Head of Research API 2003).

1.4 Objectives

The objective of this study is to find the most acceptable remediation technology to accommodate the Ronan, Montana MTBE site. Multiple technologies

11

have been researched in order to find the
most acceptable, effective, least
impaction solutions, that are at the same
time financially feasible. All objectives
have been rated either high or low.

An acceptable remediation approach
will be difficult in this case since the
multiple parties involved desire different
outcomes. The Indian reservation and
Montana DEQ wish to remove the contaminant
entirely but API wants it to remain in
order to help further understand the
natural mineralization process of MTBE
(Jeff Kuhn, Remediation Technologies Head
for Montana Department of Environmental
Quality, Personal Communication 2003). A
highly acceptable approach will please as
many people as possible and still solve
the problem. A low acceptance approach
might still solve the problem but leave
all parties unsatisfied.

For an alternative to even be
considered it needs to have the ability to
actually accomplish the task of
maintaining the State of Montana's
standards for MTBE contamination set at

12

30 $\mu g/L^1$. A highly effective technique
needs to be able to be compatible with the
site characteristics like geology,
weather, accessibility, and other items in
order to reach the standards set.

The impaction on the site also needs
to be considered since it is in the middle
of an agricultural and rural area. The
contaminate cannot be simply diluted or
transferred into different environmental
media (soil, water and air) to be
considered clean. Its presence in any
media is a problem. The alteration of the
site ecosystem must be kept to a minimum
to help prevent any further changes. A low
impaction technique will generate less
damage to the site than there would be by
leaving the contaminant at the site.

Since the State will be providing
most of the resources for the clean up,
the cost will be an important issue, as it
most always is, since the State has a
limited budget for the project (Jeff Kuhn,
Remediation Technologies Head for Montana
Department of Environmental Quality,
Personal Communication 2003). To generate

13

a highly cost effective clean up, the
project needs to be divided financially to
all of the parties involved in order of
importance to each group.

1.5 Remediation Techniques

The techniques that can achieve the
desired outcomes are: 1) Monitored Natural
Attenuation (MNA), 2) Air Stripping, and
3) Top Soil Removal. Both MNA and Air
Stripping are in-situ processes. In-situ
means that treatment occurs in place by
enhancing or just allowing natural
processes to clean the site. MNA is a
natural remedy which allows for
volatilization, biodegradation, sorption,
dispersion and dilution, and other
chemical reactions to contain and also
eliminate the contaminant[10].

Air Stripping is a combination of Air
Sparging and Soil Vapor Extraction. It
uses the volatility of a substance to take
it out of the groundwater and into the air
where it can be more easily treated. Air
stripping also increases the oxygen
content of the system which will allow for
increased aerobic mineralization of trace

14

contaminants, thus enhancing the natural removal process[11].

Soil removal, which is more commonly known as a conventional remediation, is fairly straight forward in its approach. The process involves removing the contaminant free product zone by excavation. The soil is treated through multiple processes and then returned. Another approach would to be to simply replace the material with a similar soil type after excavation and then send the contaminated soil to a landfill or treat it through land-farming[12].

Monitored Natural Attenuation, more commonly known as MNA, is a remediation process that relies heavily on natural processes to achieve remediation goals. Where applied, MNA is always used in combination with source control, that is, removal of the source of the contamination, as far as it is practicable. MNA includes a variety of physical, chemical, or biological processes that, under favorable conditions, act without human intervention

15

to reduce the mass, toxicity, mobility,

volume, or concentration of contaminants

in soil or ground water. As seen in Figure

3 below, the processes of biodegradation,

dispersion, dilution, sorption,

volatilization, and chemical reactions are

also part of MNA[10].

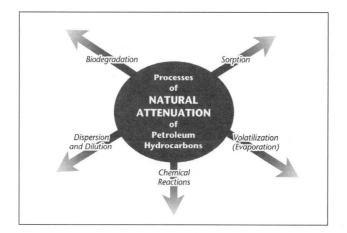

Figure 3.
Processes of Natural Attenuation
Source: USEPA-ORD, 1999

[In the next three sections, students

go on to analyze the three processes for

acceptability, effectiveness, impacts, and

cost: Section 2.0 Monitored Natural

Attenuation (MNA), Section 3.0 Air

Stripping, and Section 4.0 Soil Removal.]

16

5.0 Recommendations and Conclusions

After reviewing the possible remediation techniques related to the Ronan site, it is recommended that a combination of air stripping and monitored natural attenuation be utilized for the MTBE remediation. Air stripping technologies should be applied at the source zone and the traveling plume should be monitored as the natural attenuation is allowed to occur. Air stripping is better suited for the timely remediation of the source area and the natural processes are adequate in the remediation of the traveling plume under close monitoring.

The multiple parties involved will be satisfied with this combined approach. API can still monitor the mineralization of MTBE into CO_2. Infiltration of MTBE into Spring Creek will be avoided, satisfying the State of Montana and the Flathead Indian Reservation. The cost of MNA will be covered by API, decreasing the total cost of the project for the State to cover.

Top soil removal has been the most commonly used technique to remove MTBE

17

from the environment since it is

inexpensive and a very direct approach.

However, the ineffectiveness of the method

limits its use to very few sites. For this

reason, top soil removal was not chosen as

an alternative. The decision on the method

should not be based on past sites but on a

site-by-site basis.

References

1. Montana State Department of

   Environmental Quality. Second Quarter

   2002 Groundwater Monitoring and Task

   Order No.1: Summary Report for George's

   Conoco LUST Trust Site, Ronan (MT);

   July 2002.

2. Loustaunau PK. Transport and fate of

   Methyl tert-Butyl Ether (MTBE) in a

   floodplain aquifer and a stream

   interface, Ronan, Montana [thesis].

   Bozeman (MT): Montana State University;

   2003.

3. Keller AA, Sandall OC, Rinker RG,

   Mitani MM, Bierwagen B, Snodgrass MJ.

   An evaluation of physiochemical

   treatment technologies for water

   contaminated with MTBE. Ground Water

18

Monitoring & Remediation. 2000.
p 114-26.

4. USEPAb-Office of Solid Waste and
Emergency Response. MTBE Fact Sheet #3:
Use and distribution of MTBE and
ethanol. EPA-510-F-97-016. 1998.

5. Daubert T, Danner RP. Data compilation
tables of properties of pure compounds.
American Institute of Chemical
Engineers; 1985.

6. Squillace PJ, Zogorski JS, Wilber WG,
Price CV. Preliminary assessment of the
occurrence and possible sources of MTBE
in groundwater in the United States,
1993-1995. Enviro Sci Technol 1996;
30.5: 1721-30.

7. USEPAa-Office of Solid Waste and
Emergency Response. Fact Sheet #2:
Remediation of MTBE contaminated soil
and groundwater. EPA 510-F-98-002.
1998.

8. Kamei CR. Delay in eliminating MTBE is
going to cost the valley. San Jose
Mercury News 2003 Jan 16.

9. Barrick D. State sues oil giants over
MTBE. Concord Monitor [Internet]. 2003

19

[Cited 2003 Oct 7]. Available from:

http://www.gristmagazine.com/

forward.pl?forward_id=1584

10. USEPA-Office of Research and
    Development. Monitored natural
    attenuation of petroleum
    hydrocarbons. EPA 600-F-98-021.1999.

11. USEPAc-Office of Solid Waste and
    Emergency Response. Technology
    Innovation Office: A citizen's guide
    to soil vapor extraction and air
    sparging. EPA 542-F-01-006. 2001.

12. USEPAd-Office of Solid Waste and
    Emergency Response. Technology
    Innovation Office: A citizen's guide
    to soil excavation. EPA 542-F-01-023.
    2001.

NOTES

1. Rene Taton, *Reason and Chance in Scientific Discovery* (New York: Philosophical Library, 1957), pp. 85–88. Reprinted by permission of Philosophical Library, Inc.

2. Taton, p. 88.

3. I am indebted to Professor Judy Davidson of the Texas Tech University Geography Department for this assignment and student response.

8

Writing a Research Paper in Social Science

INTRODUCTION

The social sciences have as their goal the systematic study of human behavior and human societies. For this reason, it is particularly important for social science research to include primary research (for example, data from interviews, surveys, and questionnaires).

Social science researchers must have knowledge of current research being conducted by others in their field. That is why library work, using secondary sources, is also important. In the social science journals, researchers report their findings for scrutiny and replication by other researchers. You need to know in general how social scientists proceed when gathering information on a particular subject or issue, using both primary and secondary sources. As you become familiar with the tools used by social scientists to gain access to current research, several research principles and skills will be important to you:

1. A familiarity with primary research techniques used by social scientists
2. A familiarity with library research tools used by social scientists, including databases, bibliographies, and indexes
3. The ability to synthesize and evaluate data and opinions from a variety of primary and secondary sources
4. The ability to develop a thesis consistent with the evidence found in primary and secondary sources

5. The ability to organize and write a paper that effectively presents and supports your thesis
6. The ability to employ the formal conventions of research papers in the social sciences

THE INQUIRY PROCESS IN SOCIAL SCIENCE

Social sciences such as psychology, anthropology, political science, sociology, economics, and education developed much later than the natural and physical sciences and so are comparatively young disciplines. Because social sciences emerged after the enormously successful and influential natural and physical sciences, they understandably adopted much of the scientific method—its goals, procedures, and standards. The field of sociology, for example, has been called the science of social organization; psychology has been called the science of the mind. Many social scientists today study people using the scientific method: they develop hypotheses and design and conduct controlled experiments to test those hypotheses.

A notorious example of a controlled social science experiment was conducted by Stanley Milgram, a Yale psychologist, during the 1960s.[1] Milgram sought to determine to what extent ordinary individuals would obey the orders of an authority figure. Through his experiment, he wished to probe the psychological processes that allowed the Germans to carry out mass human exterminations during World War II. Using simulated shock experiments, which were admittedly controversial, Milgram showed that an alarming proportion of adults (65% of those tested) were willing to inflict severe and, as far as they knew, permanent damage on strangers simply because they were instructed to do so by an authority figure—in this case, the experimenter. The conclusions Milgram drew from this experiment are frightening:

> This is, perhaps, the most fundamental lesson of our study: ordinary people, simply doing their jobs, and without any particular hostility on their part, can become agents in a terrible destructive process. Moreover, even when the destructive effects of their work become patently clear, and they are asked to carry out actions incompatible with fundamental standards of morality, relatively few people have the resources needed to resist authority. A variety of inhibitions against disobeying authority come into play and successfully keep the person in his place.[2]

The research process used by Milgram closely follows that of other scientific research. His research began with a question: How could Hitler have succeeded in marshaling so much support from those who were called on to carry out his inhuman orders? After sufficient preparation, Milgram set out to determine the extent to which ordinary individuals would obey immoral orders. The psychologists were surprised by their results, which showed a large percentage of normal people obeying immoral orders from an authority figure. From the results, Milgram was able to verify that, indeed, there was something in human nature that could explain the behavior of so many Germans during World War II. Many of the people who followed orders to annihilate others were not brutal, sadistic monsters, he stated, but rather normal people who acted out of a sense of duty and obligation to their country and their leader.

The Importance of Observing Human Behavior

A great number of the experiments created by social scientists are designed to observe human behavior. Because the goal of any science is the systematic, objective study of phenomena, the social sciences must limit themselves to studying those aspects of humans that are observable. The only objectively observable part of humanity is behavior. We cannot observe human emotions or consciousness directly, but we can observe the behavior that results from feelings and thoughts. The social sciences, consequently, have focused heavily on behavior and thus have been called the *behavioral sciences*. The Milgram experiment is an example of a behavioral-science experiment. Milgram observed how his subjects behaved in a carefully controlled experimental setting to arrive at his conclusions about why people act as they do.

The Importance of Understanding Human Consciousness

Many people, both within and outside the social sciences, have felt that this objectification of observable human behavior produces a false picture of human beings. The real "inside" of a person may be missed when only outward behavior is observed. Human beings are conscious beings; we have thoughts, feelings, and intuitions that are private and never seen by others. Some in the social sciences argue that because we cannot observe consciousness directly, it is not a proper subject for scientific study at all. Others take the position that it is not only appropriate to study human consciousness but also essential, because consciousness is what makes us uniquely human. Modern social scientists have developed methods of exploring human consciousness that are admittedly subjective but nevertheless reveal important information about how people think and feel. Such methods include case studies of individuals, clinical evaluation, psychoanalysis, and hypnosis.

Social scientists also study the interaction among people in societies. A social scientist attempting to discover social rules and conventions is somewhat analogous to a natural scientist attempting to discover laws of nature. The social rules and conventions adopted by a particular society are important for understanding human behavior within that society. For example, a Polynesian native accustomed to using shells as money would have a rude awakening in an American marketplace where, by convention, slips of paper are traded for goods and services. The slip of paper Americans accept as a dollar bill has meaning only within our particular set of social conventions. Much of the work done in social sciences attempts to describe and define the social laws, rules, and conventions by which people operate within societies.

An example of a social scientist whose work has been important is the Austrian psychologist Sigmund Freud, who sought to describe and predict the complex operation of the human subconscious mind. Freud also sought to apply his theories of individuals to the operation of human beings in societies. In one of his last books, *Civilization and Its Discontents,* he expressed his views on the broad question of the human being's place in the world.[3] Freud posed this question: Why is it hard for humankind to be happy in civilization? Through his years of preparation and study, Freud was able to posit the hypothesis that unhappiness is due to the inevitable conflict between the demands of instincts (aggression and ego gratification) and the restrictions of civilized society:

> If civilization imposes such great sacrifices not only on man's sexuality but on his aggressivity, we can understand better why it is hard for him to be happy in that civilization. In fact, primitive man was better off in knowing no restrictions of instinct. To counterbalance this, his prospects of enjoying this happiness for any length of time were very slender. Civilized man has exchanged a portion of his possibilities of happiness for a portion of security.[4]

Freud's sociological theories have been as influential as his psychological theories. Verification of this particular hypothesis—that instinct and society conflict—was achieved through Freud's extensive citation of examples taken from psychological case studies and from primitive and modern societies (including the Soviet Union and the United States). Through these examples, Freud showed that human instincts are in conflict with society's constraints.

Researchers in the social sciences attempt to describe and predict human behavior and human relationships in society. Barzun and Graff, in their text *The Modern Researcher,* observe that "the works of social science that have made the strongest mark on the modern mind have been those that combined description with enumeration and imparted the results with imaginative power."[5] The work of Freud is a classic example of the way good social science research combines an understanding of individual human behavior and consciousness with an understanding of how people are organized and influenced by the societies in which they live and operate.

Objectivity versus Subjectivity

In the sciences, researchers attempt to remove their own particular preferences, desires, and hopes from the experimental process as much as possible. Scientific researchers are looking for "objective" truth. However, because each researcher as observer necessarily brings background preparation, knowledge, and experience to the situation, it is seldom possible to remove the researcher from the research altogether. But what about social science researchers? Can they be as objective as natural or physical scientists in their search for knowledge and understanding? Many would charge that subjectivity and values are inescapable and necessary parts of social science research. The social scientist studies people, social systems, and social conventions. As a person, the researcher is necessarily a part of the system being studied. Perhaps this is not altogether a bad thing. A social scientist's own beliefs, attitudes, and values can contribute to his or her understanding of what is being observed, even though he or she can, to a certain degree, demonstrate detachment from a situation and function as a relatively impartial observer. But the question of objectivity and subjectivity in the social sciences is not easily resolved, because it is not always possible to know exactly what subjective influences are affecting "objective" research. The issue of subjectivity versus objectivity is the cause of much ferment and continual debate within the social science fields as these young disciplines seek to define for themselves an appropriate method, whether it is modeled after the scientific method or something quite different.

QUESTIONS FOR DISCUSSION

1. What is the general goal of inquiry in the social sciences?

2. Why are social sciences often called *behavioral sciences?*

3. What is meant by the understanding of human consciousness?

4. What is the relationship between objectivity and subjectivity in the social sciences?

PRIMARY RESEARCH IN THE
SOCIAL SCIENCES

The social sciences have incorporated many of the research techniques of the natural and physical sciences and have developed some research methods of their own as well. Remember, the primary aim of the social sciences is to study human beings and their interactions in society and with the environment. Social scientists seek to help us understand the events that happen around us and to communicate that understanding to others. Systematic inquiry is essential in the social sciences. Because researchers must communicate the social knowledge they acquire through their research, they need a clear written form for transmitting their insights. As in the natural and physical sciences, researchers in the social sciences employ a version of the scientific method. The following steps (discussed in detail in later paragraphs) are generally utilized in the researching of a social scientific question:

1. Choosing the research problem and stating the hypothesis
2. Formulating the research design and method of gathering data
3. Gathering the data
4. Analyzing the data
5. Interpreting the results of the data analysis in order to test the hypothesis

Step 1—Problem and Hypothesis

Obviously, the first step must be preceded by extensive study and preparation in the discipline under investigation. To choose a research problem that is significant, fresh, and researchable, the social scientist must have an intimate knowledge of the field of study. Often, researchers choose a problem based on the prior research of other social scientists, or they seek to test their hypotheses against actual social reality. It is crucial for researchers to keep abreast of the current research in their fields by reading professional journals, attending national meetings of professional societies, and maintaining contacts with other researchers doing similar studies. Research problems are not formulated in a vacuum. The first two inquiry steps discussed in Chapter 1, preparation and incubation, precede the actual formulation of a hypothesis.

Once a significant research problem has been chosen, a working hypothesis can be formulated. That is, the researcher sets forth a proposition (hypothesis) that may explain the occurrence of the phenomenon observed. For example, an education researcher interested in the writing processes of children might hypothesize that the type of learning environment could influence children's willingness to write.

Step 2—Research Design

The researcher must decide how to test the hypothesis developed in step 1. To do this, he or she needs to determine which concepts or events being studied are constant and which are variable. Variables are phenomena that change or differ. Temperature, for example, is a scientific variable that differs by degrees. Thus, the variable "temperature" contains the idea of more or less heat, and this variable influences the physical world. Similarly, the social variable "religion" may be expressed differently: Protestant, Catholic, Muslim, and so on. Just as temperature influences physical nature, a social variable such as religion influences human nature. Public opinion polls have revealed that Protestants and Catholics differ predictably in their preference for political parties. Thus, the variable "religion" influences social behavior. In the example of education research mentioned on the previous page, the variable is "learning environment," which refers to the structure and atmosphere of the classroom.

Once the variables have been identified, the researcher must decide how best to measure them. The methods used by social scientists include experiments, surveys and questionnaires, interviews and case studies, and observations. These methods are discussed in detail on pages 261–271.

Step 3—Gathering the Data

The researcher gathers data (both quantitative and qualitative) based on the research design chosen as most appropriate for testing the hypothesis. Social science researchers pay close attention to matters of accurate sampling and the accurate recording of data. Table 8-1 taken from FBI Crime Reports, illustrates the kind of data often used by social scientists.

Step 4—Analyzing the Data

Researchers analyze their data quantitatively (using numbers) to discern its relationship to the hypothesis. Depending on the research method used, the researcher relies to a greater or lesser degree on statistical analyses of the data. Often, researchers code their data to make it suitable for computer processing. Computers can quickly and accurately process data and correlate variables. As an example of data analysis, students in a political science class were asked to analyze the crime statistics data in Table 8-1. First, the students were asked to compare the data for two states, in this case Alaska and Arizona, to see whether the differences were statistically significant. Then they were asked to explain or interpret their results.

TABLE 8-1 FBI Uniform Crime Reports

Area	Population	Crime Index Total	Violent Crime	Property Crime	Murder and Non-Negligent Manslaughter	Forcible Rape	Robbery	Aggravated Assault	Burglary	Larceny-Theft	Motor Vehicle Theft
ALASKA											
Metropolitan Statistical Area	231,039										
Area actually reporting	100.0%	13,746	1,025	12,721	15	154	285	571	2,113	9,491	1,117
Other Cities	168,591										
Area actually reporting	87.4%	8,100	590	7,510	9	69	62	450	1,081	5,581	848
Estimated totals	100.0%	9,267	675	8,592	10	79	71	515	1,237	6,385	970
Rural	125,370										
Area actually reporting	100.0%	5,219	691	4,528	28	108	28	527	1,743	2,319	466
State Total	525,000	28,232	2,391	25,841	53	341	384	1,613	5,093	18,195	2,553
Rate per 100,000 inhabitants		5,377.5	455.4	4,922.1	10.1	65.0	73.1	307.2	970.1	3,465.7	486.3
ARIZONA											
Metropolitan Statistical Area	2,587,955										
Area actually reporting	100.0%	204,538	17,226	187,312	206	1,208	4,262	11,550	46,196	128,869	12,247
Other Cities	422,312										
Area actually reporting	98.3%	30,282	2,267	28,015	17	139	347	1,764	6,145	20,379	1,491
Estimated totals	100.0%	30,803	2,305	28,498	17	141	353	1,794	6,251	20,730	1,517
Rural	375,733										
Area actually reporting	91.0%	7,342	1,103	6,239	27	43	66	967	2,378	3,366	495
Estimated totals	100.0%	8,064	1,211	6,853	30	47	72	1,062	2,612	3,697	544
State Total	3,386,000	243,405	20,742	222,663	253	1,396	4,687	14,406	55,059	153,296	14,308
Rate per 100,000 inhabitants		7,188.6	612.6	6,576.0	7.5	41.2	138.4	425.5	1,626.1	4,527.3	422.6

Step 5—Interpreting the Results

The relationship among variables suggested by the hypothesis is tested at this stage in the research, often through statistical measures. In the social sciences, a hypothesis can never be proved or disproved "beyond the shadow of a doubt." However, researchers can statistically calculate the probability that the hypothesis is wrong, and thus can strongly suggest the truth or validity of the hypothesis. In other words, a social scientist may be able to either reject or fail to reject a hypothesis based on a careful marshaling of the evidence. For example, in comparing the crime reports for Alaska and Arizona, the students noticed that the rates per 100,000 population differed in potentially interesting ways: Arizona had more property crimes (burglary, larceny-theft, motor vehicle theft) than Alaska did and more violent crimes (murder, rape, robbery, assault). But Alaska topped Arizona in individual crimes—murders, rapes, and vehicle thefts. The students needed first to find out whether these perceived differences were significant, using statistical tests. If so, they then could interpret their results by positing plausible explanations (hypotheses) to explore and test further. The students, for example, hypothesized that the high number of rapes in Alaska could be related to the scarcity of women. This hypothesis could be tested, perhaps by comparisons with other states with similar demographics.

Social Science Research Designs

The research designs most commonly used in social science research are the following:

1. Experiments
2. Surveys and questionnaires
3. Interviews and case studies
4. Observations

The paragraphs that follow describe these research designs. Each design has both advantages and disadvantages. Researchers must keep the relative merits in mind as they design a research project.[6]

Experiments

The social scientific experiment is a highly controlled method of determining a direct link between two variables—for example, between overcrowding and riots. The researcher must have control over the research environment so that no external variables can affect the outcome. Unlike experiments in the sciences, in social scientific research it is often difficult to control the research environment totally. A researcher who is interested in the causes of riots should not attempt to create a riot in the laboratory for study. However, social science researchers can study laboratory animals and posit hypotheses about human behavior based on their experimental results. For example, to test the hypothesis that overcrowding can cause riots, some researchers studied populations of rats and varied the population density to test their hypothesis. They found that for the rat populations, overcrowding did indeed cause antisocial behavior. From this result, the researchers hypothesized that people may be subject to a similar phenomenon—that is, overcrowded cities may contribute to antisocial behavior. Although experimental research is the best means of definitively establishing causal links (variable A causes variable B; overcrowded living conditions cause antisocial behavior), experiments may be limited in applicability. In the case of the above experiment, people may or may not behave as rats do.

Surveys and Questionnaires

Ideally, we would study an entire population to gain insights into its society; finding out how all Americans intend to vote in an upcoming election would accurately predict the outcome. However, polling an entire population is seldom feasible, so pollsters sample small segments of the entire population at random. The most frequently used sampling technique is random-digit-dialing on the telephone. Researchers have refined sampling techniques to the point that polls can be quite accurate. Thus, CBS News can announce the outcome of a presidential election hours before the returns are in for much of the country.

One particular kind of survey is the questionnaire, a form that asks for responses to a set of questions. Large numbers of people can be polled for their opinions by means of questionnaires, either over the telephone, through the mail, or in person. The advent of computers has radically changed the survey business: it is now possible to survey large populations, code their responses and enter them into a computer database, and obtain immediate analyses of the data.

The Hypothesis.   As with most other research in both the sciences and the social sciences, the first, and perhaps most important, step in survey research is the articulation of a hypothesis. "Developing the hypothesis provides the key ingredient to structure all subsequent parts of the project: the questionnaire, the sample, the coding, the tabulation forms, and the final report itself."[7] A questionnaire is not given simply to gather random facts; rather, it is a problem-solving tool. The researcher poses a hypothesis in an attempt to shed light on a particular research problem. The questionnaire works to either support or counter the hypothesis. For example, a study of the relationship between the elderly and the police might begin when researchers observed a problem, namely, that the elderly do not see the police in a positive light and therefore hesitate to call on them in an emergency situation. The researcher might then hypothesize that the real problem lies in the elderly population's erroneous perceptions of the police. A questionnaire could be designed to elicit their perceptions and to try to understand the origins of their distrust. In fact, when a study like this was conducted in a major metropolitan area, researchers discovered that an elderly person's distrust of the police was in direct proportion to the number of hours of television the person watched, in particular TV crime shows.

Question Design. The survey researcher must design each question on a questionnaire carefully to ensure that it is clear, direct, and understandable to the target population. Questions should be pretested so that initial responses can be reviewed and the questions revised to eliminate any ambiguity prior to their use in the actual study. Researchers should also design questionnaires that are reliable (measure the same thing each time) and valid (measure what they claim to measure). In addition, the population sampled should represent the larger group being studied.

Two basic kinds of questions are used on questionnaires: open-ended questions and closed questions. The open-ended questions may require an interviewer, since research has shown that self-administered open questionnaires tend to yield less usable data. Fowler says that "generally speaking, if one is going to have a self-administered questionnaire, one must reconcile oneself to closed questions, that is, questions that can be answered by simply checking a box or circling the proper response from a set provided by the researcher."[8] On the other hand, Labaw says that open questions have gotten a lot of undeserved bad press in the survey business. She says they "provide absolutely indispensable insight into how respondents interpret complex but apparently single-issue questions"[9] and, in general, recommends the strategic use of both closed and open-ended questions. She also states that "the most basic principle of question wording, and one very often ignored or simply unseen, is that only one concept or issue or meaning should be included in a question."[10]

The questionnaire below was designed by a student to discover the attitude of foreign students toward Utah State University and the education they were receiving. He hypothesized, based on his own experiences as a foreign student, that their responses would be generally very favorable. The student researcher polled sixty foreign students, representing a variety of nationalities, during several visits to the library. He found that, in general, foreign students were satisfied with university administrative policies but less satisfied with interpersonal relationships with their teachers and classmates.

Questionnaire
1. What is your nationality?
2. How long have you been a student at USU?
3. What is your native language?
4. Do you feel classes at USU are designed with consideration of the needs of foreign students?   yes   no
5. Do you feel your instructors are unbiased toward you and your nationality during class?   yes   no
6. Do you feel you have received an undeserved grade from an instructor due to a bias against foreign students?   yes   no
7. Do you feel any language difficulties (limited vocabulary, accent, etc.) cause communication barriers between you and your instructors?   yes   no
8. Do you feel accepted as an equal by your American classmates?   yes   no
9. Do you feel USU's administrative policies regarding foreign students are fair and unbiased?   yes   no
10. Do you feel USU provides an equal opportunity for a sound education for its foreign students?   yes   no

QUESTIONS FOR DISCUSSION

1. Based on the previous discussion of questionnaire design, how would you rate this student's questionnaire?

2. Do the questions asked match the hypothesis?

3. Are there any ambiguous words or phrases that could be misunderstood?

4. Do you see any way this questionnaire could be made better?

Interviews

Interviews are another type of survey. Their advantages over questionnaires include flexibility (the questioner can interact with the respondent), response rate (the questioner immediately knows the respondent's answer), and access to nonverbal behavior (the questioner can gather nonverbal as well as verbal clues). Interviews have other advantages as well, but the disadvantages are also great. Primarily, the time and expense of interviews makes them difficult to conduct. Consequently, fewer responses can be gathered. In addition, the interview is actually a complex interaction between individuals; thus, interview results can hinge on the characteristics of the individuals involved. If a respondent is put off by the interviewer, for example, his or her interview answers may be affected. Nevertheless, interviewing is an important research method in the social sciences that yields high-quality data. When designing interviews, keep the following in mind:

1. Be certain that the questions are written down and asked exactly as worded.
2. Be certain that you probe any unclear or incomplete answer.
3. Be certain that inadequate or brief answers are not probed in a directive way that may bias the results.

The interview that follows was conducted by a student who was interested in the relationship between emotions and the onset of asthma attacks in asthmatic children. Prior to the interview, she obtained the subject's permission to tape-record for later data analysis.

Interview with Dr. John W. Carlisle, September 10, 1998
(Pediatrician with extensive experience treating asthmatic children)

1. *Do emotions cause asthma?* Dr. Carlisle feels that the misconception "emotions cause asthma" is easily explained by the fact that stressful emotional situations frequently trigger asthma attacks. People who may have already been prone to asthma may experience their first attack in an emotionally stressful situation. In actuality, asthma is a physical disease that can be irritated by emotional stress or trauma.

2. *What emotional or psychological effects on your asthmatic patients have you observed?* Dr. Carlisle targeted several detrimental effects of asthma on children's emotional and psychological well-being. Older children (8–12 years) feel "defective" in some way because they are different from their peers (they often have to take medicine or other precautions to prevent an attack). Older children may rebel against parents who expect them to take on the extra responsibility for controlling their own disease. Younger children tend to regress, become very frightened, and cling to parents because they are not yet capable of understanding their disease.

3. *What suggestions do you have for treating the emotional aspects of asthma?* In Dr. Carlisle's opinion, the best emotional support parents can give childhood asthmatics is to make sure they understand the disease and what is happening to them. At the same time, try to reinforce the fact that there will always be someone there to help them if they need help. This can alleviate a great deal of the anxiety that can aggravate their condition.

Observations

The survey method is important for obtaining a person's opinion on a particular issue. Observation, on the other hand, is best suited to the collection of nonverbal data. In this method, the observer takes notes on people behaving in customary ways in a particular environment or setting. In this way, the researcher accumulates "field notes," which are used to analyze trends and discern customary behaviors. The disadvantages of observation include lack of control over the environment, lack of quantifiable data, and small sample size. Also, whenever an observer enters the environment to observe people, the participants' behavior may no longer be natural.

The goal of social research based on observation and description is a general one: to describe and perhaps evaluate a culture or subculture in as much detail as possible. An example of this type of observational research is sociologist Margaret Mead's book *Coming of Age in Samoa.* In this book, Mead describes the complex culture of the Samoan island, paying particular attention to customs surrounding the transition from adolescence to adulthood.

The following excerpt from a report written for a speech communications course illustrates an observation and description of a particular cultural setting—the country-and-Western singles bar.[11] The researcher was observing particular nonverbal behaviors exhibited by the patrons of the bar. As you read the report, notice the descriptions and categorizations of the participants in this subculture.

Red Raider Romances

by Lee Guyette

The following study was conducted at the Red Raider Club in Lubbock, Texas. The study is a brief survey of the nonverbal communication displayed in this particular club. The following observations were made by me not only in the recent few days, but also over a 7-month period in which I worked as a cocktail waitress there. I made my observations from the standpoint of a nonpatron/waitress and from the patron/female customer. The Red Raider Club is a Country and Western club that

caters primarily to a crowd of people between the ages
of 25 and 50. It is for the most part a blue-collar,
lower-middle-class crowd.

Body Types, Shapes, and Sizes

Attractiveness

A majority of the people, both male and female,
were only average in appearance. There were a few
exceptionally attractive males and females, and they
did seem to get preferential treatment; for example,
the attractive men were turned down less when they
asked a woman to dance, and the attractive women were
asked to dance more frequently.

Body Image and Appearance

Many of the individuals were slightly overweight.
They did not seem to be very aware of or satisfied
with their bodies. Their body concept seemed low.
In the more attractive individuals, the reverse was
true. The attractive individuals were more aware of
their bodies; they noticed what they were doing with
their bodies, and they smiled more and seemed in
general more comfortable with themselves. I did
notice that the less attractive people seemed to worry
less about their unsightly bodies as they became
intoxicated.

Body Messages

Most of my subjects were definitely endomorphic,
and they certainly seemed viscerotonic. Most of the men
were slightly overweight. There were women as tall as 6
feet and men as short as 5 feet. Nearly all my subjects
were white. Perhaps 2% were Hispanic and there were no

blacks. Many of the men had beards and moustaches, perhaps to indicate masculinity. Most of the women wore their hair either long and curly or short and straight.

Clothing and Personal Artifacts

Function of Dress

The main function of dress in this club was cultural display more than comfort or modesty. Nearly all of the subjects of both sexes wore jeans. The men wore Wranglers and most of the women wore designer jeans. Chic, Lee, Wrangler, Sergio, and Vanderbilt were the most commonly worn for the women. A few women wore western dresses. I did not see any man not wearing cowboy boots and most of the women also wore cowboy boots. A few women wore high-heeled shoes. All of the women wearing dresses wore heels. Most of the people, both female and male, wearing jeans and boots also had their names on the back of their belts. For the men, it was their last names on the belt; for the women, their first names.

Communication Components of Dress

It is difficult to say whether or not these people were intentionally or unintentionally communicating messages through dress. They all seemed to communicate their preference for western dress. They did not wish to communicate, however, that they were from a lower socioeconomic background by wearing western dress. Although this conception has changed in recent years, it still is thought that lower-middle-class people wear western clothes.

Personality Correlates of Dress

It is extremely difficult to assess personality types of a large group just from their clothing styles. However, I did notice that most of the women in dresses were there with dates. I also noticed that women wearing red western blouses danced more frequently. For the most part, both men and women dressed conservatively. The colors were usually solid black, brown, and white for the men, and red, purple, or blue for the women.

Perception of Dress

Most of the people were dressed in the conventional stereotype of western dress. Indeed, it was almost as if there were an unspoken dress code. The young attractive girls, wearing red and purple blouses with ruffles, tight jeans, boots, belts, and wearing their hair long, seemed to be thought the sexiest and most likeable. They were asked to dance more frequently than any others. The young attractive men with beards and moustaches wearing black or white western cut shirts seemed to be the most popular with the women. No one wore very much jewelry of any kind. A few women had small earrings or hair barrettes. Nearly everyone smoked cigarettes continuously. I saw no pipes or cigars.

The Effects of Dress

The main effect I observed was that everyone seemed able to identify with each other and feel a sense of belonging to the group because of their similar style of dress.

[The student researcher goes on to describe behaviors observed in the following categories: body movements and gestures; facial expressions and eye behavior; responses to environment; personal space, territory, and crowding; touching behavior; voice characteristics; taste and smell; culture and time.]

Discussion

I feel that the nonverbal communication that I have described may be representative of lower-middle-class Americans in Lubbock, Texas. The nonverbal communication described in this report may illustrate lower-middle-class values: the tendency to be slightly overweight in both sexes; the conservative, traditional, western-style dress; the traditional use of male/female regulators and posture; the overcontrol of masculine expressions of emotion and the lack of control in feminine emotional expressions; the environment, with its tacky chairs and dirty carpet; the use of territory by the men; the fact that women have no true territory, personal space, or value (the women are treated as possessions and property and they have only as much value as they are granted by men); the way in which the men have absolute control over when and how they will be touched, but the women have very little to say about when or how the men will touch them; the way the women plead with soft cooing pitch at the end of their voice or remain silent while the men speak loudly and uninterruptedly; the use of sub-standard speech; the accepted deception on the part of the males; the overwhelming smell of tobacco and liquor and stale urine in the restrooms; the taste of cheap wines, beer, and whisky; the time being measured by the

sets the band plays. All of these things are often
associated with lower-middle classes. Women and men may
be poorly educated and thus rely on tradition and myth.
I felt that the nonverbal communication that I observed
was representative of this particular subculture.

QUESTIONS FOR DISCUSSION

1. What is the relationship between the observer and those she is observing?

2. Observation research tends to both describe and classify behaviors of individuals in order to predict future behaviors within the setting. List the classifications used by this writer. Do they seem appropriate to the behaviors observed? Why or why not?

3. Does the writer overgeneralize from a small sample; that is, does she jump to conclusions based on insufficient data? Do her conclusions follow logically from her evidence? Why or why not?

4. Is it likely that the observer's presence changed the dynamics of the situation so that her subjects' behavior was no longer natural? Why or why not?

5. Do the writer's personal opinions and biases come through? If so, how?

6. How much can an observer infer about subjects' thoughts and emotions from observing their behaviors? For example, in the subsection "Communication Components of Dress," the author states that "they did not wish to communicate, however, that they were from a lower socioeconomic background. . . ." Is this a valid inference or a reflection of a personal bias? Justify your response.

EXERCISES

The exercises below are designed to give you an opportunity to try out some of the primary research techniques frequently used by social scientists. Or, you may wish to adapt these methods to find information pertinent to your own research topic with an eye toward incorporating the primary research data you discover into your larger research paper.

1. To understand observing and reporting, begin by observing the behavior of a particular group or subculture and report on that observation. You may find that an observation report would be a helpful component in a larger research paper project. As in the sample paper above on the country-and-Western singles bar, first choose subjects in a "field" to observe. Some possibilities include customers at a fast-food restaurant, patrons at a theater, participants in a sport, spectators at a rock concert, students in a dorm, customers in a department store elevator, and so on.

   Procedure:

   A. Identify the field you have chosen to observe. Describe the setting, location, and the time you spent observing. Describe your research method. (Are you an observer or a participant?)

   B. Take field notes as you observe the behaviors of the individuals in your chosen group. Look for verbal and nonverbal behaviors.

   C. Categorize your field notes into related behaviors and personality types.

   D. Speculate on the meaning of the behaviors you observed. What did you learn about the people in your study and how they act? Give possible reasons for why they behaved as they did.

   E. Write up your field observations in a report three to five pages long.

2. To understand the processes of interviewing and reporting, conduct an actual interview, either by yourself or with a classmate. You may find that an interview with an expert is a useful component of a larger research paper project.

   Procedure:

   A. Find someone in your intended major field. Write or phone the person to introduce yourself. Set up an interview, explaining that you want to find out what a person in your chosen career actually does.

   B. Prior to the interview, draw up a list of interview topics, including but not limited to the following:
      • education and background
      • job title and general description of the job
      • description of the company or organization
      • years at the job

- prior positions within the same company
- tasks performed in the job
- tools used in the job (for example, computers, books)
- career plans or aspirations
- job satisfaction
- advice for someone just beginning in the field

Use this topic list as a guide in developing your questions. The questions you ask will vary in accordance with your career choice. It is important to think through the questions you intend to ask your informant very carefully. If you want to tape the interview, be certain to ask for permission.

C. Once you have collected your data, analyze and categorize it in a report three to five pages long. Someone reading your report should be able to discern what the career is like for participants.

ORGANIZING AND WRITING THE SOCIAL SCIENCE RESEARCH PAPER

This section of the chapter follows the research process of Lindy Danley as she investigated the problem of electronic waste. Her research paper appears at the end of the chapter.

When thinking through her rhetorical situation for this research paper (purpose, persona, audience, subject matter, tone; see pp. 92–95), Lindy decided that she wanted to be largely informative to a general audience, helping the reader to come to a better understanding of the problems and solutions for e-waste.

Her thesis statement helped her to articulate her intentions in the paper and, at the same time, implied an organizational plan: the problem of e-waste and the possible solutions.

Lindy might have considered other possible organizational plans depending on her intentions as a writer:

Chronological: ("The problem of e-waste has accelerated over the last ten years.")

Comparison and contrast: ("E-waste differs from other environmental problems.")

Process ("The process of preventing environmental hazards includes manufacturers.")

Example ("E-waste is but one example of a larger problem of a consumer society.")

These are only examples of the possible organizational plans that you might wish to use. It is important that you pay attention to planning at this stage in your project, or the extensive materials you have gathered may seem overwhelming. It is your job to make order out of the chaos.

Organizing Your Materials

Sort your note cards or organize your research notebook by related topic areas. Group information on topics together. You may wish to write brief summaries of information in your notebook to help you understand the ideas contained in each source. Using the thesis as a guide, you are now arranging information into a logical order. The actual sorting process you use depends on the project itself. However, the main idea is to group and categorize your information.

Since Lindy had saved all her notebook information in a computer file on disk, it was a relatively easy matter for her to block related information and to move it, using her word-processing CUT/PASTE command, to the appropriate section in the paper. (Before manipulating your notebook in this way, be sure to make a backup file.)

Planning and Outlining

Now you are ready to plan and outline your research paper. Your thesis statement may help you to come up with main headings for your outline. The subpoints on your outline are the supporting points that you wish to discuss in your paper. Look through the categories you have used to sort your notes. These may make good outline headings. Carefully think through the main points you wish to cover in your paper. Consider the needs of your readers and their expectations when deciding what information to include in your paper.

Do not be overly concerned about formal outline structure. An outline should be a guide to planning and not a constraint that confines and limits your thinking. However, an informal outline is an important organizational device that can help you to construct a logically developed, unified, and coherent research paper. Your own outline will be based on the material you have discovered in your library search and in your primary research. It will describe in an organized way all the material you wish to include in your paper.

Many writers go back and forth between their outlines and their actual papers, thus in effect revising and refining their outlines as they write. Others prefer to have fairly comprehensive outlines before beginning to write. Lindy wrote the following informal outline when she was actually writing the paper. The form of the outline changed several times as she wrote and thought about the paper.

Informal Outline
  I. The Problem of E-Waste
  II. What is being done?
      A. Government
      B. Special interest groups
      C. Private enterprise
      D. Manufacturers
      E. Foreign dumping
  III. Possible solutions
      A. Government participation
      B. Collaboration
      C. Manufacturer responsibility
      D. Examples of manufacturer stewardship
  IV. Conclusion
  V. Links to more information

EXERCISE

Think through your rhetorical situation: Who is the audience for your paper and what do you wish them to learn by reading it? Arrange your source material, decide on a preliminary organizational plan, and construct an outline to guide your writing of the first draft of your research paper. Refer to Chapter 4 for help with organization (pp. 95–100).

Writing the First Draft

After you have completed your informal outline, you are ready to write the first draft of your research paper. Remember, your objective is to present to your readers the answer you have discovered to the starting question. Remind yourself at this time of the question that initially motivated your research. When writing your first draft, use concrete and simple language to explain as objectively as you can your thesis and the supporting evidence you gathered in your research. Your thesis statement and your outline will guide the writing of this first draft. You should remain flexible as you write and be open to any fresh insights you may have along the way.

As you are writing the first draft, it is important to make a note of which material comes from which sources. Do not be concerned at this point about the formal details of documentation; you can deal with that later. But do mark for yourself in the draft any ideas or words taken from your sources. Place any words you copy from a source in quotation marks, and after the quotation write down the last name and the date of publication of the source and the page number of the quoted material (in parentheses). For example:

> "First, there are a wide range of outcomes,
>
> all the way from excellent to poor" (Allen, 1985,
>
> p. 11).

Similarly, document paraphrases and restatements of ideas taken from a source even though you have recast them in your own words:

> These chemicals are of great concern because
>
> of the high potential of leaching into our
>
> groundwater (Electronics, 2003).

However, you need not document common knowledge (see pp. 103–104). That is, if three or more general sources (such as encyclopedias) agree on a certain idea, it is probably in the domain of common knowledge: anyone familiar with the topic would accept or agree to the idea, and so it does not need to be attributed to any one author.

When you are not quoting or paraphrasing from a specific page in a source, it is sufficient to include simply the author's name (or names, where there is more than one author) and the publication date:

> The real onslaught of these hazardous
>
> products has yet to hit (Bartholomew, 2001).

When you are quoting an author referred to by another source you have read, you need to acknowledge that original author in your own text. For example, if Johnson's study is referred to and discussed in Bruch, in the text you should say

```
Johnson's study (cited in Bruch, 1973, p. 89)
shows that . . .
```

[Only Bruch needs to appear on your references page.]

For general information on planning, writing, and revising your social science research paper, refer to Chapters 4 and 5. Use the following information on documentation in the social sciences to make your citations. The model paper at the end of the chapter illustrates the writing and documentation styles commonly used in the social sciences.

MANUSCRIPT PREPARATION (APA STYLE)

The *Publication Manual of the American Psychological Association* (5th ed. 2001) describes in great detail the types of articles typically written in the social sciences and the manuscript format of those articles. The major parts of a manuscript are the title page, abstract, introduction, body, references page, and appendix. Each section is described briefly here, but please refer to the APA manual for a more detailed discussion. The sample paper at the end of the chapter follows the APA style for manuscript preparation, so you may use it as a model for your own paper.

Title Page

Write a title that summarizes the main idea of the paper as simply (yet as completely) as you can. Do not use a clever or cute title, but rather an informative title that could stand alone. Lindy's title "The Problem of E-Waste" sums up quite well the main idea of her paper. You will also need to compress your title into a manuscript page header (usually the first two or three words of your title) which will serve to identify each page of your paper. Identify each page with the manuscript page header and page number in the upper right-hand corner of the page.

The title page should also present identifying information on the author (called the *byline*) and the course (when the paper is submitted as part of a course requirement). The title, author information, and course information should be centered on the page and evenly spaced. (see Lindy's title page on p. 295).

Abstract

The second page of your paper will include an abstract that briefly summarizes the essential content (about one hundred words long). The APA manual points out that an abstract should be accurate, self-contained, concise and specific, nonevaluative, coherent, and readable. From your abstract, a reader should get a clear sense of the information covered by your paper. The abstract is typed in a one-paragraph block with no paragraph indentations (see Lindy's abstract on p. 296).

Text

The text of your research paper begins on page 3. (The page number appears along with the manuscript page header in the upper right-hand corner.) Type the title, centered, in uppercase and lowercase letters. Double space after the title.

Introduction

The text of your paper should open with an introduction that makes a commitment to the reader about what is to come in the paper. A good introduction should lead the reader into the paper and usually concludes with your thesis statement. There is no need to label the introduction; just begin it immediately after your title.

Body

The body of your paper should flow logically and follow the organization set up by your outline. You may wish to divide your paper visually by using headings and subheadings. Such headings can help your reader to visually ascertain the importance of topics within your paper and their relationship to other topics covered. Your headings function much as an outline would, that is, they provide your reader with a sense of your paper's organizational structure.

The APA manual describes five levels of headings and subheadings. However, the manual suggests using just one or two levels for short papers such as your research paper. When using one level of headings, center your headings in the middle of the page (double spaced above and below), and use uppercase and lowercase letters. When using two levels of headings, use centered headings (uppercase and lowercase) for the main headings and use side headings (flush with the left margin), underlined or italicized, for the subheadings:

`What is Being Done?`   *Main heading*

`Government`   *Subheading*

See the sample student paper at the end of the chapter for an example of using one level of headings and the student paper on pp. 295–308 for an example of two levels of headings.

References Page

The references page is a listing of all the articles and books you refer to in the body of your paper. Your reference to source information in your paper helps support your own ideas and conclusions by relating them to other authors' ideas and conclusions. Each author you cite in the text of your paper (in-text citations) must appear on your reference list; similarly, each reference on your list must be cited in your text at some point. That is, do not list any sources you used for background reading but did not cite in the paper itself. These sources will be listed on your working bibliography, however, so your teacher will know the extent and breadth of your reading on the topic.

The reference list begins on a new page. Type the word "References" in upper- and lowercase letters, centered at the top of the page. Double space the entire references page.

The APA format for references is presented in the following pages. If you have a source that is not modeled there, refer to the APA manual for the appropriate style.

Appendix

Sometimes additional information is included in an appendix to a paper. If you have conducted some primary research in connection with your project, for example, the data you collected may be presented in an appendix. However, you should include an appendix only if it will help your reader understand or evaluate something that you have discussed or presented in your paper.

DOCUMENTATION IN SOCIAL SCIENCE: THE AUTHOR/DATE STYLE (APA)

In the social sciences, the author/date method of documentation is standard. This format is outlined in *The Publication Manual of the American Psychological Association*, 5th ed., Washington, DC: American Psychological Association, 2001. The citations are included in the text and thus help the reader identify authorities and the dates of the research immediately. This form of documentation is particularly useful when you are citing books and articles but are not quoting or paraphrasing from them.

Internal Citation

At the appropriate place in the text, give the author's name, followed by a comma, a space, and the year of publication:

> The therapist's goals sometimes cannot be
> reached because of the complex and diverse wants
> and needs of the child and his family (Rapoport,
> 1997).

As an alternative to prevent monotony and improve readability, you can give the author's name in the text occasionally, supplying only the year in parentheses:

> As Rapoport (1997) points out, the therapist's
> goals may conflict with the needs and wants of the
> patient and his family.

When continuing to cite the same study within a paragraph, it is not necessary to keep repeating the date, as long as there are no other studies by authors with the same name with which it could be confused:

> In a study on e-waste, Smith (1998) found . . .
> Smith also describes . . .

For paraphrases and direct quotations, follow the date with a page number:

> "Certainly our society has not confronted the
> problem at hand" (Hacking, 1995, p. 73).

If your source has two authors, list the surnames of both authors:

> Schizophrenic patients are often children of
> high intelligence (Woodman & Groen, 1987).

If your source has three, four, or five authors, list all authors the first time a reference occurs; in subsequent citations (and in citations to sources with six or more authors), use the first author's name with "et al." (abbreviation for Latin *et alii*, "and others"):

First citation:

(Giedd, Kumra, Jacobsen, & Smith, 1998)

Subsequent citation:

(Giedd et al., 1998)

If there is no author's name, use either the title or an abbreviated form of the title.

("Electronics," 2003)

If you have two authors with the same last name, use first initials:

(M. Woodman, 1989) . . . (J. Woodman, 1991)

If you have two or more works by the same author published in the same year, identify them in the text with lowercase letters using the following format:

(Bettelheim, 1993a) . . . (Bettelheim, 1993b)

If you wish to cite several articles within the same parentheses, arrange the authors' names alphabetically and use a semicolon to separate the entries:

Several studies (Werry, 1996; Geidd et al.,

1998; Sullivan & Qualley, 1994) show the effects

of childhood schizophrenia on the family.

Personal correspondence, memos, lecture notes, email, postings from electronic bulletin boards, and the like are cited in the text itself but not listed on the references page. Provide initials and surname of correspondent, plus the type of correspondence and the date.

H. J. Miller (personal communication, April,

1999)

The Reference List in APA Style

The reference list, at the end of the research paper, contains all the sources actually used in the paper. When you use this documentation style, it is titled "References" or "Works Cited." The purpose of the reference list is to help readers find the materials you used in writing your paper. You must give complete and accurate information so that others may find the works. The following principles are generally accepted in documenting social science works, although many social science journals and fields have their own particular method of documenting. These guidelines have been adopted by the American Psychological Association (APA) in its style manual.

1. Give the author's surname and initials, followed by the date (in parentheses), the title, and the publication information.
2. The publication information required is place and name of publisher and date for books; date, volume and issue number, and page numbers for articles.
3. Place periods after the three main divisions: author, title, and publication information. Within these divisions, use commas to separate information.
4. Use uppercase letters for the first word only of a book or article title or following a colon in a subtitle. Capitalize all main words in journal titles.
5. Italicize titles of books, journals, magazines, and newspapers. Also italicize volume numbers in journal references.

MODEL REFERENCES: SOCIAL SCIENCE (APA)

Type of Reference

BOOKS

1. One author

   Cantor, S. (1988). *Childhood schizophrenia*. New
      York: Guilford Press.

2. Two or more authors

   Hamilton, L., & Rimland, B. (2000). *Facing autism:*
      Giving parents reasons for hope and guidance
      for help. Blaine, WA: Waterbrook Press.

3. Two or more books by the same author

Bruch, H. (1973). *Eating disorders: Obesity, anorexia nervosa, and the person within.* New York: Basic Books.

Bruch, H. (1978). *The golden cage: The enigma of anorexia nervosa.* Cambridge, MA: Harvard University Press.

[Note: References are in chronological order.]

4. Book with editor(s)

Warloe, C. F. (Ed.). (1997). *I've always meant to tell you: Letters to our mothers.* New York: Simon & Schuster.

5. Essay, chapter, or section of an edited work

Cherns, A. (1982). Social research and its diffusion. In B. Appleby (Ed.), *Papers on social science utilisation* (pp. 316–326). Leicestershire, England: Loughborough University of Technology, Centre for Utilisation of Social Science Research.

6. Encyclopedia entry

(signed)

Davidoff, L. (1984). Childhood psychosis. In *The encyclopedia of psychology* (Vol. 10, pp. 156–157). New York: J. Wiley & Sons.

(unsigned)

Schizophrenia. (1983). In *The encyclopedic
dictionary of psychology* (Vol. 8, pp.
501-502). Cambridge, MA: MIT Press.

7. Corporate author

American Psychiatric Association. (1996).
*Diagnostic and statistical manual of
mental disorders* (4th ed.). Washington, DC:
Author.

[Note: The word "Author" at the end of the entry indicates that
the author and publisher are the same.]

ARTICLES

1. Journal article (one author)

Coyle, B. (1999). Practical tools for rural
psychiatric practice. *Bulletin of the
Menninger Clinic, 2,* 202-222.

2. Journal article (two authors)

Steinhausen, H., & Glenville, K. (1983). Follow-up
studies of anorexia nervosa: A review of
research findings. *Psychological Medicine,
13*(2), 239-245.

3. Journal article (three to six authors)

Garfinkle, P., Garner, D., Schwartz, D., &
Thompson, M. (1980). Cultural expectations of
thinness in women. *Psychological Reports, 13,*
483-491.

4. Magazine article (discontinuous pages, monthly)

Ceci, S. (2001, August). Intelligence: The surprising
truth. *Psychology Today, 8,* 50-61, 70-72.

5. Magazine article (no known author, weekly)

The sky will fall in 2016. (2001, August 6). *Time,*
158(5), 15-17.

6. Newspaper article (no author)

Eight APA journals initiate controversial blind
reviewing. (1972, June 10). *APA Monitor,* p. 1.

7. Newspaper article (discontinuous pages)

Lublin, J. S. (1980, December 5). On idle: The
unemployed shun much mundane work, at least for
awhile. *The Wall Street Journal,* pp. A1, A25.

TECHNICAL REPORTS

1. Individual author

Gottfredson, L. S. (1980). *How valid are*
occupational reinforcer pattern scores?
(Report No. CSOS-R-292). Baltimore, MD: Johns
Hopkins University, Center for Social
Organization of Schools (ERIC Document
Reproduction Service No. ED182465).

2. Corporate author

Life Insurance Marketing and Research Association.
(1978). *Profit and the AIB in United States*
ordinary companies (Research Rep. No. 1978-6).
Hartford, CT: Author.

3. Government document

National Institute of Mental Health. (1982).

Television and behavior: Ten years of
scientific progress and implications in the
eighties (DHHS Publication No. ADM 82-1195).
Washington, DC: U.S. Government Printing
Office.

OTHER SOURCES

1. Film or videotape

Maas, J. B. (Producer), & Gluck, D. H. (Director).
(1979). *Deeper into hypnosis* [Film]. Englewood
Cliffs, NJ: Prentice Hall.

2. Abstracted dissertation (in *Dissertation Abstracts;* second example,
obtained from University Microfilms International).

Foster-Havercamp, M. E. (1982). An analysis of the
relationship between preservice teacher training
and directed teacher performance (Doctoral
dissertation, University of Chicago, 1981).
Dissertation Abstracts International, 42, 4409A.

Pendar, J. E. (1982). Undergraduate psychology
majors: Factors influencing decision about
college, curriculum and career. *Dissertation*
Abstracts International, 42, 4370A-4371A. *(UMI*
No. 8206181)

3. Unpublished manuscript

Cameron, S. E. (1991). *Educational level as a*
predictor of success. Unpublished manuscript.

[Note: You may also wish to cite a university affiliation for such works.]

4. Unpublished data

```
Locke, C. (1993). [Survey of college women at
     Texas Tech University]. Unpublished raw data.
```

5. Review of book or film

```
Carmody, T. P. (1982). A new look at medicine from
     the social perspective [Review of the film
     Social contexts of health, illness, and patient
     care]. Contemporary Psychology, 27, 208-209.
```

6. Interview

(published)

```
Newman, P. (1982, January). [Interview with William
     Epstein, editor of JEP: Human Perception and
     Performance]. APA Monitor, pp. 7, 39.
```

(unpublished)

```
Hult, C. (1994, March). [Interview with Dr. George
     Emert, President, Utah State University].
```

7. Personal correspondence

Do not list personal correspondence on the references page. See the in-text citation sample on p. 281.

8. Paper presented at conference

```
Winkler, I. (1999, October). Auditory and phonetic
     representations of isolated vowels. Paper
     presented at the Society for Psychophysiologi-
     cal Research, Granada, Spain.
```

9. Television program

```
Miller, R. (Producer). (1982, May 21). Problems of

    freedom. [Television broadcast]. New York:

    NBC-TV.
```

ELECTRONIC MEDIA

The electronic documentation formats found in the *Publication Manual of the American Psychological Association,* 5th ed., illustrate the use of a retrieval statement to direct readers to the electronic source.

When citing electronic media, use the standard APA format to identify authorship, date of origin (if known), and title, just as for print material; place information about the electronic format in a retrieval statement at the end of the entry. (In case your instructor has a distinct preference as to how to list source data from online computer networks, confirm the details of electronic citation before submitting a final paper.)

1. Email communication

   Email communication from individuals should be cited as personal communication within the text and is not included in the references list. The in-text citation is formatted as follows:

   L. L. Meeks provided researchers with the pertinent information regarding teacher training (personal communication, May 2, 2000).

2. Web sites

   When referring to an entire Web site (as opposed to a specific document or page on the site), it is sufficient to give the address of the Web site within the text itself. Such a reference is not included in the references list.

   Patricia Jarvis's homepage includes a great deal of information about recent archaeological digs in the Great Basin (http://www.asu.edu/students).

3. Specific document on a Web site

```
McCarthy, B. (1997). Reflections on the Past—

    Antiques. Retrieved January 20, 1998, from the
```

```
Resources for Victorian Living Web site:
http://www.victoriana.com
```

4. Article in an online work that duplicates a printed work

```
Women in American History. (1998). In Encyclopaedia
    Britannica. Retrieved May 25, 1998, from
    http://www.women.eb.com
```

5. Article in an online scholarly journal

```
Britt, R. (1995). The heat is on: Scientists agree
    on human contribution to global warming. Ion
    Science. Retrieved November 13, 1996, from
    http://www.injersey.com/Media/IonSci/
    features/gwarm
```

6. Article in a daily online newspaper or newswire

```
Schmitt, E. (1998, February 4). Cohen promises
    "significant" military campaign against Iraq
    if diplomacy fails. The New York Times on the
    Web. Retrieved from http://www.nytimes.com/
    archives
```

[Note: When the date of retrieval is the same as the publication date, it is not necessary to reprint it in the retrieval statement.]

7. Article in an online magazine

```
Thakker, S. (1998, May). Avoiding automobile
    theft. Ontario Police Crime Prevention
    Magazine. Retrieved May 26, 1998,
    from http://www.opcpm.com/inside/
    avoidingautomobile.html
```

8. Online posting

Although unretrievable communication such as email is not included in an APA references list, somewhat more public or accessible Internet postings from newsgroups or listservs may be included.

```
Heilke, J. (1996, May 3). Webfolios. Alliance for

    Computers and Writing Discussion List.

    Retrieved December 21, 1996, from

    http://www.ttu.edu/lists/acw-1/9605/0040.html
```

EXERCISES AND RESEARCH PROJECT

Follow the procedures outlined in this chapter to research a social science topic and write a research paper. The four exercises that follow give you additional practice in skills associated with social science research projects.

1. For each entry on your research paper bibliography, write a three- or four-sentence annotation describing the contents of that source.

2. Write a review of the literature that summarizes in three to four pages the major ideas found in your sources. Often, a literature review, which lists and comments on the work to date in a particular area, is a component of a larger social science paper.

3. Write a report that details a primary research project and summarizes your findings. Use tables or graphs where possible to illustrate your results.

4. After you have completed your research paper, write an abstract of about one hundred words that succinctly summarizes what your paper is about. An abstract should accurately reflect the scope and organization of your paper.

DISCIPLINE-SPECIFIC RESOURCES
FOR SOCIAL SCIENCE

Social scientists were among the first to realize that technology could help them with their research and writing. As a student of the social sciences, you too should familiarize yourself with the available resources, particularly those in library databases and on the Internet. (Chapter 2 discusses types of library and Internet resources and how to use them.) An extended listing of useful Internet sites for the social sciences follows. Take a look, for example, at the *Social Research* site, which has many links to general social science information on the Internet. There are also numerous discussion groups, bulletin boards, and newsgroups related to the social sciences. You can find these discussion sites through an Internet search.

Resources for the social sciences

ANTHROPOLOGY
Dictionaries
Dictionary of Anthropology. Barfield, T. London: Blackwell, 1997. Information on anthropological topics.

Indexes and Abstracts
Abstracts in Anthropology
Anthropological Index Online

Web Sites
American Anthropology Association <http://www.aaanet.org>
Institute of Social and Cultural Anthropology—University of Oxford <http://www.isca.ox.ac.uk//isca/index.html>

BUSINESS AND ECONOMICS
Dictionaries
American Dictionary of Economics. D. Auld and G. Bannock. New York. Facts on File, 1983. Short, factual information on economics.
Dictionary of Business. 3rd ed. P. H. Collins. Middlesex, England: Peter Collins, 2000. Defines key terms and explains major economic theories.

Indexes
ABI-INFORM
Public Affairs Information Services

Web Sites

Library of Congress Business Resource References <http://lcweb.loc.gov/rr/business/>

ETHNIC STUDIES

Indexes

Black Index: Afro-Americans in Selected Periodicals
Index to Periodical Articles by and about Negroes
Bibliography of Asian Studies

Web Sites

University of Texas Internet Resources for African American Studies <http://www.lib.utexas.edu/subject/african/afweb.html>
University of Georgia Institute for African American Studies <http://www.uga.edu/~iaas>
Asian Studies Resources <http://www.ibiblio.org/ucis/Asian.html>
University of Texas Asian Studies Network Information Center <http://asnic.utexas.edu/asnic/index.html>

EDUCATION

Dictionaries and Encyclopedias

Dictionary of Education. Goodman, F., ed. Phoenix: Oryx, 2000. Concise definitions of terminology in education.
Encyclopedia of Educational Research. 7th ed. Alkin, M., ed. New York: Macmillan, 2001. Excellent summaries of research in education.
International Encyclopedia of Education. Husen, T., and Postlethwaite, T. N., eds. New York: Pergamon, 1994. Background information on topics related to education beyond high school.

Indexes

ERIC on Disc
Resources in Education

Web Sites

Educator's Reference Desk <http://www.eduref.org>
Department of Education <http://www.www.ed.gov>

JOURNALISM AND COMMUNICATION

Abstracts

Journalism Abstracts

Web sites

CNN <http://www.cnn.com>
The New York Times on the Web <http://www.nytimes.com>
USA Today <http://www.usatoday.com>
Wall Street Journal <http://www.wsj.com>

POLITICAL SCIENCE
Almanacs, Dictionaries, and Encyclopedias

Congressional Quarterly Almanac. Washington: Cong. Quar., annual (1945-present). Summary of the activities of Congress, including voting records and major legislation.
Dictionary of Political Thought. Scrutin, R., ed. New York: Hill & Wang, 1984.
Encyclopedia of Policy Studies. Nagel, S., ed. Public Administration and Public Policy Services. New York: Dekker, 1994. Information about public policy issues.

Indexes and Abstracts

Public Affairs Information Service Bulletin
International Political Science Abstracts

Web Sites

Political Science Resources on the Web <http://www.lib.umich.edu/govdocs/polisci.html>

PSYCHOLOGY
Dictionaries and Encyclopedias

Dictionary of Psychology. 2nd ed. Chaplin, J. New York: Dell, 1985. Concise definitions of psychological terms.
Encyclopedia of Psychology. 3rd ed. Corsini, R., ed. New York: Wiley, 1996. An overview of important terms and concepts in psychology.
International Encyclopedia of Psychiatry, Psychology, and Psychoanalysis, and Neurology. Wolman, B. B., ed. New York: Van Nostrand, 1997. 12 vols. Concise information on psychology and related fields.

Indexes and Abstracts

Psychological Abstracts
PsycLit

Web Sites

A Guide to Psychology and its Practice <http://www.guidetopsychology.com>
American Psychological Association <http://www.apa.org>

SOCIOLOGY AND SOCIAL WORK

Encyclopedias

Encyclopedia of Sociology. Borgata, E. F., and Borgata, M. L., eds. New York: Macmillan, 1999. Terms, concepts, major ideas, major theorists in sociology.

Encyclopedia of Social Work. 19th expanded ed. Edwards, R. L., ed. New York: Natl. Assn. of Social Workers, 1995. General information on a variety of topics related to social work; includes both articles and biographies.

Indexes and Abstracts

Sociological Abstracts
Social Work Research and Abstracts

Web Sites

American Sociological Association <http://www.asanet.org>
Bureau of Justice Statistics <http://www.ojp.usdoj.gov/bjs>
Bureau of Labor Statistics <http://www.stats.bls.gov>
Statistical Abstract of the United States <http://www.census.gov/statab/www>

1

SAMPLE RESEARCH PAPER: SOCIAL SCIENCE FORMAT (APA)

The Problem of E-Waste

Lindy Danley

Utah State University

Environment and Society 3350-03

Professor Mark Bransom

2

Abstract

The new and exciting technology that
we all seem to be using poses a new
environmental hazard, that of electronic
waste that seems to be ending up in local
landfills. Because electronic products
often contain chemicals and other toxic
materials, such as lead, cadmium, mercury,
and so on, there is a growing concern
about these chemicals leaching into water
supplies from landfills. It is important
that a comprehensive program that
integrates manufacturers, consumers, and
governmental agencies, be developed to
deal with this increasing threat to our
environment.

3

The Problem of E-Waste

It was not long ago that the first personal computers were hitting the shelves of America. Now nearly every middle-class American sports a cell phone, laptop, pager, palm pilot, and all the necessary accessories. But these new toys wear out, and certainly many have already found their way into the local landfill. Unfortunately, the new exciting technology of this cyber age makes for a new, not so exciting, toxic pollution. The average PC contains such toxic materials as: cadmium, mercury, chlorine, bromine, chromium, and chlorofluorocarbons (Bartholomew, 2001), not to mention the five pounds of lead in a monitor tube (Stevens, 2001). These chemicals are of great concern because of the high potential of leaching into our groundwater while the products sit in our landfills (Electronics, 2003).

With the constant push for upgrades, the turnover for these products is high. It is estimated that 125 million PCs will fill the nation's landfills by 2010 (Bartholomew, 2001). In contrast to that

4

figure, in 1998, only 11% of the 20.6 million PCs discarded were recycled (Stevens, 2001). Such numbers are alarming, but most professionals predict that we have not seen the worst yet. Most e-waste is currently held up in closets or corners, meaning the real onslaught of these hazardous products has yet to hit (Bartholomew, 2001). Certainly our society has not confronted the problem at hand, nor formulated an appropriate plan of attack. Certain current practices need to be stopped, while a comprehensive program integrating the manufacturer, consumer, and government needs to be implemented to solve the e-waste crisis.

What is Being Done?

There are efforts to solve the problem of e-waste coming from government, the private sector, and industry. However, many problems remain to be solved.

Government

Currently there are weak government regulations attempting some control of the problem. Certain programs have been established to make the public more aware

5

of the problem and what they can do with their e-waste. Most of the programs stem from the EPA, or Environmental Protection Agency. But there is a significant lack of legislation actually requiring any action of users or distributors of e-waste. In July of 2002, a legislator from California presented an initiative to fund a project in which the EPA would set up computer recycling programs across the U.S. A fee attached to all computer sales would supplement the cost of the program. The EPA would also monitor state recycling efficiencies and the output across the United States (Federal, 2003). However, the initiative has not yet passed the California legislature.

Special Interest Groups

The most effective work in e-waste recycling is being done by special interest groups. Groups across the U.S. have spent time and money researching the best methods of recycling e-waste. One example of such a group is the "Electronic Recycler's Pledge of True Stewardship." This group is made up of fifteen

6

electronic recycling firms and several
environmental groups. Their aim is to
bring attention to the lack of action by
government and electronic manufacturers.
The group also researches solutions and
sustainable methods of dealing with
the "e-waste crisis" (Electronics,
2003).

Private Enterprise

Many believe that the solution to the
e-waste problem lies in the private sector
of our economy. An excellent example of
one such private enterprise is Technology
Recycling LLC. Bob Knowles started this
company in response to the growing amounts
of e-waste. He charges corporations 35
dollars per computer, after which disabled
workers disassemble the computers. The
machine parts are then sent to different
EPA approved facilities for recycling.
Finally, the company gives its clients
proof of the recycling. These proofs can
be used as tax deductions, giving an extra
incentive for users to recycle (Maxwell,
2000).

7

Manufacturers

The fastest growing target of blame for e-waste is the manufacturers of electronic equipment. Many manufacturers and engineers of electronics are being criticized for the product's lack of sustainability, meaning that most products have a limited life. Products are designed to be engineered and reproduced as quickly as possible with little thought to any reusability (Bursky, 2000). Fortunately, some manufacturers are taking the responsibility to make their products easier to recycle and reuse. Many of these are computer producers such as Dell, Compaq, Hewlett Packard, and Apple. The necessary steps are being taken to make their products reusable, as well as offering take-back services to the public (Industry, 2003).

Foreign Dumping

Unfortunately, the idea of recycling e-waste in the U.S. and other developed countries has often been translated into shipping the products to 3rd world countries. This practice has resulted in

8

an extreme pile up of our waste in
countries such as China and India. This
recycling method was brought to our
attention in the report "Exporting Harm:
The High-Tech Trashing of Asia," by BAN
and SVTC in 2002. The report stated that
50 to 80% of e-waste collected for
recycling in North America was actually
sent to 3rd world countries. This waste
was then dumped in the environment,
causing toxic pollution and health hazards
to the people of those countries
(Electronics, 2003).

Possible Solutions

The pollution of e-waste is a threat
to the global citizen's health. Like any
hazardous threat due to pollution, the
solution will come from responsible
actions of all involved in the increasing
mass of e-waste. Indeed, a collaborative
effort will be required if this issue is
to be solved.

Government Participation

The first action against e-waste must
come from the government. Laws requiring
actual recycling of the equipment will

9

prevent the products from being simply dumped into landfills. Of course, the actual recycling process will also have to be strictly monitored and regulated. Governmental agencies, such as the EPA, would oversee the use, manufacture, and private recycling of these products. Such practices as shipping our e-waste to developing countries could be prevented and sustainable and economic practices should be expected at all levels of technology manufacturing, use, and afterlife.

Collaboration

The best and most efficient method of recycling technology equipment is a dilemma that can be answered only through careful study and analysis. Possible solutions could stem from practices already in use in the free market. One of these involves placing the recycling responsibility on the consumers. Required recycling of common hazards, such as oil and car batteries, is currently in place and readily accepted. In the situation of e-waste, users would be required to take

10

the products to private or public
recycling centers. By law, the users would
be required to recycle and possible tax
deductions could be an added incentive. If
recycling occurs through private markets,
a whole new sector of the economy is
opened with the emergence of new jobs and
opportunities.

Manufacturer Responsibility

Although the consumer and recycling
center solution offers many advantages,
there is one part of the equation absent.
Equal, or perhaps more, weight should be
placed on the actual manufacturers of the
equipment. Instead of taking the
equipment directly to the recycling
centers, users should be able to take
back the equipment to the actual
manufacturer. The manufacturers are then
responsible to either repair and reuse
the obsolete equipment or pay the cost of
a private or in-house recycling center.
Certainly as manufacturers become
responsible for the after-life of their
designs, they will have an incentive to
design a product that can be "recycled

11

more efficiently" (Electronics, 2003).
This new incentive will hopefully produce
a less toxic product and a more
sustainable technology.

Examples of Manufacturer Stewardship

Manufacturer recycling and take-back
practices are already being implemented in
the technology world. Private enterprises
such as Technology Recycling LLC have seen
great success as they provide services to
large scale and small scale users. Other
private companies have pioneered the idea
of take-back for manufacturers. Best Buy
was the first company to offer recycling
services to their customers. They offered
collection events at ten different sites,
which resulted in 250,000 pounds of
equipment being recycled in one take back
event. Other companies such as Compaq,
participate in product stewardship
throughout the life of their products.
Their engineers carefully design to
provide the least amount of environmental
damage potential within the product and
maximum ease for recycling of the product.
Compaq has also established a take back

12

program in which customers are rewarded a
discount on future purchases as they
return obsolete equipment. Such companies
are exemplary in achieving the level of
responsibility and stewardship that is
required to solve the dilemma of e-waste
(Federal, 2003).

Conclusion

Certainly the solution to e-waste is
within the public's grasp. The hazards are
large enough to call considerable
attention to the situation. With the
education and cooperation of all involved,
our obsession with technology will not
lead to destruction of our vital
resources. The progressiveness of modern
times will only be progressive if we have
the collective foresight to take
responsibility and true stewardship for
the technology of today.

Links to More Information

If you are interested in learning
more about the e-waste problem or what you
can personally do, please visit the
following links:

13

- http://www.epa.gov/
- http://www.svtc.org/

References

Bartholomew, D. (2001, March). Where have
    all the PCs gone? *Industry Week,*
    250(3), 34. Retrieved February 27,
    2003, from http://search.epnet.com/
    direct.asp?an=4213920&db=afh

Bursky, D. (2000, January). Rethink your
    designs to keep our planet green.
    Electronic Design, 48(2), 44.
    Retrieved February 27, 2003, from
    http://search.epnet.com/direct.asp?an
    =2751259&db=afh

Electronics recyclers pledge: No export,
    no dumping, no prisons. (March,
    2003). *Silicon Valley Toxics*
    Initiative. Retrieved March 2, 2003,
    from http://www.svtc.org/media/
    releases/2003/ctbc225_pledge.htm

Federal initiatives. (2003, March).
    Environmental Protection Agency.
    Retrieved March 2, 2003, from
    http://www.epa.gov/epr/products/
    efed.html

14

Industry initiatives. (2003, March).

Environmental Protection Agency.

Retrieved March 2, 2003, from

http://www.epa.gov/epr/products/eindu

st.html

Maxwell, J. H. (2000, March). P.C.s. *Inc,*

22(4), 25. Retrieved February 27,

2003, from http://search.epnet.com/

direct.asp?an=2901593&db=afh

Stevens, M. (2001, June). Old boxes pose

hazard. *EWeek, 18(24),* 62. Retrieved

February 27, 2003, from http://

search.epnet.com/direct.asp?an=474557

5&db=afh

NOTES

1. Stanley Milgram, *Obedience to Authority: An Experimental View* (New York: Harper & Row, 1974).

2. Milgram, p. 6.

3. Sigmund Freud, *Civilization and Its Discontents,* edited and translated by James Strachey (New York: W. W. Norton, 1961).

4. Freud, p. 62.

5. Jacques Barzun and Henry F. Graff, *The Modern Researcher,* rev. ed. (New York: Harcourt Brace and World, 1970), p. 245.

6. Kenneth D. Bailey, *Methods of Social Research,* 2nd ed. (New York: The Free Press, 1992).

7. Patricia Labaw, *Advanced Questionnaire Design.* (Cambridge, MA: ABT Books, 1981) p. 35.

8. Floyd J. Fowler, Jr. *Survey Research Methods,* 2nd ed. (Newberry Park, CA: Sage Publications, 1993) p. 57.

9. Labaw, p. 134.

10. Labaw, p. 154.

11. I am indebted to Professor John Deethardt of the Texas Tech University Speech Communications Department for passing on to me this assignment and student response.

9

Writing a Research Report in Business

INTRODUCTION

In business, writers often produce research reports in order to become "experts" on particular topics and to communicate that expertise to other concerned individuals. The businessman or woman must have knowledge of the business world in general and should be familiar with library tools used by those in business to gain access to current information in the field.

In the business report, your task is to summarize for your readers the present situation in a particular field or market. Your contribution, then, is to interpret and organize the information you find, thus making it easily accessible to your readers. Generally, in a business report, through paraphrase and summary, you are reporting on the information you discovered in your research as objectively as you can.

Some business research reports use primary research, such as marketing reviews, surveys, technical studies, or computer data. For many business research projects, library research is also involved. The following library research principles and skills will be important for you as you investigate your chosen topic:

1. Familiarity with library resources, including bibliographies and indexes used in business.
2. The ability to understand and evaluate data from a variety of sources.

3. The ability to paraphrase and summarize information in your own words.
4. The ability to synthesize the information gathered into an organized presentation of the data.
5. The ability to employ the formal conventions of business reports.

THE INQUIRY PROCESS IN BUSINESS

Since many business researchers also have as their overall goal the systematic study of human behavior, business research has adopted many of the inquiry processes used in the social sciences. Also like the social sciences, business has adopted much of the scientific method—its goals, procedures, and standards. Many business researchers today study people and systems using the scientific method: they develop hypotheses and design and conduct controlled experiments to test those hypotheses. Some businesses even establish their own in-house laboratories to conduct scientific research that may prove relevant to new product development. In the business arena, this kind of research is often called *Research and Development*, or *R&D*. Although the objective of academic research is typically to obtain new knowledge, the objective of R&D is "to obtain new knowledge *applicable to the company's business needs,* that eventually will result in new or improved products, processes, systems, or services that can increase the company's sales and profits."[1]

Three Types of R&D

According to the National Science Foundation (NSF), there are three types of R&D: basic research, applied research, and development. Basic research seeks to increase understanding of a subject without specific regard to its application; applied research is aimed directly at meeting a specific business need; development is the systematic use of the knowledge gained by both the basic and applied research. However, the distinctions between these three types of research are often blurred: some companies rely heavily on research for the eventual development and deployment of new products, while others rely on research that has been generated in the public domain but conduct little basic research themselves. As technology becomes increasingly proprietary, more companies have had to develop their own R&D operations.

[1]Information for this section of the chapter is adapted from John G. Maurer, Joel M. Schulman, Marcia L. Ruwe, and Richard D. Becherer, "Research and Development," "Organizational Theory," "Sales Forecasting," and "Marketing Strategy," in *The Encyclopedia of Business* (New York: Gale Research, 1995).

Other Types of Business Research

Marketing Research

Business researchers also study the behavior of people who make up particular markets. They analyze markets to come up with effective marketing strategies that will optimize the sales of their product or service. Marketing strategies are often developed using computer technologies that apply marketing models and concepts.

Organizational Research

A business researcher attempting to discover rules and conventions within organizational structures is somewhat analogous to a natural scientist attempting to discover laws of nature. Based on such studies, researchers have posited organizational theories that explain the dynamics within business organizations. Much of this research is based on "human factors," that is, the human influences that result in changes within an organization. The focus on human interaction was articulated most productively in Maslow's "hierarchy of human needs," which was also integrated into organizational theory (Maurer et al. 1113). Though organizations differ greatly, they all have in common the features of a division of labor, a structure for making decisions, and a system of policies or procedures. Businesspeople try to take into account all that is currently known about organizational theory when making decisions about a company.

QUESTIONS FOR DISCUSSION

1. What is the general goal of inquiry in business?

2. What is R&D, and what kind of research is conducted in an R&D effort?

3. Describe some other kinds of business research.

PRIMARY RESEARCH IN BUSINESS

Just as the social sciences have incorporated many of the research techniques of the sciences, so the field of business has adopted many of the research techniques and methods of the social sciences. The types of research questions commonly asked in business situations have immediate and practical consequences: Should Company A take on a new product? How can Company B improve its image? How well do customers understand the sales offer of Company C? Does bottle color affect customer perception of beer taste? Such questions arise out of particular business needs and concerns. But to answer these questions, researchers use familiar research techniques.

For example, if Company A wants to know whether it should take on a new product, it might conduct a consumer survey using questionnaires or interviews to ascertain the market potential. Company A might also wish to compare the market shares of competitors and perhaps field-test its product with samples to consumers, monitoring their reactions. Or if a company wishes to discover whether bottle color influences perceptions of the taste of beer, an experimental design (using taste tests) might be in order. These research techniques should sound familiar, since they are those customarily employed in the social sciences: surveys, questionnaires, interviews, and experiments.

Researchers in business, just like their counterparts in the social sciences, are especially interested in statistical compilations of information to help with decision making. There are many government and corporate agencies that provide information to researchers in business. For example, Table 9-1, produced by the U.S. Department of Commerce, might be of interest to businesspeople in the grocery business.

Presenting Business Information

Much of the research information in business is presented in the form of tables, graphs, flow charts, or diagrams for easy access. The flow chart, in Figure 9-1, for example, outlines the process by which a researcher in business would conduct a skills survey. The purpose of such a survey would be to determine the level of employees' skills, knowledge, and ability so that they could be utilized more fully to meet the employment objectives and the staffing needs of a particular organization. As you look over the flow chart, notice its similarity to the five research steps outlined previously for the social sciences: formulating a problem or hypothesis, developing a research design, gathering data, analyzing results, and interpreting results.

Conducting a Survey in Business

Mike Smith, a student in business administration, encountered a problem at his place of employment and decided to investigate the extent of the problem by conducting a survey. As a line supervisor at a computer manufacturing plant, Mike had become aware that the workers he supervised were under considerable occupational stress. He wondered just what the origins of that stress were and how the workers were coping with it. First, Mike defined the problem: line workers at Bourn Enterprises seemed to be working under considerable occupational stress. Second, Mike designed a survey questionnaire and tested

TABLE 9-1 Weekly Food Cost for Families, by Type of Family: 1975 to 1988 (in dollars, as of December, except as indicated. Based on moderate-cost food plan; assumes all meals are eaten at home or taken from home)

Urban Family Type	1975	1980	1981	1982	1983	1984	1985	1986	1987	1988 Jan.	1988 May
Couple, 25–54 years old*	37.10	52.00	53.40	54.60	54.70	56.50	58.30	60.40	63.50	63.90	64.20
Couple, 55 years and over*	32.40	45.90	47.10	48.10	52.00	53.90	55.70	57.80	60.70	61.40	61.70
Couple with children:											
1 child, 1–5 years old	44.90	62.90	64.70	66.00	66.90	69.20	71.30	73.90	77.50	78.10	78.60
1 child, 15–19 years old	53.50	74.80	76.80	78.50	77.80	80.50	83.00	85.50	90.10	90.90	91.40
2 children, 1–5 years old	51.80	72.60	74.70	76.20	77.80	80.50	82.90	85.80	90.00	90.70	91.40
2 children, 6–11 years old	63.00	88.10	90.70	92.60	93.50	97.10	99.80	103.30	108.30	109.20	110.00
2 children, 12–19 years old	67.20	93.80	96.50	98.60	98.00	101.60	104.60	108.20	113.50	114.50	115.20

*Beginning 1983, costs based on revised food plans with age groups 25–50 years old and 51 years old and over.
Source: *Statistical Abstract of the United States*, 1989. U.S. Department of Commerce, Bureau of the Census (Washington, DC: Government Printing Office, p. 100.)

Reprinted from U.S. Dept. of Agriculture, Human Information Service, *News*, monthly.

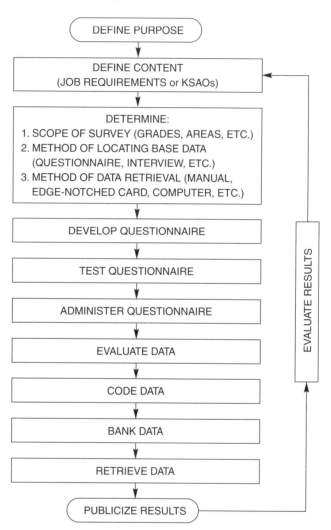

Skills Survey Process Flow Chart

FIGURE 9-1   Skills Survey

Source: U.S. Civil Service Composition, *The Skills Survey: What It Is and How It Works* (Washington, DC: U.S. Government Printing Office, October 1977), p. 24.

it on ten workers at Bourn in order to refine the questions and eliminate any ambiguities. Mike then gathered his data by having sixty-nine of the line workers at Bourn write their answers to nine questions before their work shifts began. Then, once his data was gathered, Mike began to analyze it by compiling the results on each question (see below).

Mike presented the information gathered in his survey to his business administration class in the form of an oral report.

In his data analysis, Mike pointed to the high percentage of his sample who felt stressed because of work: 82%. Responses to question 7 yielded some explanations of where that job stress originated. Respondents mentioned their job duties and tasks as the number-one cause of their work stress. In follow-up interviews, Mike learned that many of the workers felt stressed by the repetitive nature of their work tasks and by the limited variety and lack of creativity in their jobs.

Respondents mentioned their supervisors as the second largest reason for stress on the job. Mike speculated that there is often a lack of communication between line workers and supervisors, causing a disparity between what the supervisor expects and what the worker is attempting to perform. Respondents listed equally stress from machines and stress from coworkers. Having to put up with machines that are broken or under repair is a frustrating stressor for production workers. Similarly, workers who have trouble getting along with others will find their job situation stressful. Again, Mike pointed to the need for supervisors to encourage communication between themselves and workers and among coworkers.

The respondents to Mike's survey also listed their three main ways of coping with stress in the workplace: relaxation, exercise, and talking to coworkers. Interestingly, the majority (70%) of the respondents all indicated that they thought a certain amount of stress was beneficial because it could motivate them to do better. Mike concluded from this survey that rather than eliminating stress altogether, the workplace goal probably should be to lessen unproductive stress and to provide an outlet for excessive stress through relaxation breaks, exercise programs, and effective communication.

Questionnaire Results
(69 people were surveyed)

1. Average years of service = 27 months
2. Average time assigned to present task = 47 weeks
3. Percentage of respondents who are main source of income for their household = 44%
4. The three main reasons for working: a. money; b. benefits; c. diversity of life (something to do)
5. Percentage of respondents who feel stress because of work = 82%
6. Percentage of respondents who feel stress: a. At work: 60%; b. At home: 34%; c. Neither: 6%
7. Three main stressors at work: a. job duties (assigned tasks and responsibilities); b. supervisors; c. machines and coworkers (equal number of responses)

8. Three ways to cope with stress: a. relaxation; b. exercise; c. talking
9. Percentage of respondents who think stress is beneficial = 70%

QUESTIONS FOR DISCUSSION

1. What was Mike's purpose in conducting the survey?

2. What is the nature of the workplace problem Mike described?

3. Do you think the information Mike gathered is representative, complete, accurate, fair? Why or why not?

4. Do you agree with Mike's suggested solutions to the problem of workplace stress? Do you have other suggestions?

5. Have you experienced workplace stress yourself? Does your experience correspond with that described in Mike's report? How is it similar or different?

EXERCISES

To practice some of the research techniques we have been discussing in this chapter so far, prepare a written proposal to an employer or organization outlining a study of current procedures. The outcome of this assignment could be the proposal itself, or you could follow up the proposal by actually conducting the study described and reporting on its results.

1. Think of a problem or question about work procedures that arose at a current or previous place of employment. Describe as clearly as you can the nature of the organization where you were employed and the specifics of the problem or question. Perhaps your employer implemented a new procedure that caused workers to lose productivity (drive-in workers at a fast-food restaurant being required to wash their hands after serving each car, for example); or perhaps your coworkers are taking long coffee breaks in an effort to evade the work; or maybe the scissors at the fabric store where you work are never kept sharp enough to cut the cloth cleanly, resulting in waste.

2. Write a short proposal in the form of a memorandum to the logical recipient (supervisor, employer, business owner). In your memorandum, outline the problem and propose a study to determine the exact nature and extent of the problem in an effort to discover an acceptable solution. For the coffee break example, you might propose to your employer an anonymous observation by an unbiased observer of length of coffee breaks. Or, for the ex-

ample of dull scissors, you might propose an experiment comparing the fabric remnants left over by one employee using a recently sharpened pair of scissors with those left by one whose scissors have not been sharpened.

3. (optional) Conduct the study proposed in 2 above. Write a short report in which you interpret the results of the study and draw conclusions from your data or make specific suggestions to the organization in question that will remedy the identified problem.

ORGANIZING AND WRITING THE BUSINESS REPORT

A major task in writing a business report is organizing the material you have gathered. It is your job to make sense of the information you have found and to present it logically for the reader in an objective, comprehensive manner. For this chapter, we will follow the research of Brent Lot, whose report on consumer privacy appears at the end of the chapter. When Brent narrowed his topic to consumer privacy, he decided to report on the state of consumer privacy: defining what it is and how it is protected, describing some applications to ensure privacy in business and industry, and indicating the future of consumer privacy. He outlined a preliminary plan that would cover these major sections, as follows:

Introduction to consumer privacy

Background

Main arguments in favor of protecting privacy

Counterarguments from business, which desires consumer information

Conclusion

After you have completed your outline, you are ready to write the first draft of your report. Remember, you are writing to report to your readers the current status of a particular issue or topic. Remind yourself at this time of your general understanding of your topic. When writing your first draft, use concrete and simple language to explain as objectively as you can your understanding of the topic. Your outline will guide the writing of this first draft.

As you write the first draft, it is important to note down which material comes from which sources. Do not be overly concerned at this point about the formal details of documentation, which can be dealt with later, but do mark for yourself in the draft any ideas or words you take from your sources. You should place any word or sentence you copy from a source in quotation marks, followed by the last name, the date of publication, and the page number of the source (in parentheses):

> "The drafter can produce finished drawings in much less time" (Stanton 1985, 3).

Similarly, document paraphrases and restatements of ideas taken from a source even though you have recast them in your own words:

> Reasons for the low cost include ease of setup and less user training (Teicholz and Smith 1987, 25).

When referring generally to a source, it is not necessary to provide a page reference:

> Zinsmeister (1987) reports that microCADD is used to test designs instead of building a costly prototype.

For general information on planning, writing, and revising your business report, refer to Chapters 4 and 5. Use the following information on documentation in business and economics for the correct form for citations. The sample research report at the end of this chapter can serve as a model for a business report.

DOCUMENTATION IN BUSINESS AND ECONOMICS

In business and economics, it is common to use the same general author/year system used in the social sciences. This system includes (1) in-text citations giving the author's name and the publication year of the source, and (2) an alphabetized list of references at the end of the paper.

Internal Citations

In business and economics, the citations within the text provide enough information to refer the reader to the complete list of references on the references page. The following principles should be observed:

1. When an author's work is cited in general, you list the author's name and the year of publication in parentheses at the end of the information or use the author's name to introduce the information:

   ```
   Today there are nearly 200 microCADD vendors

   (Goetsch 1988).

   Goetsch (1988) states that today there are

   nearly 200 microCADD vendors.
   ```

2. When an author's words or ideas are directly quoted or paraphrased, a page number should be included (without p.):

   ```
   User training takes "less than a month to

   learn" (Teicholz and Smith 1987, 25).
   ```

3. When a work has more than three authors, use "et al." ("and others") for the in-text citation. Thus, a work by Schulz, Chote, Horn, and VanDevener would be listed as follows:

   ```
   (Schulz et al. 1988)
   ```

4. When two or more references are given together, they are separated by semicolons:

   ```
   (Kalb 1987; Woodcock and Binsacca 1987)
   ```

5. When no author is given for a work, use the title of the sponsoring group or organization, such as (Federal Reserve Bank of Boston 1976); in the case of magazines, use an abbreviated form of the title (Applications still flood in 1983).

The Reference List

The reference list in business and economics (like that used in the social sciences) is an alphabetized list of all the sources actually cited in the paper. It is titled "References." The actual format of the entries differs somewhat from that used in the social sciences. The following principles are generally accepted in business and economics journals:

1. Authors are listed by complete name (when known) or by surname and initials.

2. Capitalize only the first word in the title of a magazine, newspaper, or journal article, and do not use quotation marks.
3. Names of books and journals are underlined. Names of journals may be abbreviated.
4. For books, the title is followed by the date, the place of publication, and the publisher.

```
Melman, Seymour. 1987. Our depleted society. New

     York: Dell Publishers.
```

5. For articles, the date, volume number, and the inclusive page numbers follow the name of the journal:

```
Powell, Gary N. 1983. Sexual harassment: Confront-

     ing the issue of Definition. Business Horizons

     9 (July-August): 24-28.
```

6. The first word of the entry is typed at the left margin. Subsequent lines of the same entry are indented five spaces. The entire reference page is double-spaced.

If you are writing a research paper for a class in business or economics, it is important to ask your instructor which documentation form he or she prefers. A style manual frequently used in business and industry is *The Chicago Manual of Style,* 15th ed., published by the University of Chicago Press (2003). You may wish to refer to this manual for your papers in business courses. The model references and sample paper below use the author/year style (and a few of the models) outlined in *The Chicago Manual.*

MODEL REFERENCES: BUSINESS AND ECONOMICS (CHICAGO)

Type of Reference

BOOKS

1. One author

```
Cole, Robert H. 1976. Consumer and commercial

     credit management. 5th ed. Homewood, IL:

     Irwin.
```

2. Two or more authors

> Weston, J. Fred, and Eugene F. Brightman. 1975.
> *Managerial finance.* 5th ed. New York: Dryden
> Press.

[Note: Include the names of all authors listed on the title page. Use "et al." only with in-text citations.]

3. Book with editor

> Rathe, Alex W., ed. 1961. *Gantt on management.* New
> York: American Management Association.

4. Essay, chapter, or section of edited work

> Ogilvy, David. 1965. The creative chef. In *The*
> *creative organization,* edited by Gary
> Steiner. Chicago: University of Chicago
> Press.

5. Corporate author

> International Monetary Fund. 1977. *Survey of*
> *African economies.* Vol. 7, *Algeria, Mali,*
> *Morocco, and Tunisia.* Washington, D.C.:
> International Monetary Fund.

ARTICLES

1. Journal article (one author)

> Boyer, Ernest. 1983. The recovery is shaping the
> economy. *Fortune* 108 (October): 60-65.

2. Journal article (two or more authors)

> Lear, Ronald, and C. Groneman. 1983. The corporate
> Ph.D.—humanities scholars bring new
> perspective to business problems. *Management*
> *Review* 72 (September): 32-33.

3. Journal and magazine (no known author)

> The applications still flood in, but slight rise
> in vacancies cheers graduate recruiters. 1983.
> *Personnel Management* 15, August, 12-13.

OTHER SOURCES

1. Dissertation or thesis

> King, Andrew J. 1976. Law and land use in Chicago:
> A pre-history of modern zoning. Ph.D. diss.,
> University of Wisconsin.

2. Paper presented at conference

> Saunders, Robert. 1983. Today's manager. Paper
> presented at the Annual Meeting of the
> American Institute of Industrial Engineers,
> New York, N.Y.

3. Personal communication (letters and interviews)

> Ewing, Nancy. 1985. Letter to author. 24 January.

> Hughes, Howard. 1970. Interview with author. Las
> Vegas, Nev., 15 July.

4. Public documents

> U.S. Department of Justice. Law Enforcement
> Assistance Administration. 1970. *Criminal*
> *justice agencies in Pennsylvania.* Washington,
> D.C.: GPO.

ELECTRONIC MEDIA

Because *The Chicago Manual of Style,* 15th ed. primarily covers citation formats for electronic journals with a print equivalent, researchers continue to adapt to new electronic formats by modifying some of the basic CMS conventions. Melvin E. Page of East Tennessee

State University has developed a CMS-based style sheet for citing Web sources and other online material <http://www2.h-net.msu.edu/~africa/citation.html>. This section reflects features of that style sheet, which has been recommended by I I-Net, a consortium of email lists. One feature of Page's proposed style is the convention of enclosing URLs within angle brackets. Another is the provision of any publicly recorded email addresses (but not privately recorded ones) as part of the author's identification. The date of posting, if available, follows the Internet address without parentheses; a date of access is provided when no date of posting is available.

1. Online professional or personal site

   ```
   Academic Info. "Humanities," <http://
       www.academicinfo.net/index.html>. 1998-2000.

   Trayor, Michelle "Michelle Trayor Data Services."
       <http://www.mtdsnet.com>, 1989-1998.
   ```

2. Electronic book

   ```
   Aristotle. Rhetoric. Trans. W. Rhys Roberts. New
       York: The Modern Library, 1954. The English
       Server (Carnegie Mellon Univ.), <http://
       www.rpi.edu/~honey/Rhetoric/index.html>.
       8 April 1997.
   ```

3. Electronic journal article

   ```
   Herz, J. C. "Surfing on the Internet: A Nethead's
       Adventures Online." Urban Desires 1.3 (1995),
       <http://www.desires.com>. 21 July 1996.
   ```

4. Electronic correspondence (email, bulletin boards, listservs)

   ```
   Heilke, James. "Webfolios,"
       <http://acw-lattacs.ttu.edu>. 3 May 1996.
       Archived at <http://www.ttu.edu/lists/acw-1/
       9605>.
   ```

Ellsworth, Peter. "WWW Devalues Writing."

<http://news.alt.prose>. 7 November 1997.

EXERCISES AND RESEARCH PROJECT

Complete the exercises in this chapter as you research and report on a business topic. The exercises below will give you additional practice with skills associated with business reports.

1. For each entry on your bibliography, write a three- or four-sentence annotation describing the contents of that source.

2. Write a review of the literature that summarizes in three to four pages the major ideas found in your sources. Often, a literature review, which lists and comments on the work to date in a particular area, is a component of a larger paper. The review of the literature proceeds in chronological order based on the publication date of the sources and thus will differ from the report itself, which may be organized around concepts or categories.

3. When you have finished writing your report, write a synopsis (fifty to one hundred words long) in which you summarize the main points of your paper. A *synopsis* is a brief, general condensation of the report. See the section on abstracts in Chapter 5.

4. When you have finished writing your report, write a table of contents for your report. See the model paper at the end of the chapter.

DISCIPLINE-SPECIFIC RESOURCES FOR BUSINESS AND ECONOMICS

Technology and Business

Like the social scientists, businesspeople were among the first to see that technology could help them with their research and their writing. Students of business should familiarize themselves with the available resources, particularly those on the Internet. Take a look, for example, at the *Business Resources on the Internet* site. Here you will find many links to general business information on the Web. There are also numerous discussion groups, bulletin boards, and newsgroups related to business. You can find these discussion sites through an Internet search. The list below provides useful Internet sites related to business.

Resources for Business

BUSINESS, GENERAL
Dictionaries and Encyclopedias
Dictionary of Accounting. 2nd ed. R. Hussey, ed. New York; Oxford UP, 1999.
Dictionary of Business. 3rd ed. P.H. Collins. Middlesex, England: Peter Collins, 2000.
Encyclopedia of Business Information Sources. 16th ed. Detroit: Gale, 2001.

Indexes and Abstracts
ABI-INFORM
Business Education Index
Business Index
Business Periodicals Index
Public Affairs Information Index (PAIS)

Web Sites
Business Ethics <http://www.ethics.ubc.ca/resources/business/>
Business Resources on the Internet <http://www2.gsu.edu/~librab/business/>
InfoWorld.com <http://www.infoworld.com>
International Business Resources on the WWW <http://globaledge.msu.edu/ibrd/ibrd.asp>
Library of Congress Business Resource References <http://lcweb.loc.gov/rr/business/>
MoreBusiness.com <http://www.morebusiness.com/>

ECONOMICS, COMPUTERS, AND TECHNOLOGY
Dictionaries and Encyclopedias
Mathematical Dictionary for Economics and Business Administration. W. Skarpek et al., eds. Boston: Allyn & Bacon, 1978.
Encyclopedia of Banking and Finance. 10th ed. C.J. Woelfel. New York: McGraw-Hill, 1996.

Indexes and Abstracts
Wall Street Journal Index
Index of Economic Articles

Web Sites
Byte Magazine <http://www.byte.com>
Electronic Frontier Foundation <http://www.eff.org.>
Internet Society <http://www.isoc.org.>
Internet.com <http://www.internet.com>
MIT Laboratory for Computer Science <http://www.lcs.mit.edu.>
Virtual Computer Library <http://www.utexas.edu/computer>

GOVERNMENT RESOURCES

Statistical Abstract of the United States, 1879–present (annual). Washington, DC:
U.S. Bureau of Census.

Web Sites

Bureau of the Census <http://www.census.gov>
Bureau of Justice Statistics <http://www.ojp.usdoj.gov/bjs>
Bureau of Labor Statistics <http://stats.bls.gov>
FedWorld <http://www.fedworld.gov>
Government Information Sharing Project <http://govinfo.kerr.orst.edu>
The Internal Revenue Service <http://www.irs.gov>
Library of Congress <http://lcweb.loc.gov>
Population Index <http://popindex.princeton.edu>
STAT-USA <http://www.stat-usa.gov/stat-usa.html>
Thomas (congressional legislation) <http://thomas.loc.gov>
Vote Smart <http://www.Vote-smart.org>

SAMPLE RESEARCH REPORT: BUSINESS AND ECONOMICS FORMAT (CHICAGO)

Consumer Privacy

Presented To:

Professor Susan Larsen

Business Information Systems 255

Presented By:

Brent Ito

2 December 2000

Contents

Title: Consumer Privacy

Introduction   2

Background   3

Protecting Privacy   5

Business Point of View   9

Conclusion   10

References   12

2

Introduction

How much is too much? That is, how much personal information do you think is appropriate for others, such as banks and retailers, to know about you? With the help of computers and recent technology, institutions such as banks and marketing companies collect detailed personal information to create profiles of or dossiers on the unknowing and oftentimes unwilling members of the public. These companies know our purchasing preferences, credit history, where we live, and how much income we earn. With the rapid rise of e-commerce on the Internet, combined with increasingly sophisticated data-mining software, retail stores can record every sale, banks can capture each push of the button on an ATM, and telephone companies can keep track of every phone call. Personal privacy is at risk as never before. According to John Markoff (1999), the author of *The Privacy Debate*, the emergence of government surveillance known as "Big Brother" during the '70s and '80s

3

has given way to the "Little Brother" of the '90s, the database administrator who has access to all the details of your life as a consumer.

Background

Personal identifying information, such as your name, email address, and postal address, along with demographic information, such as your gender, zip code, and preferences are being collected, shared, and even purchased through partnerships with companies that have access to this information without the knowledge or consent of the individual. According to the Georgetown Internet Privacy Policy Survey, a progress report to the Federal Trade Commission, 92.8% of the Web sites in its sample collected at least one type of personal identifying information. Fifty-six percent of the sites collected at least one type of demographic information. And 56.2% of the sites collected both personal identifying and demographic information (Culnan 2000). Surprisingly, only 6.6% of the sites collected neither type of personal

4

information. Web sites have "cookies,"
which track the IP address of the computer
that visits them and the "footsteps" of
other sites this computer visited.
Doubleclick.com is a company notorious in
the computer world for tracing these
"footsteps" and selling this information
to companies that send you individualized
electronic advertising while you are
surfing the net.

Credit card companies are the most
direct and accurate method of tracking
buying patterns of a consumer. First Data
Corporation, a giant Atlanta-based
company, records eight of every ten times
a credit card is used at stores,
restaurants, and hotels across the nation
in a huge database. First Data knows the
who, what, when, and where of each
transaction and uses this information, in
partnership with a number of banking
clients, to send out millions of
promotional mailings related to your
buying patterns.

Wireless companies are also capable
of obtaining personal information, via

5

cell phone use, on the places that you
frequent. By tracking where you make your
cell phone calls, these companies get a
good idea of where you like to shop and
eat, and they actively pursue ways of
using this information for commercial
purposes or selling it to third parties.
Before long, your cell phone will be a
digital dog tag (McCarthy and Mills 1999).

Protecting Privacy

With technology growing at a rapid
rate, information can be obtained simply by
the push of a button. Whether it is the
Internet, cell phones, or credit cards,
this technology comes with a high price,
the loss of privacy. First of all, it is
unethical for companies to compile and sell
our personal information without our
knowledge. Also, in the wrong hands, this
information puts us at risk of falling
victim to numerous crimes and various forms
of discrimination. Why should we, the
consumers, put ourselves at risk and pay
the price for gross negligence and obvious
lack of consideration just to increase the
monetary gains of these large corporations?

6

The underlying question of this
controversy deals with ethics. Is it moral
for businesses and companies to collect
and maintain personal profiles of members
of the public and sell or share this type
of personal information without the
knowledge or consent of the individuals?
Shouldn't we, as individuals, have the
right to control information about
ourselves, the right to have our own
personal space, and the right to be left
alone, both as consumers and individuals?
Toysmart.com recently announced that it
would be closing up shop and would sell
its customer list. This incident created a
stir of controversy and led to a lawsuit
from thirty-nine state attorneys general
that said "the sale would not only be
unethical, but that it would violate the
retailer's customer-privacy policy"
(Verdisco 2000, 15). Toysmart.com is not
the only organization selling personal
information. The state of Maryland already
earns approximately $13 million a year
selling driver's license records. The
state of Texas also earns revenue by

7

selling information on voter registration,
driver's licenses, and eviction papers to
a company in the West Indies, which then
sells this information to the public over
the Internet (Verdisco 2000).

Besides the ethics of selling
personal information generally, it scares
me to imagine what would occur if my
personal information landed in the wrong
hands. Joe Harris, systems administrator
for Blarg Online Services, a company that
hosts e-commerce sites for other
companies, recently discovered that more
than one hundred online stores hosted by
Blarg were inadvertently revealing
consumer information such as names,
addresses, credit card numbers, and other
purchasing information. Internet users
could access this information by inputting
certain keywords or doing searches on
these sites. Imagine if your sensitive
medical records, including information on
genetic predisposition to certain
conditions, fell into the hands of
insurance companies or prospective
employers. In fact, it was recently ruled

8

in a British court that British insurers
may use the results of genetic tests for
Huntington's disease, a degenerative brain
disorder, in deciding to refuse to
underwrite life insurance policies. This
should be of no surprise in that bankers
are also using this type of electronic
information to turn away prospective
borrowers who were monitored for credit
risk (Aldred 2000).

Another serious problem that occurs
as a direct result of information being in
the wrong hands is cyberstalking. Amy
Boyer, age 20, from New Hampshire, was
shot by a man who had been stalking her
for some time. The man, who killed himself
after killing Boyer, acknowledged that he
had obtained details about Boyer such as
her Social Security number, which he had
used to track her, from brokers on the
Internet. "Nanci," a woman from Worcester,
Massachusetts, was also a victim of
cyberstalking. In an article entitled
"Cyberstalking" in the July/August 2000
Medford Mail-Tribune, J. A. Hitchcock
reported that her harasser began emailing

9

her information he obtained over the
Internet, such as her father's name and
where she lived. He later became more
aggressive, making death threats and
telling her what kind of car she was
driving, where she was earlier in the day,
and the name of her daughter.

Business Point of View

Businesses feel that having access to
information regarding consumer buying
preferences and economic status is not
only essential to maximizing profits for
them, but is also beneficial for
consumers. Companies argue that their
knowing where you like to shop, what you
frequently buy, or where you prefer to eat
benefits consumers because they can be
easily targeted with coupons or specials
pertaining to their preferences. For
example, if a business knows you live in a
city with a high mean income, it will
likely send you magazines or coupons
targeted at wealthy families. Or, suppose
a company knows that you always eat at a
certain restaurant. You may receive
coupons for this eatery or maybe even
coupons for one of its competitors.

10

However, there are various other methods businesses can use to collect this type of information. Surveys, polls, or questionnaires are all ways companies can use to gather consumer information voluntarily and, most importantly, with the consent of an individual, rather than, in essence, "spying" on consumers through hidden means.

Conclusion

As this debate heats up, the federal government is getting more and more involved, with numerous bills being introduced in the Senate pertaining to various privacy issues such as selling customer data, obtaining personal information without the consent of an individual, cyberstalking, and privacy regulations, to name just a few. The government should be responsible for ensuring our personal privacy by enacting and monitoring regulations against these types of unethical actions that are potentially dangerous and discriminatory. Ask yourself, if government intervention does not happen now, how far will this consumer profiling go in the coming years?

11

References

Aldred, Carolyn. 2000. Insurers to use
genetic information. *Business
Insurance* 15 (October):60-65.

Culnan, Mary J. 2000. "Georgetown Internet
Privacy Policy Survey Executive
Summary." 2000. <http://www.msb.edu/
faculty/culnanm/grippshome.html>. 21
November 2000.

Markoff, John. 1999. *The privacy debate*.
Homewood, IL: Irwin.

McCarthy, Jack, and Elinor Mills. 1999.
"E-commerce Sites Exposing Consumer
Information." *InfoWorld.com* (1999).
<http://www.infoworld.com>. 3 May
2000.

Verdisco, Bob. 2000. Consumer privacy is
coming to a boil. *DSN/Retailing Today*
25 (March):15-17.

Index

Abbreviations, of journal names in CBE
    documentation, 222
ABI-INFORM, 39
Abstracts, 27–28
    in APA documentation, 278
    business, 327
    defined, 24
    example of from social science
        research paper, 296
    humanities, 188, 191
    locating, 27
    in MLA documentation, 177
    science and technology, 228, 229
    social sciences, 291, 292, 293, 294
    writing, 126
Academic American Encyclopedia, 26
Academic Info, 45
Acknowledgment, required, 71
*The ACS Style Guide: A Manual for
    Authors and Editors*, 222
Active voice, versus passive voice, 117
Almanacs
    defined, 24
    social sciences, 293
AltaVista, 41, 42
Altick, Richard, 152
American College of Physicians, 226
American Heritage College Dictionary, 25
American Medical Association, 226
American Psychological Association
    (APA). *See* APA documentation
Analysis
    comparative, 15–16
    critical, 6
    process, as organizational pattern, 99
Anderson, Frank Maloy, 153
Animal science
    discipline-specific resources for, 228
    Web sites, 228
Annotated bibliography, 127
Annotation
    bibliography, 127
    example of Internet printout, 57
    of text while reading, 18–19
Anonymous works
    in APA documentation, 285

in CBE documentation, 225
in CMS documentation, 324
in MLA documentation, 180
Anthropology
    discipline-specific resources for, 291
    Web sites, 291
APA documentation
    abstracts, 278
    appendix, 279
    author/date style, 279–281
    authors, 280, 281, 282–283
    body, 278–279
    books, 282–283
    chapters, 283
    dissertations, 286
    edited works, 283
    electronic media, 288–290
    email messages, 281, 288
    encyclopedia entries, 283–284
    essays, 283
    films or videotapes, 286
    government documents, 286
    internal citation, 280–281
    interviews, 287
    introduction, 278
    journal articles, 284
        online, 289
    lecture notes, 281
    magazine articles, 285
        online, 289
    manuscript preparation, 277–279
    newspaper articles, 285
        online, 289
    papers presented at conferences, 287
    personal correspondence, 281, 287
    postings from electronic bulletin
        boards, 281
    reference list, 282–290
    reviews, 287
    sample research paper: social science
        format, 295–308
    technical reports, 285
    television programs, 288
    text, 278
    title page, 277
    unpublished manuscripts, 286

Web sites, 288–289
Appendix
  in APA documentation, 279
  in research papers, 128
Applied research, 312
Argumentative research papers,
  92–93, 96
Art and architecture
  discipline-specific resources for, 188
  Web sites, 188
Art criticism, 151–152, 154
Articles
  in APA documentation
    journals, 284
    magazines, 285
    newspapers, 285
    online, 289
  in CBE documentation, 222
    journals, 224–225
    newspapers, 225
  in CMS documentation
    journals, 323, 324
  in MLA documentation
    journals, 175, 176–177
    newspapers, 177
  in serials, locating
    popular periodicals, 35–37
    professional journals, 37–38
AskERIC Virtual Library, 45
Astronomy
  discipline-specific resources for,
    231
  Web sites, 231
Atlases, 24
Audience(s)
  identifying, for research papers,
    93–94
  target, for journals and magazines, 68,
    70
Author(s)
  in APA documentation, 280, 281,
    282–283
  in CBE documentation, 219, 220, 221,
    223
  in CMS documentation, 322, 323
  discerning organizational plan of, 76
  evaluating credentials of, 67
  in MLA documentation
    books, 175–176
    journal articles, 176–177
    online catalog searches for, 33–34
Author/date style, in APA
  documentation, 279–281

Barzun, Jacques, 256–257
Basic research, 312
Behavioral sciences, 255
Bibliographic Index, 27
Bibliographies, 27
  annotated, 127
  defined, 25
  word-processing features to help
    with, 120
  working, 35
    example of, in CBE documentation,
      58–59
Bibliography cards
  for books or journals, 60–61
  example of, 60
  information to include on, 57–58
  note cards and, 59–60
Biographies
  defined, 25
  general, 26
*Biography and Genealogy Master
  Index*, 26
Biological and Agricultural Science Index,
  32
Biology
  discipline-specific resources for, 228
  Web sites, 228
Block quotes, 121
Bookmarks, saving Web sites with, 48
Book Review Digest, 27
Book Review Index, 27
Books
  in APA documentation, 282–283
  bibliography cards for, 60–61
  in CBE documentation, 222, 223, 224
  in CMS documentation, 322–323
    online, 325
  locating library, 29–35
  in MLA documentation, 173–174,
    175–176
    online, 180
Boolean operators, 43–44
  tips on, 43
Botany
  discipline-specific resources for, 228
  Web sites, 228
Brackets
  angle, to enclose URLs, 325
  insertion in quotations of, 122
British Journal of Experimental Pathology,
  205
Browsers, 52
Bulletin boards, online, 70

in APA documentation, 281
in CMS documentation, 325
Bureau of Justice Statistics, 46
Bureau of Labor Statistics, 46
Bureau of the Census, 46
Business
   conducting surveys in, 316–318
   discipline-specific resources for,
      291–292, 327
   documentation in, 320–322
      internal citation, 320–321
   information, presenting, 314
   inquiry process in, 312–313
   marketing research, 313
   organizational research, 313
   primary research, 313–318
   reference list, 321–322
   research and development (R&D), 312
   research reports. *See* Business research
      reports
   technology and, 326
   Web sites, 292, 327
Business research reports
   documentation, 320. *See also* CMS
      documentation
      internal citation, 320–321
      reference list, 321–322
   example of, in CMS documentation,
      329–340
   first drafts of, 319–320
   organizing and writing, 319–320
   outlining, 319
Business Resources on the Internet, 326

Call number searches, 34
Capitalization
   for business and economics reference
      list, 322
   in CBE documentation, 221, 223
   and direct quotations, 122
   in MLA documentation, 174
Card catalogs, 29
   conversion of, into computerized
      systems, 29
Cause/effect organizational pattern, 97
CBE documentation
   books, 223, 224
      online, 226
   capitalization in, 221, 223
   chapters, 224
   content notes, 221
   dissertations, 225
   edited works, 224

electronic media, 226–227
email messages, 227
example of working bibliography in,
   58–59
government documents, 224
internal citation, 219–221
journal articles, 224–225
   online, 226
listservs, 227
magazine articles, 225
name/year system, 219–220
newspaper articles, 225
   online, 226
number system, 220–221
online professional or personal sites,
   226
periodicals, 224–225
personal letters, 225
position of date in, 223
reference list, 221–222
unpublished interviews, 225
unpublished manuscripts, 225
CD-ROMs
   in MLA documentation, 181
   and other electronic databases, 39–40
Chapters
   in APA documentation, 283
   in CBE documentation, 224
   in CMS documentation, 323
   in MLA documentation, 176
Chemistry
   discipline-specific resources for,
      228–229
   Web sites, 229
The Chicago Manual of Style, 322. *See also*
   CMS documentation
Citations. *See also specific documentation
   styles*
   components of complete, 37
   listing, on working bibliography, 62
Citation-sequence system. *See* Number
   system (CBE documentation)
Civilization and Its Discontents (Freud),
   256
Classification/definition organizational
   pattern, 98
Closed questions, 263
Closings, for research papers, 106–107
CMS documentation
   authors, 322, 323
   books, 322–323
   chapters, 323
   corporate author, 323

dissertations, 324
edited works, 323
essays, 323
interviews, 324
letters, 324
public documents, 324
sample research report (business and economics format), 329–340
CNN Interactive, 47
Coleridge, Samuel, 152
Collaboration, 108–109
example of report using, 211–214
for research and written reports, 210
team writing, 108–109
working with a group, 108
College research, 1–21
Colons, to introduce quotations, 122
Commas, quotation marks and, 122
Common knowledge, 72, 103–104
Communication
discipline-specific resources for, 292–293
Web sites, 293
Compare/contrast organizational pattern, 97–98
Computer(s)
data analysis using, 259
developing research notebook on, 55
discipline-specific resources for, 229, 327
drafting with, 109–110
formatting and printing using, 123
in lab environment, 110
Web sites, 229, 327
wise usage of, 110
Computer research notebooks, 55
Conclusions, for research papers, 106–107
Conrad, Joseph, 157
Content notes
in CBE documentation, 221
in MLA documentation, 173
Content, of sources, 70
Corporate authors
in APA documentation, 185
in CBE documentation, 224
in CMS documentation, 323
Council of Biology Editors (CBE), 218–219. *See also* CBE documentation
Council of Science Editors (CSE), 219
Counterarguments, presenting, 92–93
Creative writing, 150

Credibility, establishing, 93
Critical reading, 15–16
checklist for evaluation during, 16
Critical thinking, 5–8
analyzing topic, 6
establishing purpose and raising questions, 5–6
evaluation, as part of, 7–8
making inferences, 7
synthesizing, 7
Criticism
art, 151–152, 154
literary, 151–152, 154
Critiquing
of sources, 81–83
using outline for, 82
Cross-referencing, of sources, 68
Current Biography, 26

Danley, Lindy ("The Problem of E-Waste"), 295–308
Databases
CD-ROMs and other electronic, 39–40
computerized library, 32–33
full-text electronic, 40
in MLA documentation, 179
specialized, 32
Department of Education, 46
"Diary of a Public Man" (Anderson), 153
Dictionaries
business, 327
defined, 25
economics, computers, and technology, 327
humanities, 188, 189, 190
looking in, for word divisions, 126
science and technology, 228, 229, 230, 231
social sciences, 291, 292, 293
suggestions for, 25
using, 14, 124
Dictionary of American Biography, 26
Directories, search, 52
Direct quotations
in APA documentation, 280
brackets and, 122
capitalization and, 122
colons introducing, 122
ellipses and, 122
incorporating, 121–123
introduced by commas, 123
in MLA documentation, 170
punctuation of, 122

Discovery Channel, 228
Dissertation Abstracts International, 28
Dissertations
    in APA documentation, 286
    in CBE documentation, 225
    in CMS documentation, 324
    in MLA documentation, 178
Documentation
    of paraphrasing, in review
        paper, 218
    in science and technology, 218–219
    in social sciences: author/date style
        (APA). *See* APA documentation
Domain types, 67
Drafting
    with a computer, 109–110
    in humanities, 169–170
    questions to help with, 113
    research papers, 102–105
    strategies, 104–105
Drafts
    of business reports, 319–320
    in humanities, 169–170
    rereading and reviewing, 112
    rough, 113
    in science and technology, 218
    in social sciences, 275–277

Easterbrook, Gregg, 73, 74
EBSCOHost, 40
Ecology
    discipline-specific resources for, 230
    Web sites, 230
Economics
    discipline-specific resources for,
        291–292, 327
    documentation in, 320–322
        internal citation, 320–321
        reference list, 321–322
    Web sites, 292, 327
Edited works
    in APA documentation, 283
    in CBE documentation, 224
    in CMS documentation, 323
    in MLA documentation, 176
Editing, 112
    for grammar, punctuation, and
        spelling, 117–118
    with word processing, 119
Editorial Research Reports (ERR), 52
Education
    discipline-specific resources for, 292
    Web sites, 292

Education Index, 32
Educator's Reference Desk, 45
Einstein, Albert, 207
Electronic bulletin board postings, in
        APA documentation, 281
Electronic communication. *See* Email
        correspondence
Electronic Library, 47
Electronic media
    in APA documentation, 288–290
    in CBE documentation, 226–227
    in MLA documentation, 178–183
    style CMS-based style for, 324–326
Electronic sources, evaluating, 65–71
Ellipses
    within brackets, 122
    at end of quoted material, 122
Email correspondence
    in APA documentation, 281, 288
    in CBE documentation, 227
    in CMS documentation, 325
    in MLA documentation, 182–183
*Encyberpedia: The Living Encyclopedia from
        Cyberspace*, 26
Encyclopaedia Britannica, 26
Encyclopedia Americana, 26
Encyclopedia of American History, 26
Encyclopedia of Education, 52
Encyclopedia of Psychology, 52
Encyclopedias
    in APA documentation, 283–284
    defined, 25
    economics, computers, and
        technology, 327
    general, 26
    humanities, 188, 189, 190
    in MLA documentation, 176
    science and technology, 228, 229, 230,
        231
    social sciences, 292, 293, 294
    specialized, 26, 52
Endnotes
    format for, 126–127
    in MLA documentation, 184
    word-processing features to help
        with, 120
Engineering
    discipline-specific resources for,
        229
    paper: science format, example of,
        233–251
    Web sites, 229
English literature and language

discipline-specific resources for,
188–189
Web sites, 189
Environment
discipline-specific resources for, 230
Web sites, 230
Essays
in APA documentation, 283
in CMS documentation, 323
in MLA documentation, 176
Ethnic studies
discipline-specific resources for, 292
Web sites, 292
Evaluation
in critical thinking process, 7–8
of periodicals, 37
of print and electronic sources, 65–71
in reading process, 15–16
Evidence, acceptable, in humanities,
153–154
Excite, 41, 42, 48
Exclamation points, quotation marks
and, 122
Executive summary, example of, 217
Experiments
behavioral-science, 255
controlled, conducted by business
researchers, 312
laboratory, 208–209
social scientific, 261–262

Favorites, saving Web sites with, 48
Field observations, 210–211
Films
in APA documentation, 286
discipline-specific resources for,
191
Web sites, 191
in MLA documentation, 178
First drafts
of business reports, 319–320
of research papers
in humanities, 169–170
in science and technology, 218
in social sciences, 275–277
Fisheries
discipline-specific resources for, 231
Web sites, 232
Fleming, Alexander, discovery of
penicillin by, 205
Flow charts, 314
skills survey process, 316
Footnotes

in MLA documentation, 183–187
word-processing features to help
with, 120
Freewriting, 107
Freud, Sigmund, 256

Garber, Eugene K., 156–157
General Sciences Index, 32
General to specific organizational
pattern, 99
Geography
discipline-specific resources for, 230
Web sites, 230
Geology
discipline-specific resources for, 230
Web sites, 230
*Geowriting: A Guide to Writing, Editing,
and Printing in Earth Science*, 223
Google, 36, 41
Government documents
in APA documentation, 286
in CBE documentation, 224
Internet sites for, 46
locating, 38–39
searching, 47
Graff, Henry F., 256–257
Grammar-checking software, 120, 123
Grammar, editing for, 117–118
Guide to Reference Books, 27
Gutch Memorandum Book (Coleridge), 152
Guyette, Lee ("Red Raider Romances"),
266–271

Handbooks
defined, 25
science and technology, 228, 230
*Hard Times: An Oral History of the Great
Depression* (Terkel), 163–165
Hawthorne, Nathaniel, 156–157
Headings, in APA documentation,
278
Health sciences
discipline-specific resources for, 230
Web sites, 231
Historical research, 152–153
acceptable evidence in, 154
History and classics
discipline-specific resources for,
188 189
Web sites, 189
H-Net, 325
HotBot, 41, 42
Humanities

acceptable evidence in,
153–154
discipline-specific resources for,
188–191
documentation in. *See* MLA
documentation
importance of texts in, 150–151
inquiry process in, 149–150
literary and art criticism in, 151–152
model notes, 185–187
primary research in, 156–157
reports, 148
research, 151
historical, 152–153
philosophical, 152
research papers, 147–200
example of, 192–200
first drafts of, 169–170
organizing and writing, 166–170
outlining, 167–169
technology and, 188
Humanities Index, 32
Hypotheses
developing, 53–54
development, by business researchers,
312
reassessing working, 96–97
scientific
importance of formulating and
testing, 205–206
reporting on findings of, 207
in social sciences
articulation of, 262–263
discerning relationship of data to,
259
interpreting results of, 261
problem and, 258
testing, 254
testing, 10–11

Illumination stage, of research, 10
Incubation stage, of research, 9–10
Indentation
for business and economics reference
list, 322
for long quotations, 173
for research papers, 126
Indexes
business, 327
defined, 25
of government documents, 39
humanities, 188, 189, 190, 191
newspaper, 36

periodical, 36–37
of reviews, 27
science and technology, 228, 229, 230,
231
search directories, 41–42
of serials, 38
social sciences, 291, 292, 293, 294
Index to U.S. Government Periodicals, 39
Inferences, making
in critical thinking process, 7
in reading process, 14–15
Infomine Scholarly Resource Collections, 45
Information
communicating, 103
presenting business, 314
timeliness of, 67–68
Informational research papers, 92, 96
Inquiry process
in business, 312–313
in humanities, 149–150
in science and technology, 204–208
in social sciences, 254–257
Intentional plagiarism, 72–73
Interlibrary loan, 33
Internal citation
in APA documentation, 280–281
in business and economics, 320–321
in CBE documentation, 219–221
in MLA documentation, 170–173
Internet. *See also* Internet resources;
Internet sources; Web sites
obtaining articles from another
library, using, 33
research, time-consuming aspects of,
63
searching, phrases for, 43
sites for online periodicals, 47
sites related to business, 326–328
Internet Public Library, 45
Internet resources, 41–48. *See also*
Internet sources
bookmarking sites, 48
evaluation of, 65–71
library and periodicals collections,
44–45
search tools, 41–44, 52
Boolean operators, 43–44
sites for government documents,
46
Internet sources. *See also* Internet
resources
downloading, 56–57
making photocopies and database

printouts of, 56
printing, 56
special criteria for, 70
Interviews
in APA documentation, 287
in CBE documentation, 225
in CMS documentation, 324
designing, 165
life-history, 163
Emma Tiller (transcribed tape, by
Studs Terkel), 163–165
in MLA documentation, 178
in social sciences, 264–265
example of, 265
Introductions
in APA documentation, 278
for research papers, 105–106
Ixquick, 41, 42

James, William, 154
Jargon, replacing, 115
Journalism
discipline-specific resources for,
292–293
Web sites, 293
Journals
in APA documentation, 284
online, 289
bibliography cards for, 61
in CBE documentation, 224–225
online, 226
in CMS documentation, 323, 324
online, 325
professional, locating articles in,
37–38
target audiences for, 68, 70

Kershisnik, Kauleen ("Is Your Ch'i in
Balance?"), 129–144
Keyword searches, 34, 42–43
advanced, 35
Knowledge
common, 72, 103–104
communicating scientific, 207
gained by basic and applied research,
312
personal, 103
source, 103
"Kubla Khan" (Coleridge), 152

Lab experiments, 208–209
Laboratory notebook, 208–209
Language

appropriate, for research paper, 95
English literature and, discipline-
specific resources for, 188–189
need for clarity of, 114
Web sites, 189
Letters
in APA documentation, 281, 287
in CBE documentation, 225
in CMS documentation, 324
in MLA documentation, 178
Lexis-Nexis, 40
LibCat, 44, 45
Librarian's Index to the Internet, 45
Libraries. *See also* Library research
accessing information from other, 40
computer cataloging systems in. *See*
Online catalogs
general reference works in, 25–29
Internet, 45
reference area in, 24–25
searching virtual, 44–45
time needing for searching in, 63
Library of Congress, 30
Library of Congress, 45, 46
*Library of Congress Subject Headings
(LCSH)*, 30–32
Library research. *See also* Libraries
beginning, in library reference area,
24–25
developing search strategy for,
61–62
involved in business reports, 311–312
locating articles for, 35–38
locating government documents,
38–39
other technologies used in, 39–40
reference librarians, 24, 52
skills for scientific review papers, 204
in social sciences, 253
tools of
computer cataloging systems,
29–35
reference sources, 24–29
using OCLC in, 40
LibWeb, 44
Life on the Mississippi (Twain), 149–150
Lincoln, Abraham, 153
Line spacing, for research papers, 125
Links, 45, 47
Listservs
in APA documentation, 290
in CBE documentation, 227
in CMS documentation, 325

in MLA documentation, 183
Literal meaning, reading for, 14
Literary criticism, 151–152, 154
Lord Jim (Conrad), 157
Lot, Brent ("Consumer Privacy"),
    329–340
Lowes, John Livingston, 152
Lycos, 41, 42
Lycos News, 47

Magazine Index, 36
Magazines
    in APA documentation, 285
        online, 289
    in CBE documentation, 225
    in MLA documentation, 177
        online, 180–181
    target audiences for, 68, 70
Magazines for Libraries, 37
Maitre, H. Joachim, 74
Margins, for research papers, 125
Marketing research, 313
Maslow, Abraham, 313
Mathematics
    discipline-specific resources for, 231
    Web sites, 231
Medved, Michael, 74
Microforms, 35
    newspapers stored on, 36
Milgram, Stanley, 254–255
MLA documentation
    abstracts, 177
    articles, 175
    authors, 175–177
    books, 173–174, 175–176
        online, 180
    CD-ROMs, 181
    chapters, 176
    databases, 179
    dissertations, 178
    edited works, 176
    electronic media, 178–183
    email messages, 182–183
    encyclopedia entries, 176
    endnotes, 184
    films or movies, 178
    footnotes, 183–187
    humanities research paper
        example of, 192–200
        sentence outline for, 167–169
    internal citation, 170–173
    interviews, 178
    journal articles, 176–177

listservs, 183
    magazine articles, 177
    newspaper articles, 177
    periodicals, 176–177
        online, 180–181
    reference list, 173–175
    television programs, 178
    translated works, 174
    Web sites, 179
    work from subscription services, 181
*MLA Handbook for Writers of Research
    Papers*, 170, 175
Modern Language Association (MLA),
    66, 170. *See also* MLA
    documentation
The Modern Researcher (Barzun and
    Graff), 256–257
*Monthly Catalog of United States
    Government Publications*, 39
Movies. *See* Films
Music
    discipline-specific resources for,
        189–190
    Web sites, 190
"'My Kinsman, Major Molineux': Some
    Interpretive and Critical Probes"
    (Garber), 156–157

Name/year system (CBE
    documentation), 219–220
    articles, 222
Narration/description organizational
    pattern, 99
NASA, 46
National Institutes of Health, 46
National Library of Medicine, 46
National Science Foundation
    (NSF), 312
The News Directory, 48
News Directory, 47
Newsgroups, online, 70
    in APA documentation, 290
    in MLA documentation, 183
Newspaper Index, 36
Newspapers, 36
    in APA documentation, 285
        online, 289
    in CBE documentation, 225
        online, 226
Newton, Isaac, 207
New York Times, 47
New York Times Index, 36
Nicolle, Charles ("The Mechanism of the

Transmission of Typhus"), 11–12
Nominalizations, 116–117
North American Review, 153
Note cards, 59–60
  example of, 60
  sorting, by related topic areas, 274
Notes
  laboratory, taken during experiments,
    208
  numbering of, 59–60
  taking accurate and careful, 77–83
  taking, with photocopies and
    printouts, 56–58
Nouns, complete, 116
Number system (CBE documentation),
    220–221
  articles, 222
  example of paper using, 233–251

Objectivity, versus subjectivity, 257
Observation
  example of report using, 266–271
  of human behavior, 255
  importance in sciences of, 204–205
OCLC (Online Computer Library
    Center), 40
Online catalogs, 29–30
  databases, 32–33
  how to search, 32–35
  locating articles in serials from, 35–37
  major parts of, 32
  methods of searching, 29
  recording bibliographic information
    from, 35
  searches
    advanced keyword, 35
    call number, 34
    keyword, 34
    subject, 34
    title and author, 33–34
  subject headings in, 30–32
Online publications
  in APA documentation
    journals, 289
    newspapers, 289
  in CBE documentation
    books, 226
    journals, 226
    newspapers, 226
  in MLA documentation
    books, 180–181
    periodicals, 180–181
Open-ended questions, 263

Openings, for research papers, 105–106
Organization
  of humanities research paper, 166–170
  patterns for, 97–99
    cause and effect, 97
    classification and definition, 98
    compare and contrast, 97–98
    general to specific, 99
    narration and description, 99
    problem and solution, 98
    process analysis, 99
    question and answer, 98
  of research paper, 95–100
  of social sciences research paper,
    273–275
    materials, 274
Organizational research, 313
Outlines
  of business report, 319
  constructing, for research papers,
    101–102
  of critiques, 82
  of humanities research paper, 167–169
  reconstructing author's
    organizational plan with, 76
  of research time frame, 63–65
  reverse, 114
  for review papers, 217
  of social sciences research paper, 275
  of synthesis, 80
Owen, Stephanie J. ("Jim as a
    Romantic"), 157–162

Page, Melvin E., 324–325
Paragraphs, revising, 114
Paraphrasing, 20–21
  in APA documentation, 280
  appropriately, 73
  documentation of, 276
  in review papers, 218
  examples of acceptable and
    unacceptable, 74–75
  in MLA documentation, 170
Pascale, Richard, 74
Passive voice, active voice versus, 117
Peer review, 66
Periodicals
  in APA documentation, 284, 285
    online, 289
  in CBE documentation, 224–225
  evaluating, 37
  finding, 36–37
  locating articles in, 35–37

in MLA documentation, 176–177
searching online, 47–48
Periods, quotation marks and, 122
Persona, 93
Philosophical research, 152
acceptable evidence in, 154
Philosophy
discipline-specific resources for, 190
Web sites, 190
Photocopies, of sources, 56
Physics
discipline-specific resources for, 231
Newtonian, 207
Web sites, 231
Plagiarism
avoiding, 20–21, 71–76
defined, 20
intentional, 72–73
unintentional, 72
Plant genetics
discipline-specific resources for, 228
Web sites, 228
Point of view, changing, 107
Political science
discipline-specific resources for, 293
Web sites, 293
Preparation stage, of research, 9
Previewing, in reading process, 17
Primary research, 203
in business, 313–318
field observations and reports,
210–211
in humanities, 156–157
lab experiments and reports, 208–209
in sciences, 208–211
in social sciences, 258–259, 261
time allowance for conducting, 64
used in business reports, 311
Primary texts
example of interpretation of, 157–162
skills for using, 147
using, 156–157
Print sources
elements to examine in, 69
evaluating, 65–71
Problem/solution organizational
pattern, 98–99
Process analysis organizational pattern,
99
Process and Reality (Whitehead), 152
ProFusion, 41, 42
Proofreading, 112, 123–124
strategies for effective, 124

Psychology
discipline-specific resources for, 293
Web sites, 293
Public Affairs Information Services (PAIS),
39
Publication information
in CBE documentation, 221, 222
in MLA documentation
articles, 175
books, 174
*Publication Manual of the American
Psychological Association*, 223, 277,
279
Punctuation
of direct quotations, 122
editing for, 117–118
Purdue University Libraries, 45
Purpose
having clear sense of, in critical
thinking, 5–6
of research paper, 92–93

Question/answer organizational
pattern, 98
Question marks, and quotation marks,
122
Questionnaires, 262–264
design of, 263–264
example of business, 317–318
example of social sciences, 264
questions used on, 263
relationship to hypothesis of, 263
Questions
asking research, 53
closed, 263
design of, in questionnaires, 263
to help with drafting, 113
to help with grammatical errors,
118
interpretive, connected with
humanities, 150
open-ended, 263
for paragraph revision, 114
raising, in critical thinking process,
5–6
research, commonly asked in business
situations, 313–314
for sentence revision, 115
Quotation marks
in Boolean searching, 44
brackets and, 122
commas and, 122
for copied sources, 71

ellipses and, 122
exclamation points and, 122
for incorporating direct quotations, 121–123
periods and, 122
question marks and, 122
use of, for sources, 276
Quotations. *See also* Direct quotations; Quotation marks
indentation for long, 173

Random House Unabridged Dictionary, 25
Readers
being compliant, 14
reconstruction of meaning by, 95
shifting roles from writers to, 111
supplying source information to, 21
Readers' Guide to Periodical Literature, 36
Reading process, 13–19
annotating text during, 18–19
reading critically, 15–16
reading for interpretation, 14–15
reading for literal meaning, 14
reading for meaning, 70–71
structuring, 17–19
previewing, 17
rereading, 17–18
reviewing, 18
Reason and Chance in Scientific Discovery (Taton), 205
Reference librarians, 24, 52
Reference list
in APA documentation, 282–290
in business and economics, 321–322
in CBE documentation, 221–222
in MLA documentation, 173–175
Reference sources, 24–25
incorporating, 120–121
Relevance, of sources to research, 66
Religion
discipline-specific resources for, 190
Web sites, 190
Reports. *See also* Research reports
excerpt from collaborative student, 211–214
field observations and, 210–211
humanities, 148
lab experiments and, 208–209
technical, in APA documentation, 285
Research, 1–21
applied, 312
basic, 312
collaboration on, 210

critical scientific, 206–207
defined, 2
design, in social sciences, 259, 261–264
developing search strategy for, 61–62
in the disciplines, 2–3
in humanities, 151
historical, 152–153
philosophical, 152
importance of, 4–5
library. *See* Library research
marketing, 313
materials, gathering, 54–55
organizational, 313
outlining time frame for, 63–65
primary, 64, 156–157, 203
in sciences, 208–211
in social sciences, 258–259, 261
principles and skills for social sciences, 253–254
process, 8–12
example of physician's use of, 11–12
illumination stage, 10
incubation stage, 9–10
preparation stage, 9
steps in scientific, 205
verification stage, 10–11
questions, asking, 53
topic, choosing, 52
Research and development (R&D)
objective of, 312
types of, 312
Research notebook, 54–55, 76
computer, 55
organizing, by related topic areas, 274
Research papers
abstract, 126
acknowledgments in, 21, 71
annotated bibliography, 127
appendix, 128
argumentative, 92–93
constructing outline or plan for, 101–102
difference between reports and, 148
drafting, 102–105
editing for grammar, punctuation, and spelling, 112–114, 117–118
endnotes, 126–127
formal details, 124 128
humanities, 192–200
example of, 129–144
first drafts of, 169–170
incorporating reference materials,

120–121
indentation, 126
informational, 92
introductions and conclusions,
    105–107
line spacing, 125
margins, 125
numbering of, 126
organization of, 95–100
planning, 91–100
preparation of, with word processor,
    125
references page, 127, 279
rewriting, 111–119
    using word processing, 119–120
science and technology
    first drafts of, 218
in social sciences, 273–279
    example of (APA documentation),
        295–308
    outlining, 275
    planning, 274
title page, 125
word spacing, 126
writing working title for, 105
Research process, 58–62.
Research reports, 92. *See also* Reports
    business. *See* Business research
        reports
    business and economics format:
        sample, 329–340
    collaboration on, 210
    description of, 203
Resources
    discipline-specific
        for humanities research papers,
            188–191
        for science and technology papers,
            228–232
        for social sciences, 291–294
    government, 328
    Web sites, 328
Resources in Education (RIE), 39
Reverse outlining, 114
Reviewing
    in reading process, 18
    of sources, 76
Review of the literature, 148. *See also*
    Reports
Review papers
    description of, 203–204
    library research skills necessary for,
        204

organizing, 216–218
    arranging materials, 217
    in science and technology, 203–251
        example of engineering, 233–251
    writing, 216–218
Reviews
    in APA documentation, 287
    defined, 25
    indexes providing access to, 27
Revising, 111. *See also* Rewriting
    gaining distance needed for, 112
    paragraphs, 114
    sentences, 114–115
    for structure and style, 112–114
    with word processing, 119
Rewriting. *See also* Revising
    research papers, 111–119
    using word processing, 119–120
Rhetorical situation, 92–95
    appropriate language or tone, 95
    identifying audience, 93–94
    persona, 93
    subject matter, 94–95
    writer's purpose, 92–93
Rhetorical stance, 68, 70
"The Rime of the Ancient Mariner"
    (Coleridge), 152
Roget's Thesaurus, 25

Science. *See also* Technology
    discipline-specific resources for,
        228–232
    documentation in, 218–219
    forums of, 208
    inquiry process in, 204–208
        critical scientific research, 206–207
        formulation and testing of
            hypotheses, 205–206
        importance of replicability and
            scientific debate, 207–208
        observation, 204–205
    primary research in, 208–211
        field observations and reports,
            210–211
        lab experiments and reports,
            208–209
    review papers in, 203–251
        example of engineering,
            233–251
    technology, as branch of, 203
Scientific method
    adoption of, by social sciences, 254
    business adoption of much of, 312

employed by laboratory researchers, 209
need for understanding of, 208
steps in, 206
Scientific Style and Format: The CBE Manual for Authors, Editors, and Publishers, 218–219, 222, 226
Search directories, 52
Search engines, 41
news tracker services of, 36
Searches. *See also* Search engines
call number, 34
of government documents, 47
keyword, 34, 42–43
advanced, 35
of online periodicals, 47–48
subject, 34
title and author, 33–34
tools used for, 42
using Boolean operators, 43–44
using online catalogs, 32–35
using subject directories, 41–42
Secondary sources, 71
in social sciences, 253
Sentences, revising, 114–115
Serials
defined, 25
indexes of, 38
listing, 37
locating articles in
popular periodicals, 35–37
professional journals, 37–38
Smith, Maure, 166
"Cathy, the 'Eve' of Eden," 192–200
sentence outline for, 167–169
Social sciences, 253–308
discipline-specific resources for, 291–294
experiments, 261–262
inquiry process in, 254–257
objectivity versus subjectivity, 257
observing human behavior, 255
understanding human consciousness, 255–257
interviews, 264–265
observation in, 266
example of report using, 266–271
human behavior, 255
primary research, 258–259, 261
analyzing data, 259
gathering data, 259
interpreting results of, 261
problem and hypothesis, 258

research design, 259, 261–264
questionnaires, 262–264
research papers
organizing, 273–274
outline for, 275
planning, 274
writing, 275–277
research principles and skills for, 253–254
sample research paper (APA documentation), 295–308
surveys, 262–264
Social Sciences Abstracts, 38
Social Sciences Index, 32
Social work
discipline-specific resources for, 294
Web sites, 294
Society for Engineering Educators, 66
Sociological Abstracts, 27–28
Sociology
discipline-specific resources for, 294
Web sites, 294
Software, bibliography and footnote, 120
Sources
documenting, in first draft of business report, 320
elements to examine in electronic, 69
evaluating electronic and print, 65–71
knowledge from, 103
making photocopies and database printouts of, 56
peer-reviewed, 66
printing Internet, 56
publisher or sponsor of, 66
reference, 24–25
relevance of, 66
responsible use of, and avoidance of plagiarism, 20–21
saving online, 57–58
secondary, 71
working with, 70–71
writing from, 77–83
Spell checkers, 118, 119, 123
Spelling
editing for, 117–118
using spell checkers, 118, 119, 123
Statistical Abstract of the United States, 46
Statistics
compilations of, in business, 314
discipline-specific resources for, 231
Web sites, 231
Style Manual: For Guidance in the

Preparation of Papers for Journals Published by the American Institute of Physics, 223
Subheadings, in APA documentation, 278
Subject directories, searching via, 41–42
Subjectivity, objectivity versus, 257
Subject matter, in research papers, 94–95
Subject searches, 34
Summaries. *See also* Summarizing
  executive, example of, 217
  first drafts of, 78–79
  making section-by-section, 75–76
Summarizing, 20–21, 78–79. *See also* Summaries
main point in form of thesis statement, 78
Surveys
  in business, conducting, 314, 316–318
  interviews, 264–265
  questionnaires and, 262–264
  skills, 314, 316
Syntax, 118
Synthesizing
  in critical thinking process, 7
  materials from sources, 79–81

Taton, Rene, 205
Team writing, 108–109
Technology. *See also* Science
  as branch of science, 203
  and business, 326
  discipline-specific resources for, 228–232, 327
  documentation in, 218–219
  humanities and, 188
  proprietary aspects of, 312
  review papers in, 203–251
    example of engineering, 233–251
  Web sites, 327
Television programs
  in APA documentation, 288
  in MLA documentation, 178
Tense, consistency of verb, 121
Terkel, Studs, 163–165
Text(s)
  annotating, while reading, 18–19
  in APA documentation, 278
  changing look of research paper, 112
  changing notion of, using computer, 109–110
  creating professional looking, 123
  in MLA documentation, 183–187

primary. *See* Primary texts
types of, in humanities, 150–151
Thacker, Rebecca A. ("Innovative Steps to Take in Sexual Harassment Prevention"), 84–89
Theater
  discipline-specific resources for, 191
  Web sites, 191
Thesaurus
  Roget's Thesaurus, 25
  word processor's, 119
Thesis
  argumentative, 96
  informational, 96
Thesis statement, 78, 79
  referring to, as organizational guide, 167
  writing, 96–97
Thomas (congressional legislation), 46
Time frame
  for research project, 63–65
  sample, 64–65
Timeliness, of information, 67–68
Title page
  in APA documentation, 277
  of research papers, 125
Titles
  online catalog searches for, 33–34
  writing working, 105
Tone, appropriate, for research papers, 95
Topic
  analyzing, in critical thinking process, 6
  areas, sorting note cards and research notebook by related, 274
  finding, 52
  information, using search tools to locate, 41–44
  narrowing and focusing, 53–55
  selecting specific, 53
Transitions, between paragraphs, 114
Translated works, in MLA documentation, 174
Twain, Mark (*Life on the Mississippi*), 149–150

Unintentional plagiarism, 72
University of California–Riverside Infomine, 45
Unpublished works
  in APA documentation, 286, 287
  in CBE documentation, 225

in MLA documentation, 178
URLs
    enclosed in angle brackets, 325
    information to be gleaned from, 67
    noting complete, 56
    rapid change of, 48
U.S. Fish & Wildlife Service, 46
*U.S. Government Reports, Announcements
    and Index* (*NTIS*—National
    Technical Information Service),
    39

Verbs
    action, versus nominalizations,
        116–117
    active voice versus passive voice, 117
    content, versus empty, 116
    tense of, quotations and consistency,
        121
Verification stage, of research, 10–11, 218
Virtual Information Center, 45
Virtual libraries, 44–45
Visualization, 107

Wall Street Journal Index, 36
Ward, Samuel, 153
Web sites. *See also* Internet
    in APA documentation, 288–289
    bookmarking, 48
    clue to sponsoring organizations for,
        67
    CMS-based style for citing, 325–326
    for government documents, 46
    for government resources, 328
    humanities, 189, 190, 191
    for libraries and collections, 45
    in MLA documentation, 179
    for online periodicals, 47
    printing parts of, 56
    science and technology, 228, 229, 230,
        231, 232
    for search engines, 36
    social sciences, 291, 292, 293, 294
Webster's Collegiate Dictionary, 25
Webster's Dictionary, 25

Whitehead, Alfred North, 152, 154
White House, 46
Wildlife
    discipline-specific resources for, 231
    Web sites, 232
*Wilson Guide to Applied Science and
    Technology Index*, 32
Wilson Guide to Art Index, 32
Wilson Guide to Business Periodicals, 32
Word processors, 55
    bibliography and footnote software,
        120
    editing with, 119
    formatting features of, 123
    grammar-checking software of, 120
    power of functions in, 112
    preparing research papers with, 125
    revising with, 119
    rewriting using, 119–120
Words, improving, 115–117
Working bibliography, 35, 58–59
    example of CBE citation style in,
        58–59
World Association of Medical Editors,
    226
World Wide Web, 41
Writer's block, 107
    suggestions for overcoming, 107
Writers, to readers, shifting roles from,
    111
Writing
    creative, 150
    habits, adapting, 109
    humanities research paper, 166–170
    role of, in scientific method, 208–209
    from sources, 77–83
        critiquing, 81–83
        summarizing, 78–79
        synthesizing, 79–81

Yahoo!, 41, 42
Yahoo Today's News, 47

Zworks, 41, 42